SOA Governance in Action

SOA Governance in Action

REST AND WS-* ARCHITECTURES

JOS DIRKSEN

MANNING

SHELTER ISLAND

Manning Publications Co.
20 Baldwin Road
PO Box 261
Shelter Island, NY 11964

Development editor:	Scott Meyers
Technical proofreader:	Niek Palm
Copyeditor:	Linda Recktenwald
Proofreader:	Melody Dolab
Typesetter:	Marija Tudor
Cover designer:	Marija Tudor

ISBN: 9781617290275
Printed in the United States of America
1 2 3 4 5 6 7 8 9 10 – MAL – 18 17 16 15 14 13 12

To my wife Brigitte, my daughter Sophie, and my parents

brief contents

PART 1 INTRODUCTION 1

      1 ▪ Introducing SOA governance   3

      2 ▪ Setting up the SOA governance environment   27

      3 ▪ Using a case study to understand SOA governance   60

PART 2 DESIGN-TIME POLICIES 79

      4 ▪ Service design and documentation policies   81

      5 ▪ Security policies   116

      6 ▪ Testing, performance, and the cloud   156

PART 3 RUNTIME POLICIES 187

      7 ▪ Using tools for runtime governance   189

      8 ▪ Lifecycle support and discovering resources   212

      9 ▪ Integrating SOA governance tools with existing tools and technologies   235

contents

preface   xv
acknowledgments   xvii
about this book   xix
about the cover illustration   xxiii

PART 1   INTRODUCTION.. 1

1   *Introducing SOA governance   3*

1.1   What is SOA governance?   4

*Definition of service-oriented architecture   4 ▪ Introducing
governance   7 ▪ Defining SOA governance   10*

1.2   How using SOA governance can help   13

*Keeping track of how services are used   13 ▪ Keeping uniformity
among services   14*

1.3   Common pitfalls when introducing SOA governance   14

1.4   Requirements of an SOA governance solution   15

*Creating and maintaining policies   16 ▪ Applying policies at
design time   17 ▪ Applying policies at runtime   18*

1.5   Getting started with SOA governance   18

1.6   Getting an overview of the available policies   20

       Design and documentation policies   21 ▪ *Security policies   21*
       Testing and performance policies   22

1.7   SOA governance and open source   22

       Where is open source at the moment?   22 ▪ *Open source
       tools   24*

1.8   Summary   25

2   **Setting up the SOA governance environment   27**

2.1   Architecture of the SOA governance environment   28

       Services architecture   29

2.2   Setting up the Eclipse environment   31

2.3   Introducing the traffic avoidance example   32

2.4   Configuring the general services and database   34

       The data model used in this service   34 ▪ *Setting up the data
       access layer   35* ▪ *Setting up the logic layer   37*

2.5   Checking out and configuring the REST services   38

       Overview of the REST layer   38 ▪ *Implementation of the
       REST layer   40* ▪ *Testing the REST layer   41*

2.6   Checking out and configuring the SOAP services   43

       Overview of the WS-* layer   43 ▪ *The WSDL-based contract
       for this service   44* ▪ *Implementation of the WS-* layer   47*
       Testing the WS-* remoting layer   48

2.7   Setting up the SOA registry   49

       Running the SOA registry for the first time   49 ▪ *Registering a
       service manually in the registry   50* ▪ *Accessing the WSO2
       Governance Registry   51*

2.8   Setting up the BAM application   53

       Installing BAM tools and checking out the code from SVN   53
       Attaching an event sender to the service   54 ▪ *Setting up the
       widget to visualize the statistics   57*

2.9   Summary   59

3   **Using a case study to understand SOA governance   60**

3.1   Getting to know OpenGov   61

       The organizational chart of OpenGov   61 ▪ *The stakeholders
       of OpenGov   63*

3.2 Explaining SOA governance using OpenGov
products   64

GovForms: permit registration   65 ▪ *GovTraffic: the traffic
avoidance system   66* ▪ *GovMobile: registering your complaint
using mobile devices   66* ▪ *GovPortal: information about city
services   67* ▪ *GovData: OpenGov's open data portal   67*

3.3 Overview of the available services   68

3.4 Defining policies for the OpenGov organization   69

Service design and documentation policies   70 ▪ *Security
policies   72* ▪ *Performance and testing-related policies   75*

3.5 Summary   77

PART 2 DESIGN-TIME POLICIES 79

4 *Service design and documentation policies   81*

4.1 Complying with the self-documenting service policy   82

Documenting a REST-based service   83 ▪ *Documenting a WS-*
based service   88* ▪ *Adding documentation to the service
repository   92*

4.2 Following existing standards and definitions   95

Including an existing XML schema in a WSDL   95 ▪ *Using an
existing XML schema in a REST resource   98* ▪ *Using a
REST-based search definition   99*

4.3 Creating a reusable service   103

Define the correct level of granularity   103 ▪ *Decoupling the
transport layer from the logical layer   104* ▪ *Service
discovery   104* ▪ *Versioning, documentation, and using
standards   106*

4.4 How to version services   107

Versioning a WS-* based service   107 ▪ *Versioning a REST
service   111*

4.5 Summary   115

5 *Security policies   116*

5.1 Encrypting a communications channel for sensitive
data   117

Using HTTPS with Jetty   118 ▪ *Using HTTPS and client-side
SSL with Jetty   119*

5.2   Validating message integrity and non-repudiation   120

Applying WS-Security to SOAP messages   121 ▪ *Using HMAC for message integrity and non-repudiation   126*

5.3   Using a centralized identity system   131

Installing the authentication provider   133 ▪ *Configuring the authentication provider   133* ▪ *Creating the authentication façade   134* ▪ *Creating the authentication filter   137*

5.4   Using OAuth to allow other services to access your service   141

5.5   Reusing existing authorization services   149

Configuring the OpenAM entitlement service   150 *Creating an authorization filter   153*

5.6   Summary   155

6   **Testing, performance, and the cloud   156**

6.1   How to test your service   157

Logic layer and data layer testing   158 ▪ *Remoting layer testing   161* ▪ *Integration testing   167*

6.2   Using quality management tools   170

Running a maven build for Sonar   172

6.3   Developing for the cloud   174

Different types of cloud services   174 ▪ *Requirements for the cloud provider   175* ▪ *Creating a service that can run in the Amazon cloud   176*

6.4   Summary   185

PART 3   **RUNTIME POLICIES** 187

7   **Using tools for runtime governance   189**

7.1   Runtime governance   189

Gadget   191 ▪ *Gadget server   191* ▪ *Event producer   192* *Event service   193* ▪ *Event processor   194*

7.2   Monitor performance and service usage   195

Average response time   196 ▪ *Report usage based on service   199* ▪ *Report usage based on location   202* *Number of requests per time period   206*

7.3   Security and documentation   208

Failed authentication and authorization   208 *Documentation compliance   211*

7.4   Summary   211

8 *Lifecycle support and discovering resources* **212**

    8.1   Defining the lifecycle of a service   213

         Standard service lifecycle   213 ▪ OpenGov service lifecycle   214

    8.2   Creating a custom view for the policy   217

    8.3   Defining the lifecycle of a policy   225

    8.4   Discovery of a service and a policy in the service repository   227

         Searching the repository from the web application   227
         Searching the repository from the repository client   229

    8.5   Visualizing the information from the registry   230

         Creating a gauge that shows the documentation percentage   231 ▪ Creating a pie chart that shows the lifecycle stages   232

    8.6   Summary   234

9 *Integrating SOA governance tools with existing tools and technologies* **235**

    9.1   Enterprise integration   236

         Provisioning a WSDL from the repository   236 ▪ Provisioning the configuration from the repository   238 ▪ Sending events from Mule   241 ▪ Loading the Mule configuration from the repository   245 ▪ Sending events to Nagios from the Bamos event server   246

    9.2   BPM engine integration   251

         Monitoring average task execution   251 ▪ Monitoring which processes are started   255

    9.3   Language integration   257

         C#   257 ▪ Ruby   260 ▪ Python   261

    9.4   What you should remember from this book   263

    9.5   Summary   264

appendix   *Installing tools, libraries, and frameworks   265*
         index   277

preface

A few years ago, I wrote a book with a colleague about open source ESBs (Enterprise Service Buses), *Open Source ESBs in Action* (Manning, 2008). In that book we wrote about using open source tools to integrate applications and expose legacy systems as services. In the years that followed, ESBs were seen as one of the cornerstones of developing Service Oriented Architectures (SOAs). In 2008, when people talked about SOA, especially in the enterprise world, they meant the traditional SOAP-over-HTTP-based services. Everyone was doing this, the big vendors promoted it, and it finally looked like we had a way to create services that could be used by other departments and multiple users.

Over the next couple of years I wrote many services myself and was part of many projects that tried to use SOA concepts to create reusable services. What I noticed was that every company and every department had their own standards, tools, technologies, and a set of principles they used to determine how a service should be written. For one project we created a RESTful service using Scala without writing any documentation; for another project, we meticulously documented each element and operation of a SOAP/HTTP-based service. But the goals for both projects were the same: we wanted to create a service that would have a long life, would be used by many consumers, and was easy to maintain and possibly extend.

One thing I know is that developers and architects want to create good services, but what is almost always missing is a solid set of rules and standards to follow when developing a service. In our projects we often create a set of coding standards that are enforced through an IDE plugin, as well as some coding guidelines and dos and don'ts. While that assures the quality of the code, it isn't enough to create an easy-to-use service. For this you also need a set of rules, a set of principles that determines how your client interacts with your service. In other words, it is good to have a set of policies that help you define the contract of your service.

And what happens after a service is in production? I know from experience that measuring who is using a service and garnering insight into the business processes using your service can give you valuable information. This information can help you determine where to focus your development, where to add resources, and much more.

What I needed was a form of SOA governance. I wanted a set of policies we could use while creating the service (design-time governance) and a way to measure how our services were being used (runtime governance). Most books on SOA governance focus on the process, which is also very important, but they often lack practical examples. This book tries to provide you both with a set of guidelines for and practical examples of how to apply SOA governance.

I hope this book will show you that getting started with SOA governance isn't that hard and that it provides many advantages—and that there are plenty of open source tools that can help you take the first steps.

acknowledgments

Writing a book is a long and difficult effort. I couldn't have done this without the support and hard work of many others. There are many people I'd like to thank:

- Michael Stephens at Manning who helped me with the initial proposal. Without his help this book wouldn't have seen the light of day.
- My technical proofreader, Niek Palm, who worked tirelessly during the holiday period to meticulously work through the examples and the content. I appreciate that he always spoke his mind, and didn't always agree with me or with what I'd written.
- My copyeditor Linda Rechtenwald for her hard work translating my non-native written English to readable text. You wouldn't believe how many times she corrected my errors.
- Katie Tennant and Melody Dolab for proofreading the book and making my work easier by ensuring that everything was consistent.
- All the other people at Manning who helped me get this book published. Thanks for believing in this book and helping me all along the way.
- I'd also like to thank my development editors who guided me through the many stages of the book: Scott Meyers, Jeff Bleiel, and Dean DeChambeau.
- Thanks to the following reviewers who read the manuscript at various stages of development. Your valuable and sometimes critical comments made this a better book: Alberto Lagna, Andy Verberne, Barry Polley, David Dossot, Hemant Bedekar, Jason Coates, Javier Carro, Jeroen Benckhuijsen, Padmavathy Ramesh, Roy Prins, Sander Rossel, Senaka L. Fernando, Tijs Rademakers, and Tray Scates.

- Thanks to the guys at WSO2 for creating such great 100% open source products.
- Special thanks to Edwin Damen and Jac Speelman at JPoint (my employer), for giving me the time to finish the last couple of chapters, instead of sending me out to clients.
- A final thank-you to my wife who, once again, had to endure many long days and evenings without me while I sat at my laptop. And I couldn't have done this without my daughter who always succeeds in cheering me up when I'm down.

about this book

Welcome to *SOA Governance in Action*. The main goal of this book is to introduce you to SOA governance and provide you with a set of guidelines and policies you can use to get started introducing SOA governance to your organization.

The book is divided into three parts. In the first part you'll be introduced to the theory behind SOA governance and you'll set up an environment that you can experiment with. In the second and third parts of the book, we look at and discuss various concepts you can use to start governing your SOA.

Audience

This book is intended for software developers and architects who want to better understand SOA governance and use it to create great services.

The focus of this book is on the practical side of SOA governance. It shows you how to apply the principles of SOA governance to your own services and organization. There are many great books published that also cover SOA governance, but none that focus on the practical side of things.

Even though this book has many examples using Java, XML, and JSON, you don't have to be an expert in these technologies to benefit from this book. If you've got a basic understanding of programming, you'll be able to read the examples and implement them using the technology of your choice.

Experience with SOA, or with governance, is helpful but isn't required for this book.

Roadmap

This book is divided into three parts:

- In the first part of the book, you'll get an introduction to SOA concepts and governance tools, as well as the environment and policies that we're going to discuss.
- In the second part, we look at the policies you can use during the development phase.
- In the last part of the book, we focus on how to work with SOA governance when your services are deployed and running.

The first part consists of the following chapters:

- Chapter 1 starts with an introduction to SOA Governance. It includes a simple explanation of SOA and an explanation of governance. In this chapter you'll see why SOA Governance is important and what problems SOA governance solves. This chapter also describes how open source tools can help you get started with SOA governance.
- Chapter 2 shows you how to set up a complete SOA governance environment where you can experiment with the examples from this book. This chapter also includes an example of the basic architecture that we'll use throughout this book for REST and WS-*-based services.
- Chapter 3 presents a scenario that we'll use throughout the book—a fictional company that provides a number of applications and services to its customers. This company faces a number of problems that we'll use as input to define a set of policies. In later chapters you'll see how to use various open source tools to comply with these policies.

The second part contains the following chapters:

- Chapter 4 looks at the policies related to service design and documentation. This chapter will show how you can make your services self-documenting and how to correctly version your services.
- Chapter 5 stresses the importance of taking security into account during the design phase of a project. This chapter explains how tools can help you implement security-related policies such as centralizing authentication and authorization.
- Chapter 6 discusses how testing and SOA Governance work together. You'll see how you can test all the layers from a service using different tools and technologies. You'll also see how you can create a service that can easily run in the cloud. For this last example, we'll use Amazon as the cloud provider.

The last part consists of the following chapters:

- Chapter 7 shows how you can use the Bamos runtime governance environment to monitor your services in real time. It provides a number of examples on how you can visualize key metrics of your service landscape.

- Chapter 8 looks at how a service and a policy both have a lifecycle. You'll be introduced to a standard lifecycle you can use for services and for policies. This chapter also shows how the WSO2 registry can help you keep track of all the services and policies used in your organization or department.
- Chapter 9 discusses how you can integrate the tools and technologies shown in this book with your existing components and services. It includes examples to get you started in a number of languages and also shows you how to integrate with ESBs and BPM engines.

The appendix contains installation instructions for the tools used throughout the book. If you work through chapter 2, you'll see references to the appendix on how to install specific components.

Code conventions and downloads

All the code in the examples used in this book is presented in a `monospaced font like this`. This code, except for the code in chapter 9, is written in Java. Even though Java is used for the code samples, all the concepts that are explained also apply to other languages. For longer lines of code, a wrapping character may be used to keep the code technically correct while conforming to the limitations of a printed page.

Annotations accompany many of the code listings and numbered cueballs are used if longer explanations are needed. Longer listings of code examples appear under clear listing headers; shorter listings appear between lines of text.

The source code for all of the examples in the book is available for download from the publisher's website at www.manning.com/SOAGovernanceinAction. You can also download the latest sources from the Google code project. How to get the latest code is explained in the appendix.

Software and hardware requirements

The examples in this book use various tools and libraries. Each chapter explains which specific tool is used to implement a policy or show a concept. The appendix explains all the tools that you will need and how to install them. The easiest way to play around and experiment with the examples in this book is by configuring an Eclipse installation. The appendix also explains how to install and configure Eclipse to work with the examples from this book.

Author Online

Purchase of *SOA Governance in Action* includes free access to a private web forum run by Manning Publications where you can make comments about the book, ask technical questions, and receive help from the author and from other users. To access the forum and subscribe to it, point your web browser to www.manning.com/SOAGovernancein Action. This page provides information on how to get on the forum once you're registered, what kind of help is available, and the rules of conduct on the forum.

Manning's commitment to our readers is to provide a venue where a meaningful dialog between individual readers and between readers and the author can take place. It's not a commitment to any specific amount of participation on the part of the author, whose contribution to the AO remains voluntary (and unpaid). We suggest you try ask the author some challenging questions lest his interest stray!

The Author Online forum and the archives of previous discussions will be accessible from the publisher's website as long as the book is in print.

about the cover illustration

The figure on the cover of *SOA Governance in Action* is captioned "A Fisherman." The illustration is taken from a 19th-century edition of Sylvain Maréchal's four-volume compendium of regional dress customs published in France. Each illustration is finely drawn and colored by hand. The rich variety of Maréchal's collection reminds us vividly of how culturally apart the world's towns and regions were just 200 years ago. Isolated from each other, people spoke different dialects and languages. On the streets or in the countryside, it was easy to identify where they lived and what their trade or station in life was just by their dress.

Dress codes have changed since then and the diversity by region, so rich at the time, has faded away. It is now hard to tell apart the inhabitants of different continents, let alone different towns or regions. Perhaps we have traded cultural diversity for a more varied personal life—certainly for a more varied and fast-paced technological life.

At a time when it is hard to tell one computer book from another, Manning celebrates the inventiveness and initiative of the computer business with book covers based on the rich diversity of regional life of two centuries ago, brought back to life by Maréchal's pictures.

Part 1

Introduction

In the first part of this book I'll talk about the theory behind SOA governance and help you set up an environment you can use to play around and experiment with the concepts explained in this book. I'll explain what SOA governance is by looking at the following subjects:

- What is SOA and what is governance?
- What are the advantages and disadvantages of SOA governance?
- How can tools and open source help in applying SOA governance?

After this introduction we'll take a look at how you can set up an environment that you can use to experiment with. This environment contains all the tools you need for a minimal SOA governance solution. I'll also show you, based on a complete case study, how the various tools and components work together.

The last subject in this first part deals with the case study that we'll work with throughout the book. First, I'll introduce an organization with multiple departments that provides a number of applications to its customers. Based on this case study, we'll arrive at a set of policies that are important for this organization. In the rest of the book I'll show you how you can use various tools and techniques to implement services that comply with these policies.

Introducing
SOA governance

This chapter covers

- The core concepts of SOA governance
- Why SOA governance is important
- What roles tooling and open source play in SOA governance
- How SOA governance can be applied on the organization level

Service-oriented architecture, or SOA, governance involves the process of creating a set of guidelines with which your services need to comply. When you apply good SOA governance practices, you can create high-quality services that can be easily used by your consumers and that behave exactly as expected. With SOA governance it's easier to create new services, upgrade existing ones, and monitor the customer and business use of your services.

When people first hear about SOA governance, they often think of large organizations, heavy processes, and lots of paperwork that pretty much prevents you, as a developer, from getting any work done. If you've read any of the books that have *SOA governance* in the title, this view will be somewhat confirmed. SOA governance, especially the *governance* part, sounds heavy and restrictive, and this can quickly scare people. But don't worry; as you'll see in this book, applying SOA governance principles is easy and not so different from the normal way you design or monitor the services you've created.

Governance isn't something exclusive to IT, as you'll see in this chapter. It's applied throughout the industry. Let me give you an example of what happens in the aviation industry. In this industry governance is the most important way to make sure that airplanes are safe and don't drop out of the sky on a regular basis. In the aviation industry everything from construction, to maintenance, to flight monitoring happens under the strictest regulations. Every screw and bolt needs to be accounted for, and even the smallest component of the plane is validated and exhaustively tested before it can be used. For this the industry uses a strict set of governance guidelines to control and validate that the aircraft is constructed in a safe and controllable manner using materials they know the exact properties of. The services and applications you're developing most likely won't cause airplane crashes or nuclear explosions, but having a good set of guidelines, or *policies* as I'll call them, is important to make sure your services comply with the guidelines defined by your organization and behave as you expect.

When you look at the organizational part of SOA governance, you have to deal with various administrative processes and follow regulations, and all this doesn't have much to do with actual software development. But this is only one part—and an important one—of SOA governance. During this phase the policies will be defined that you as a software developer will have to follow. Many people think that you only need SOA governance when you have heavy, traditional, SOAP-based architectures, where you follow the various web service standards (I'll call these WS-*). This isn't the case; regardless of the technology you use for creating your SOA, be it REST-based or WS-* based, you need some sort of governance to assure that all your services follow the same security, quality, and performance requirements mandated by your organization.

In this first chapter we'll dive directly into the details of SOA governance. I'll explain why SOA governance is important and what the benefits are when you have SOA governance in place, and I'll give an overview of how you can deal with SOA governance in a practical and pragmatic manner. In the following chapters I'll show you how to start using it.

1.1 What is SOA governance?

To understand what SOA governance is, you first have to look a bit deeper at what SOA is and what governance is. We'll start with the definition of SOA.

1.1.1 Definition of service-oriented architecture

Let's start by looking at what Wikipedia has to say about this. Although not an authority on the subject of SOA, it gives a good idea of what a lot of people think about when talking about SOA.

> DEFINITION "Service-oriented architecture (SOA) is a flexible set of design principles used during the phases of systems development and integration in computing. A system based on a SOA architecture will provide a loosely-

coupled suite of services that can be used within multiple separate systems from several business domains."

—Wikipedia: http://en.wikipedia.org/wiki/Service-oriented_architecture

What you see in this quote is that it focuses on only the technical aspect of SOA; it talks about service design principles, systems development, and integration. Although this is an important part of SOA, there's more to it. When we talk about SOA we should look at it from a couple of different angles (including the technical angle). To really define SOA we should look at more than just the technical aspect. When I talk about SOA, I include the following different views:

- *Business view*—This view focuses on the value and advantages SOA offers for the business. This is an important view because ultimately you adopt a SOA architecture to improve the way you do business. From this perspective it's important to be able to quickly create new products, adapt to changes in the market, reduce costs, and improve the return on investment (ROI).
- *IT view*—This view shows how SOA can help IT quickly adapt to changes. Using SOA, the IT department can save costs by reusing services and can better determine who needs to be billed for the usage. By correctly applying SOA, IT can optimize the way it provides services to the business.
- *Technical view*—The final view is the one also referenced in the Wikipedia quote. The services provided to the business need to be designed following a set

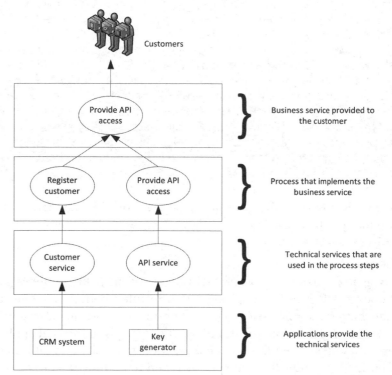

Figure 1.1
The various views of SOA combine to provide a product to a customer.

of SOA best practices. There needs to be a solid technical architecture from which services can be provided, and standards need to be defined and followed.

In figure 1.1, you see a simple use case where an organization wants to make it easy for its customers to request access to a specific service for which they need an API key.

You can compare this with the process you have to go through to get an API key for the services Google provides. The business point of view here is that the business wants to provide this functionality to its users to get as many users as possible. More users means more custom mashups, and in the case of Google, ultimately more advertisement revenue. From the IT point of view, the department wants to provide a simple set of reusable services, so that the next time the business wants to make some small changes or to provide another product to their customers, they can do so as quickly and efficiently as possible. And finally, from a technical viewpoint, for this scenario you need to provide the actual implementation of the services provided. And you want to do this following best practices and standards.

SOA != WS-* + SOAP + UDDI + WSDLs

As you've probably read from the table of contents or the introduction to this chapter, when I talk about SOA or services in general in this book, I don't necessarily mean the traditional web services stack. Even though SOA is often equated with using the standards-based WS-* stack, this is only one possible solution. When you look at what's currently deployed in the enterprise, you mostly see the traditional WS-* approach. In the Web 2.0 space, to give it a name, you see the opposite. When web services first became popular, you saw a rise of public APIs based on SOAP, WSDLs, and XML. The last couple of years, though (especially in the public space), these types of services have pretty much all disappeared or have been replaced with REST-based services. A similar trend is going on in the enterprise space. It's not as drastic as on the internet, but in the enterprise the value of a REST architecture has been accepted. We're now slowly moving to a situation where the best solution is used for a problem. This doesn't mean the WS-* stack is going anywhere soon. What you'll see is these two architectural types running side by side. In this book we'll look at both WS-* and REST and show how governance can be applied to these kinds of services.

Before looking a bit deeper at the governance part, I'll quickly summarize what the advantages are that can be gained by correctly applying SOA. The following list shows some of the advantages SOA offers.

ADVANTAGES OF SOA

- *Business agility/reduced time to market*—This is one of the main advantages a company hopes to achieve when applying SOA principles. With more agility a company can better respond to changes in the market and quickly launch new products and services. Note that this doesn't only apply to internal applications and services; with all the REST and cloud services available today, it's much easier for businesses to quickly create products and reuse functionality.

- *Reduced costs*—This is one of the other main business reasons. When everything was going well, for instance, during the dot-com boom, money wasn't that hot an issue. Technology companies and IT departments received all the funding they wanted, whether the business, or the venture capitalists, really knew what to expect. With SOA, businesses want to reduce costs by reuse, standards-based development, and a clear view of what services are available and the functionality they provide.

- *Improved reuse of services*—If the services are better defined, and a clear inventory of the services is kept, it's much easier to start reusing existing services. This is once again an example of where SOA is not just about internal services but also about reusing existing services on the web. In this last category you can think about the cloud-based services provided by Amazon, Microsoft's Azure platform, and Salesforce. A nice overview of available services can be found at http://www.programmableweb.com/.

- *Improved software quality*—A SOA contains a set of defined standards and best practices. It tells you how to build services, what to do, and what not to do. This will lead to a higher quality of software. Another advantage is that because you're reusing existing services you don't have to reinvent the wheel every time, assuming the service you're reusing is being well maintained.

- *Better interoperability*—Whether you're building a REST-based service or a WS-* based service, in both cases you have a well-defined contract, based on standards to help you in the interoperability area.

Now that we've looked a bit at what SOA is, let's look at the governance part of the concept.

1.1.2 *Introducing governance*

Most people have probably heard the term *governance* in one way or the other. Usually when people talk about governance they mean corporate governance. Corporate governance defines a set of rules, laws, policies, and regulations that affect how a corporation should be run. Corporate governance should make sure that corporations are run correctly, efficiently, and responsibly. Well-executed corporate governance makes sure that all the stakeholders in a corporation are represented properly.

CORPORATE GOVERNANCE

When you look back at the last couple of years, you've seen a lot of things go wrong in this area. The crisis in the financial market, various stock market scandals, and large corporations going bankrupt are all examples. This, however, doesn't mean corporate governance has failed; what this means is that even though you can define all the processes, regulations, and laws, you still need some way to enforce and control the policies in place.

IT GOVERNANCE

Another area where governance has become more important the last decade or so is in the area of IT governance. During the big dot-com bubble and the Y2K problems, IT

The Enron scandal

One of the main reasons governance has become an important part of how a business operates is because of the scandals at the beginning of the last decade. The most prominent was the Enron scandal. Enron, which was an energy corporation from Houston, at its peak had a value of $111 billion; a year later it filed for bankruptcy. In the nineties the energy market in California was deregulated, and Enron quickly became one of the largest energy companies in the United States. But in 2001 investigations were initiated to look into the financial position of Enron, and all kinds of fraudulent practices were discovered. For instance, Enron stored its debts in foreign accounts and used its political influence to raise the price of energy. To makes matters even worse, high-ranking Enron executives sold most of their stock when the shares were at $90, the highest the shares reached. They did this because they knew Enron was accruing massive losses. On the other hand, the public was encouraged to buy Enron stock, which within a few months dropped to 30 cents per share. The Enron executives were charged with bank fraud, securities fraud, wire fraud, money laundering, conspiracy, and insider trading. As a result of the Enron scandal, the federal government passed the Sarbanes-Oxley act (SOX for short), which forces companies to follow a set of policies with regard to reporting information to their investors and mandates that companies have strict internal financial control mechanisms in place.

spending went through the roof. It was hard for the business to see where the money was going and what IT was doing. The goal of IT governance is to minimize the risks of IT projects and make sure that IT provides actual business value. If you consider that, depending on who you believe, almost two-thirds of all IT projects fail, you'll understand the need for a good governance body. A more reasonable percentage was given by Standish Group International and is shown in figure 1.2.

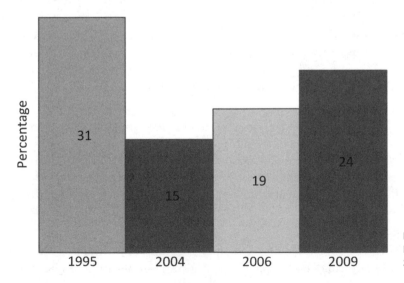

Figure 1.2
Failed projects in 1995, 2004, 2006, and 2009

IT project failures

In the previous sidebar I used Enron as an example of why governance within a company is needed. IT projects also have a tendency to go seriously wrong if there isn't a good governance or control mechanism in place. One of the most talked-about examples is the Denver International Airport's automated baggage system. This baggage system, created for the new airport, was designed to route all the passenger's bags to and from aircraft without human intervention. Even though this system was eventually completed ($55 million over budget) it didn't work. The carts that were used to automatically transfer the bags couldn't cope with sharp corners, sensors lost track of where bags were in the system, and more problems were present in the system. All this caused the Denver airport to open 16 months late so that the system could be fixed and added a total of $560 million to the cost of the airport. After a couple of years, though, the system was abandoned completely. Another example is the automated fulfillment system developed for Sainsbury's, a British supermarket. Sainsbury's wanted a new system for its main distribution center. This barcode-based system was designed to save a huge amount of money and increase efficiency because a lot of human tasks could be automated. In the end though, the system, installed in 2003, failed because of apparent barcode-reading errors. After two years of bug fixing, Sainsbury's wrote that the system worked as intended. In 2007, however, the complete system was scrapped. Total write off: £150 million.

If you ever need to set up IT governance, there are a number of frameworks that can guide you. I've listed a few of them in table 1.1 and provided links to additional information.

Table 1.1 IT governance frameworks

Name	Description
ITIL	The Information Technology Infrastructure Library defines a set of best practices and concepts you can use to set up the IT governance processes within your organization. For instance, it defines best practices for security management, ICT infrastructure management, software asset management, and much more. More information can be found on the official ITIL website: http://www.itil-officialsite.com/home/home.asp.
CMM	The Capability Maturity Model defines the level of maturity an organization is on with regard to software development. It defines five levels, where on level one (called *initial*) software development is done without any process and control and on level five (called *optimizing*) the software development process is already mature and only small parts can be optimized. Although it's not specifically an IT governance framework, you can use CMM to measure the maturity of your current governance-related processes and best practices. Information on CMM can be found at http://www.sei.cmu.edu/cmmi/start/.
COBIT	Control Objectives for Information and Related Technology is a framework that can help you set up IT governance for your organization. It provides tools, models, and methodologies for this. More information on COBIT can be found at the official COBIT website: http://www.isaca.org/Knowledge-Center/COBIT/Pages/Overview.aspx.

What you see in both corporate governance and IT governance is that governance will fail if not all the stakeholders are involved with the critical decision making. That's the main reason why scandals such as Enron happen and why so many IT projects go wrong.

1.1.3 Defining SOA governance

The goal of applying governance to SOA is to get the most out of your SOA. You do this by listening to the stakeholders and, based on that information, defining a number of policies.

This requires taking the following steps:

1 Define the policies you want to apply.
2 Apply these policies during design time.
3 Monitor and enforce the policies during runtime.

It's important to know that SOA governance should be applied as an iterative approach. When you've executed these steps, you aren't finished. Based on the information you learn from step 3 and other inputs, you might want to adjust the policies that you've defined.

Let's look a bit closer at the first item on the list.

DEFINE THE POLICIES YOU WANT TO APPLY

This step is mostly an organizational step where you get all the stakeholders together (for instance, in a SOA governance board) and, based on the strategy and goals of the company, coordinate and control the various SOA efforts. The organizational part of SOA, which is the subject here, is an important part of SOA governance. If there's no backing from your stakeholders, it's hard to apply SOA governance effectively and define the correct policies to implement and enforce. This means that besides the technical aspect of applying the policies you define, you also need to take into account the roles the process and the people play in regard to SOA governance. These concepts are sometimes called the three Ps: people, processes, and policies.

- *People*—To effectively apply SOA governance you need to know who the business owners of your services are. Who is using your services, why are your services being used, and who is technically responsible for keeping your services up and running?
- *Processes*—What processes are in place to define your policies? Do you have life-cycle processes in place for your services? What business processes depend on your services? Is there a process in place to determine whether your services implement the defined policies?
- *Policies*—What policies are defined for your service, and how are they applied during design and runtime?

A number of books have been written on these specific topics that dive into the details of the process and people parts of SOA governance. This book focuses on the practical approach of SOA governance. I do look at the lifecycle of a service and the lifecycle of a policy, but I won't dive into the details of the processes and people aspects.

When the policies have been defined, you can look at how you apply those during design time. For instance, let's assume your organization has defined the following policy regarding the documentation of your services:

"All the services that are provided to external clients must have documentation explaining all the service operations. This documentation must explain what the operation does, must explain all the arguments the operation takes, and must describe the results of the operation. Furthermore, if there's a logical sequence in which operations need to be called, this flow should be described as well."

What's a policy?

In this book I'll often talk about policies. When I talk about a policy, I mean a policy as defined by OASIS in its SOA Reference Model (you can find more on this model here: http://www.oasis-open.org/committees/tc_home.php?wg_abbrev=soa-rm). You can read the complete definition if you follow this link, but I'll summarize the most important parts here. A policy consists of three parts: the policy assertion, the policy owner, and policy enforcement. The assertion of a policy could be, for instance, "All the messages are encrypted." This assertion can be measured; it's either true or false. The second part of a policy is its owner. In the previous example, a service consumer can make this assertion and enforce it independent of the provider. Finally, a policy may be enforced; this can be done technically, but it can also be done through reviews.

In the second section of the book I'll elaborate on specific policies regarding documentation, but for now this small summary will suffice.

APPLY THESE POLICIES DURING DESIGN TIME

During design time you have to take these policies into account and provide an adequate design. Let's look back at the aviation example from the introduction to this chapter. Design-time policies also apply to the aviation industry. When an airplane is being designed, it has to comply with all different kinds of government legislation and safety protocols. For instance, it must have multiple backups for the primary system, it should emit only so much CO^2, and it must be able to land on just two engines.

Let's assume you're working at the IT department of your hometown and you're asked to create a service that allows the clients to retrieve a list of all the provided building permits for a specific area. Because this is a public service you decide to use a REST-based service for this (the technical type of service to provide in a specific scenario could also be a specific policy). Now you need to make sure you can fill in the requirements of the policy for this service. An example of the supplied documentation could be the following (which could be provided on the city's website as a simple HTML document):

Name: City of Seaford: Building Permits service.
Description: This document describes the operations provided by the City of Seaford to its residents. This service can be used to retrieve information about the currently approved building permits for a specific region within the city limits.

```
URI: {serviceURI}/permits?postalCode=?{postalCode}&range={range}
Method: GET
Example: http://api.seaford.org/services/public/permits?postalCode=90210
       ➥ &range=300
Description: This URI can be used to find a set of permits that match the
       provided search criteria.
Arguments: {postalCode} the postal code that serves as the center of the
       search region. If no postal code, or a postal code outside the city, is
       provided, this search will yield no results. {range} the range in yards
       to search for. If a negative range is used no results will be returned.
       If no range is provided, the search will default to a one-mile radius.
Result: The result of this operation will be a list of permit resources. The
       media type of this resource is application/vnd.seaford.org.permit+xml.
Links: In the returned list of permits you'll find a number of links to
       resources. These possible links are described below.
Self: Points to the permit resource itself. This resource is of the type
       application/vnd.seaford.org.permit+xml.
Location: Points to the exact location of this permit. This resource is of
       the type application/vnd.seaford.org.location+xml.
Owner: Points to the owner of the permit. This resource is of the type
       application/vnd.seaford.org.permit.owner+xml.
Status: Shows the current status of this permit. This resource is of the type
       application/vnd.seaford.org.permit.status+xml.
```

If you had decided to do this service as a WS-* based service, you would have annotated the WSDL with the correct information on the provided operations. You can find more on this subject starting in chapter 4.

MONITOR AND ENFORCE THE POLICIES DURING RUNTIME

The third part of SOA governance deals with enforcing and checking the policies at runtime. If you just spend time defining policies but have no means of checking whether they're followed, it's little use defining the policies in the first place. For this you need a mechanism to check whether the policies you defined are followed. For an airplane, you want to measure the fuel consumption to see whether it's within defined parameters, to check whether the backup systems are functioning, and so on.

To make it clearer, we'll have a quick look at a simple security policy: "All calls to the publicly provided services should be made over a secure channel."

This is a simple security policy, and you'll probably know how to comply with this service. If you look back at the previous service we discussed, the service providing information on permits, you'll see that this service should comply with the policy you defined. At design time you don't have to worry about this policy, whether you're running securely or not; your service interface and implementation don't have to comply with this policy. This is a

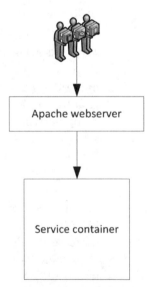

Figure 1.3　A basic implementation showing how you can make sure all the calls to the publicly provided service are done over a secure channel

Apache webserver

Service container

policy you have to enforce at runtime. Following this particular policy isn't that hard. If you can force all the calls to your service to be done over HTTPS, you'll comply with this policy. What you can see in figure 1.3 is that by using Apache as a filter, you can make sure all calls are done over HTTPS.

You could also configure Apache in such a way that calls made over normal HTTP are redirected to HTTPS, making sure you comply with the requirements set out by the policy.

In part 3 of the book we'll dive a lot deeper into the details of runtime policy enforcement, and I'll show you the tools you can use to check policies at runtime.

In this first section we've looked at SOA, at governance, and finally at what SOA governance entails. In the next section we'll look in more detail at why you need SOA governance and the advantages it offers.

1.2 How using SOA governance can help

As you've seen in the previous section, the goal of SOA governance is getting the most out of your SOA. I've already touched on some of the reasons why applying SOA governance is a good thing. In this section I'll give an overview of reasons why you need to apply SOA governance. I'll keep away from the business reasons such as total cost of ownership, time to market, and other buzzwords, and look at some of the most important reasons why SOA governance is needed. As a software developer or architect, you're faced with a lot of different challenges when designing and implementing services. Whether you're creating a public REST-based service that provides social networking functionality or you're building an internal WS-* based service to provide accounting information to another department, you have a number of challenges to deal with. The following sections give you an overview of a couple of these challenges and explain how applying SOA governance can help you in solving them.

1.2.1 Keeping track of how services are used

The first challenge we'll look at is when your service isn't used in the way you intended. When you create a service and other people start using this service, they expect a certain level of performance and reliability. When you designed this service you probably took this into account, but it's hard to plan for everything.

The service that couldn't keep up

A couple of years ago I worked on a large project for a public agency. For this project our team created a service that served as a web service facade to a document management system. During our tests everything was fine; during a customer's tests some small issues were found but nothing that we couldn't quickly fix. During production, though, we noticed that the usage pattern of our service wasn't as we expected. Instead of small documents being added, very large documents were added. Because of this change of usage, our service was becoming unusable, not just for this client but also for the other clients of our service.

On the other hand, it's possible that your team has created a great service, but no one is using it. How can SOA governance help in this scenario? It can help you do the following:

- *Define a lifecycle for your service*—Part of SOA governance is defining the lifecycle for your service. This means describing the phases a service goes through from inception to retirement. Included in the lifecycle are, among others, processes defined that describe how the availability of your service is communicated to the other departments or possible clients.
- *Apply and enforce runtime policies*—Without metrics it's impossible to determine if your service is being used as you imagined, how much it's being used, and whether you provide the performance your clients expected. When you apply policies at runtime, you can use those metrics to quickly find out if your service is struggling.

Another important part of developing services is making sure you have uniformity among your services. In the next section we'll look at how SOA governance can help you in maintaining a good level of quality when you're developing your services.

1.2.2   Keeping uniformity among services

If five services are written by five different teams in an organization, they should follow the same principles with regard to documentation, message design, interoperability, and security. SOA governance can help you in this area:

- *Define design-time policies*—If you define a set of design-time policies and create a reference architecture based on these policies, you provide the developers with the information they need to define consistent services.
- *Set up service review boards*—Just defining these policies isn't enough; you have to set up regular review sessions to make sure the services that are designed follow the principles defined through the policies.
- *Standardize messages and facilitate reuse*—An important tool to support SOA governance is a service repository. Within this repository you can, for instance, define the messages for your domain, define the canonical data model, and register the services that are available.
- *Enforce policies at runtime*—With runtime SOA governance you can enforce certain policies at runtime. You can make sure the correct security levels are used and add additional input validation.

Besides the advantages mentioned above, SOA governance introduces a number of common pitfalls.

1.3   Common pitfalls when introducing SOA governance

The following is a list of issues you'll see at a lot of companies that introduce SOA governance:

- *Introducing governance processes that are too complex*—If you've look at any of the other SOA governance books available, you've probably noticed that they all focus on the governance processes and on the organizational part of SOA governance. Even though those aspects are important, many SOA governance initiatives get buried under too many rules, governance boards, and regulations. It's often easier to start small, be successful, and work from that. The information in this book can help you with this.
- *Introducing governance processes that are too simple*—On the other hand, there are numerous organizations where there are almost no governance processes or governance boards present. They might have some standards and perform an occasional service review, but the organizations don't have a structure in place. Just as doing too much doesn't work, doing too little also doesn't work. You need some sort of structure and processes to at least handle the reviews and allow you to check whether the policies you set out are followed.
- *Placing too much reliance on tools*—If you listen to the big tool vendors, and even some open source ones, you can buy SOA governance. Just buy their SOA registry and you have a SOA governance solution. Unfortunately, that isn't the case. Tools can help immensely in applying SOA governance, but they'll always support the policies that have been designed, the reference architecture that has been defined, and the processes that have been put into place.

Quickly looking back at these sections, you can see that applying SOA governance provides a lot of advantages. It will help you create better software, allow you to better control how your services are used, and promote reuse and standardization. What you can also see is that SOA governance isn't the silver bullet and that there isn't a tool you can just buy to implement it. It takes effort, both on the technical and organization levels. In the next section we'll look at how to get started with SOA governance.

1.4 Requirements of an SOA governance solution

So far we've looked at what SOA governance is and why it's important. In this section we'll look at what a complete SOA governance solution should do and how this can help you apply SOA governance in practice.

A SOA governance solution should help you in

- Creating and maintaining a set of policies
- Applying these policies at design time
- Applying these policies at runtime

In figure 1.4 you can see an overview of the functionality a SOA governance solution should provide. Here stakeholders are defining policies that need to be stored and managed by the SOA governance solution. When the policies have been defined, they're consumed by various other parties. Developers need to be able to access the policies so they know what the services they're developing need to comply with. System admins access the runtime information from the SOA governance solution to see

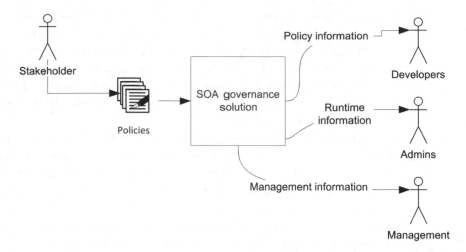

Figure 1.4   The information a SOA governance solution should provide to the various actors

if everything is running according to the policies that have been defined, and finally management wants to see if, for instance, orders are completed within the defined time.

Let's look a bit closer at these three points. We'll start by looking at how such a solution should help you in creating and maintaining your policies.

1.4.1   Creating and maintaining policies

The first thing a complete SOA governance solution should provide is a way to register your policies. Often, when I talk about policies, people automatically think about WS-Policy and automatic enforcement. This isn't a requirement when you talk about policies or when you want to register them. In section 1.1 I mentioned the OASIS SOA Reference Model, which defines a policy in the context of a SOA. Its definition mentions the following with regard to how SOAs should be written.

> **DEFINITION**   "Policy assertions SHOULD be written in a form that's understandable to, and processable by, the parties to whom the policy is directed. Policies MAY be automatically interpreted, depending on the purpose and applicability of the policy and how it might affect whether a particular service is used or not. A natural point of contact between service participants and policies associated with the service is in the service description. It would be natural for the service description to contain references to the policies associated with the service."
>
> —Reference Model for Service Oriented Architecture 1.0

What you can read in this quote is that policies should be written in a format that can be understood and processed by the parties to whom the policy is directed. In most cases the party to whom a policy is directed is a human party. It's directed at developers, at administrators, at information analysts, and so on.

You can use many different tools to register your policies. Commercial tools allow you to register your policy, but because we're talking about human consumers, a shared Word document or a Wiki is also a good, maybe even a better, option depending on the environment you're in. If you have only a small set of service consumers from within your own organization, a shared document or Wiki will probably be more accessible than a (complex) commercial or open source tool.

1.4.2 Applying policies at design time

Besides helping you define the policies, the solution should also help communicate these policies. You can see this in figure 1.4, where the designers and administrators need information regarding the policies and the available services. For the policies part you need the same functionality as you did in the previous section: a tool to register and view the policies. But you also need access to the list of services that are already defined. You need this not only to determine whether functionality requires a new service but also to determine the functionality you can reuse. For this you need a central place to store the contract of your service and its other metadata. In the most basic sense this can once again be a Word document or a wiki page describing the service, but usually a service repository is used for this purpose.

Repository versus registry

The words *SOA repository* and *SOA registry* are often used to mean the same thing— a place where you can register your services so that all the information regarding those services can be easily found and the services themselves can be easily located. When you really look at the definitions, though, there's a difference between a repository and a registry. A repository is the place where you register a service and its metadata and where you can also register other artifacts, whereas a registry helps in locating a specific service. In the beginning of web services and SOAP, people often also mentioned UDDI. A UDDI registry provided a phone book/yellow pages–like interface that you could use to look up a specific service, either at runtime or at design time. It didn't allow you to register other metadata or artifacts. That made it a registry, which often used a repository as its backend. Most of the current repositories started their lives as registries. They later gained the ability to register other metadata and artifacts, and that turned them into repositories. Today these terms are still used interchangeably.

Figure 1.5 shows an example of a SOA repository with a service registered. Note that in the screenshot you see that the product calls itself a registry. In this specific case there's a good reason. The WSO2 Governance Registry provides all the specific features of a registry: a governance API, a yellow pages–like interface, and artifact classification. It also presents itself as a repository, because you're pretty much free to register everything you want. The reason for calling this product a registry instead of a repository is that even though it provides a resource-oriented repository interface, it provides all the features and APIs to also serve as a full-fledged repository.

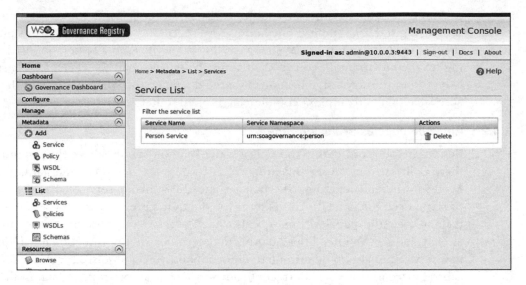

Figure 1.5 In this SOA repository you can register services, policies, and other structured and unstructured content.

The final item a SOA governance solution should help you with is applying these policies at runtime.

1.4.3 *Applying policies at runtime*

The final aspect a SOA governance solution should cover is how to apply and enforce the policies you've created at runtime. Not all the policies lend themselves to being enforced automatically but a number of them do. For instance, you can easily monitor whether the minimum response time is less than two seconds. Just register the time the service was called and the time the service responded. Calls that take longer than two seconds are logged and reported for further analysis.

Again, there are many different tools to help you with this. Active monitoring tools (gateways) monitor incoming and outgoing data and can check whether the data complies with your policies. Those tools can restrict or deny calls that don't follow your policies. Reactive tools monitor the events and the performance of your service and provide reports on their usage. These reports can then be analyzed to determine whether the service follows the policies defined for it. Into this latter category falls the WSO2 Business Activity Monitor, shown in figure 1.6.

In this section we've looked at the parts of a SOA governance solution. Now let's look at some simple policies you can apply to get started with SOA governance.

1.5 *Getting started with SOA governance*

As you've read so far, SOA governance encompasses a large area. You need to define a set of policies, you need a reference architecture that can serve as an example for the

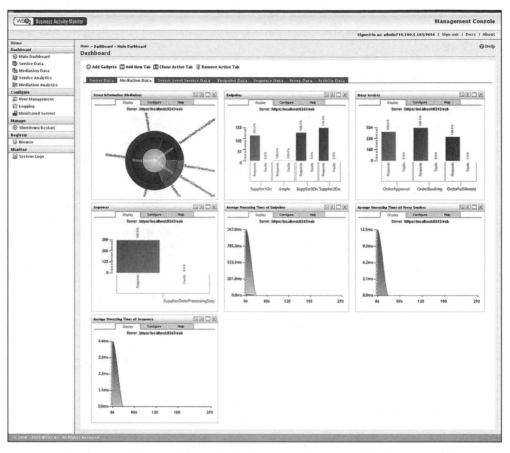

Figure 1.6   An example of reactive monitoring. With this information the IT department or business can determine whether the service complies with the policies set out for it.

services that will be created, and you need to set up all kinds of control mechanisms to make sure the policies you've set out are followed. All this can be a bit overwhelming and might make it seem impossible to get started with SOA governance.

To get a feeling for SOA governance and create awareness within your organization, you can start with some simple policies within your own department and let the results speak for themselves. If you're successful within your department and can show results like better services, lower costs, and more predictability, other departments will follow suit.

So how do you begin? The first thing to do is define two or three simple policies, which you'll follow throughout the process of creating new services. A good starting point would be at least one policy you follow during design time and one policy you can enforce during runtime. This way you'll get experience with following and enforcing policies, and you'll quickly see the advantages of applying SOA governance.

Table 1.2 shows a number of good design-time policies to follow when you're just getting started. In the other parts of this book, we'll dive deeper into the details of these policies.

Table 1.2 Basic design-time policies to get started with

Name	Description
No duplicate services	This might seem like a no-brainer, but it's a good policy to start with. Even within a department much functionality is duplicated between services. Formalizing this in a policy and checking this policy before you start work on a new service can save you a lot of duplicate work.
Technology standardization	This policy can sound something like this: "All services provided to the general public, for example, over the internet, must follow the REST paradigm. Services offered exclusively for B2B purposes must use a WS-* architecture." Again, this is a basic policy but one that will prevent designers of projects from doing what they think is best without looking at the bigger picture.
Validate message content	This policy can help you in creating a uniform service landscape. When you look deeper at this policy you'll probably also need to define the type of validation that's required. This could, for instance, mean that all the message formats of this service should be XML accompanied by a schema. But this could also imply that all the JSON messages that are sent can be validated using a JSON schema.

Let's also look at a couple of simple runtime policies that can form a good starting point for SOA governance; see table 1.3.

Table 1.3 Basic runtime policies to get started with

Name	Description
Services should be available from 9 a.m. to 5 p.m.	With the tools used in this book you can check whether your service is available. This is one of the easiest runtime policies to start with. Set up the tools, and you'll get a nice graphic of when your service was available and when it was not.
Services calls should be made over a secure channel.	Another basic one to get started. If one of your policies is that all communications should be over a secure channel, you can easily enforce this with Apache, for example.
Services should be self-describing.	When a service is deployed it should be self-describing. You shouldn't need a big book describing the service and how to interact with it. For REST there's an example in section 1.1.

The next section provides an overview of the policies discussed in this book.

1.6 *Getting an overview of the available policies*

For this book I divided the policies into three main categories:

- *Design and documentation policies*—These policies define certain rules you must follow when you're designing and implementing your services.

- *Security policies*—Security is always a hot topic. Security policies deal with how a service should be accessed, audited, and secured.
- *Testing and performance policies*—This category includes policies that require execution of a specific operation within a certain time.

Let's look a bit closer at these categories.

1.6.1 Design and documentation policies

Table 1.4 shows an overview of the policies discussed in this book that fall into the design and documentation category.

Table 1.4   Design and documentation policies

Name	Policy description
Create self-documenting services.	All services should be self-documenting. You should be able to use a service without having to check a manual.
Reuse existing message standards.	If there's a standard or de facto model that's used within your organization or business domain, you should use that model in your services.
Design for reusability.	Before starting work on a new service, you must make sure that there isn't a service already available that provides the same functionality or that can be easily modified to provide the required functionality.
Support multiple versions of services.	It must be possible to support multiple versions of the same service next to each other. Changes in versions should affect the consumer as little as possible.

In part 2 of this book we'll look at how you can take these policies into account during design time and how you monitor compliance at runtime.

1.6.2 Security policies

Table 1.5 gives an overview of the security-related policies covered in this book.

Table 1.5   Security policies

Name	Policy description
Encrypt a communications channel for sensitive data.	All communication with your service must be done over a secure channel.
Validate message integrity and non-repudiation.	You must make sure you can guarantee a message's integrity and origin of data.
Use a centralized identity system for authentication.	When a consumer needs to authenticate for your services, they should only have to authenticate one time, not separately for each service.
Use a centralized identity system for authorization.	Authorization is something all services need. To avoid having to implement this for each service separately you should use a centralized identity system.

The last set of policies we'll look at are those defined for the testing and performance category.

1.6.3   *Testing and performance policies*

Table 1.6 gives a short description of the policies in this category discussed in this book.

Table 1.6   Testing and performance policies

Name	Policy description
Process messages within 10 ms.	A service should always respond within a minimum amount of time.
Monitor services in real time.	If you want to monitor your services effectively, you need to be able to measure the performance in real time.
Provide a flexible view for how services are used.	Depending on the requirements from the analysts, you need to be able to show different views of how your services are used.
Run services in the cloud.	All the services that are developed must be horizontally scalable to avoid a large investment in hardware and allow linear growth
Enforce code quality and test coverage.	All of your services must comply with a specific percentage of code coverage and have a predefined minimal level of quality.

I'll show you throughout the following chapters how to implement these policies and how you can set up and configure a runtime environment to monitor and check whether your services comply with these policies. For now, let's continue with this introduction and dive somewhat deeper in what open source can offer in this area.

1.7   *SOA governance and open source*

In this book I focus on using open source tools to help you apply SOA governance. In this section we'll look a bit deeper at the open source developments in the SOA governance area and how these tools can help in creating your own open source–based SOA governance solution. Before we look at specific developments in SOA governance, we'll first have a quick look at open source itself.

1.7.1   *Where is open source at the moment?*

I don't need to explain to the readers of this book what open source is, but for completeness let's look at the official definition from the Open Source Initiative (OSI). OSI defines *open source* using the following criteria:

- *Free redistribution*—This criterion is what most people associate with open source. You're free to redistribute the open source product either in its entirety or as an aggregate of another product.
- *Source code*—Together with the free redistribution criterion, this is the other one most people think about when talking about open source. This criterion states that you must be able to access the source code of the product.

- *Derived works*—The license attached to the software product must also allow you to make derived works or modifications to the original from it.
- *Integrity of the author's source code*—The license may require that any derived works use a different name and version number from the original. For example, this is the case for projects from the Apache Software Foundation.
- *No discrimination against persons or groups*—You can't say that only left-handed people with red hair can use your software. Everybody can use your software.
- *No discrimination against fields of endeavor*—This is pretty much the same as the previous criterion. You can't specify in your license that your software can only be used by financial institutions, for example. Regardless of the field of endeavor, anybody can use your software.
- *Distribution of license*—If a product is redistributed, the original license still applies.
- *License must not be specific to a product*—This criterion means that you can't say in your license that it may only be distributed as part of a specific software distribution. For instance, you can't say that your piece of software may only be distributed as part of Fedora.
- *License must not restrict other software*—The license can't put any restrictions on other software it's distributed with.
- *License must be technology neutral*—You require that your product only be used with a specific technology or on a specific platform.

If a piece of software fulfills these criteria, it can be classified as open source. The tools used in this book all follow these criteria.

If you look at open source these last couple of years you see that the types of open source projects have been slowly moving up the stack. Figure 1.7 shows a software stack for open source.

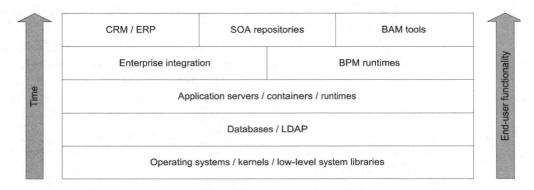

Figure 1.7 Open source software in its early days focused on offering technical functionality and low-level services. In recent years open source software has been offering products that also offer lots of business and end-user functionality.

In figure 1.7 you can see that in the beginning of its development, most open source software was low-level software such as operating systems and databases. In the last couple of decades open source has matured, and you can see this in the type of applications that can be found in the open source community. In the last couple of years a number of tools have appeared in the open source community that can help in applying SOA governance. In the following sections we'll look at these tools.

1.7.2 Open source tools

In this section we'll look at two different types of tools: the available open source SOA repositories and the BAM (Business Activity Monitoring) tools that have been made available by the open source community.

SOA REPOSITORIES

When you look at the open source SOA repositories, your choices at the moment are still a bit limited. There are various open source UDDI registries, but as I mentioned before, a registry isn't a repository. So what open source SOA repositories are available?

- *Mule Galaxy*—Mule Galaxy is a mature SOA registry brought to you by MuleSoft, the people who created the great open source ESB Mule. Mule Galaxy provides all the features a SOA repository requires. You can manage different kinds of artifacts and apply a lifecycle to these artifacts. Mule Galaxy also provides service discovery functionality, flexible reporting on services, and easy customization. If you're already using Mule as your ESB, using Mule Galaxy as a SOA repository is a good option. More information on Mule Galaxy can be found at http://www.mulesoft.org/galaxy.
- *WSO2 Governance Registry*—The SOA registry from WSO2 is also a standalone product with which you can manage different kinds of artifacts and apply a lifecycle to these artifacts. This is the registry used in the examples for this book. More information on this product can be found at the WSO2 website: http://wso2.com/products/governance-registry/. Besides a registry, WSO2 also offers a complete set of other products, for instance, a great ESB that integrates with this repository.
- *Petals Master*—Petals Master calls itself a complete SOA governance solution. It allows you to categorize your services and endpoints based on a UDDI registry. Just like the previous two registries, Petals Master allows you to add comments to your artifacts and share these with all the users of the registry. Besides the registry-oriented functionality, Petals Master allows you to manage your organization because it includes a UDDI-based identification system. More information on this solution can be found at the OW2 website: http://petalsmaster.ow2.org/.

For a list of commercial SOA repositories see the appendix. Besides the registries we've looked at here, for a complete SOA governance solution you also need some way to monitor and manage your runtime environment.

OPEN SOURCE BAM TOOLS

In section 1.4, I mentioned that for runtime monitoring you need to be able to monitor service actively (for example, through an XML gateway) and reactively (using some sort of BAM tool). For actively monitoring services there are many different options available, and this depends heavily on the architecture you use for your services. If you have an ESB-based architecture, your ESB will normally enforce these policies, and if you run inside a service container, this container will often provide this functionality.

So in this section let's focus a bit more on the BAM tools. Normally when you start looking for a certain piece of software in the open source community, you'll quickly find many different mature solutions. But this isn't the case for BAM tools. There are one or two tools, which I'll show you next, but the main issue with these tools is their inflexibility. The currently available BAM tools are bound to a specific technology stack, are limited in their reports, or cover only a specific framework. So what's out there?

- *WSO2 Business Activity Monitor*—I've already shown an example in this chapter of what this application looks like. This tool provides beautiful diagrams of usage stats, error reports, and business diagrams. The problem is that customizing the graphs or monitoring non-WSO2 servers is nigh impossible. This tool uses fixed reports, and if you have a WSO2-only landscape, this tool is a good way to go. More information can be found on the WSO2 website: http://wso2.com/products/business-activity-monitor/.

- *Esper*—Esper calls itself a complex event processor. It's great for handling, analyzing, and correlating events. Because a BAM tool needs to be able to correlate events and show the end user only useful data, this is a great feature. The issue, however, is that that's all Esper is. It doesn't provide a reporting environment with which you can monitor or view these correlated events. More information on Esper can be found at http://esper.codehaus.org/.

So within the open source community there isn't a great BAM tool that allows you to monitor (and analyze) events and show them in a customizable way to the end user. Luckily, though, all the various components that you need to build such a solution are available. In the following chapters I'll show how you can combine tools such as Esper and WSO2's gadget server to create an easy-to-use and flexible BAM tool. I'll also show how you can use this tool, whose code is also made available as open source (http://www.smartjava.org/bamos), to monitor your services so that you can easily check whether you comply with the specified runtime policies.

1.8   *Summary*

- SOA governance is all about defining the policies that are important for the various stakeholders within your organization, applying these policies during design time, and monitoring and enforcing these policies at runtime.

- SOA governance isn't scary. The goal of SOA governance isn't to set up a mammoth process you need to follow; the goal is to make sure your services are a certain level of quality and follow the policies set out by your company. If you follow the guidelines set out in this book, you'll see how easy it is to get started with SOA governance and get the advantages from applying SOA governance.

- SOA isn't just exposing services using a specific technology. If you want to get the most out of your SOA, you need to set the business goals first. The business goals should lead to the specific services that need to be developed, and when services are developed, reuse needs to be taken into account. With SOA governance you're presented with a set of tools and best practices that can help you in getting the most out of the services you've defined.

- SOA governance can be divided into two distinct areas: SOA governance during design time and SOA governance during runtime. The first focuses on making sure all the services are created and defined consistently and follow a set of predefined policies. The second makes sure that the policies you've defined, and those that can be monitored, are enforced during runtime.

- Tools can help you make sure policies are followed. In addition to many commercial offerings there are a number of mature open source tools that can help you apply SOA governance. This book offers a pragmatic approach using open source tools. There's no good open source BAM tool; this we'll create ourselves.

Setting up the SOA
governance environment

This chapter covers
- Basic architecture of the services
- Components of the SOA governance environment
- Setting up an Eclipse-based environment to use with the examples in this book
- Installing tools that make up your SOA governance environment
- Details of the REST and WS-* based architectures

In the previous chapter we looked at the theory behind SOA governance. You learned what it is and why it's needed and looked at the advantages it provides to an organization. We also looked a bit at how to apply this within your organization or department. In this chapter I'll show you how to set up your local environment so you can easily run the various examples from this book and get a feel for the tools and techniques explained in the latter chapters of the book. The example used in this chapter shows how to create a REST- and a WS-* based service that stores and retrieves information from a NoSQL database.

As you can see, the focus of this chapter is on getting all the various tools and components together and making sure you have an environment to run the examples in and to play around with. To make this experimentation easier, it's good to have an integrated development environment (IDE). There are many good IDEs, but I had to choose one. I've chosen to use Eclipse, because it provides a well-supported platform with good integration with Maven and SVN. If you want to use another IDE (for example, NetBeans or IntelliJ) you can do so. All the projects are Maven projects and available through SVN, and using those in your browser of choice shouldn't be that hard.

2.1   *Architecture of the SOA governance environment*

Let's start by looking at the complete overview of your SOA governance environment. In figure 2.1 you can see what the environment looks like.

You can see that you have three services; these services will register information in the SOA repository and use this same repository to look up resources. You can also see the Business Activity Monitoring (BAM) application. Your services will provide information such as load, number of calls, faults, and execution times to the BAM application. The BAM application can then visualize this information so that at runtime you can see whether your services are behaving as they should.

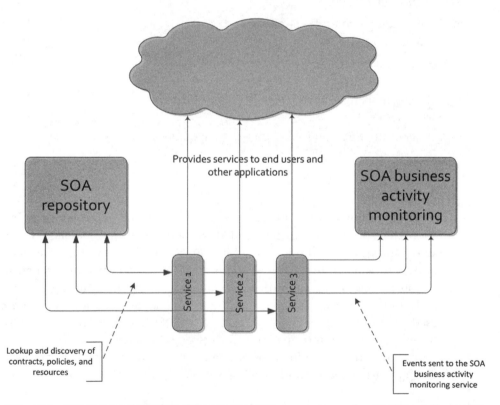

Figure 2.1   This high-level overview of the complete SOA governance environment shows the services providing information to the various tools in this environment.

2.1.1 Services architecture

Before you install the various tools, let's have a quick look at what the architecture of your services looks like; see figure 2.2.

Here you can see the basic architecture for the services you'll work with in this book. It's a straightforward architecture consisting of a logic layer for the business logic and a data layer that handles the communication with the data store. The service remoting layer is where you put your REST and WS-* functionality. The reason for this is that you want to reuse the functionality from the logic and database layers for both of these remoting technologies.

Before we dive into the installation instructions, let's have a quick look at the various technologies I've used to create these services. Note that these tools and frameworks are mostly a personal preference. There are many other great tools, frameworks, and languages that you can use to create the services explained in this book. We'll start at the bottom, the data layer.

DATA LAYER

As you can see from figure 2.2, the data layer is responsible for the lifecycle of the objects you work with. This layer handles the creation of new objects, handles updates to these objects, and allows you to find objects using specific criteria. As you probably know, there are many different tools and standards that can help with this, such as Hibernate, JDO, and JPA. To keep it simple we'll use NoSQL for the data layer. We'll use Apache Cassandra as the data store because one of the policies is that the service should be able to run in the cloud. To make communicating with Cassandra easier, we'll use the Hector client library.

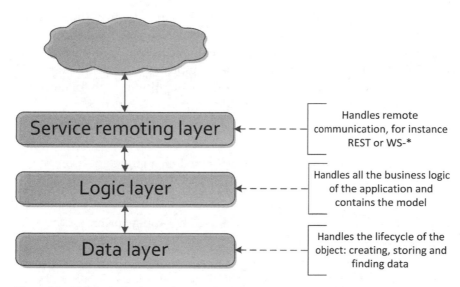

Figure 2.2   This is the basic architecture for the example services in this book. It's a basic three-layered architecture.

What's a NoSQL database?

When people think about databases they usually think about the traditional relational databases. These databases are great for storing data for transactional systems and provide extensive query possibilities using SQL. Besides this, they maintain data integrity and have many options to validate and enforce the relations between various tables. These advantages, however, come at a cost. When these databases grow very large, searching through indexes, enforcing relations, and such can have a significant impact on performance. Another issue is that you lose some flexibility when you choose a traditional relational database. You define the model (the tables) up front, and making changes to this model, for instance, letting the user add an extra column, isn't easily done.

With a NoSQL database you don't have the set of tables, relations, and foreign keys that you have with a relational database. Instead, you have a distributed multidimensional key/value store (there are other NoSQL types such as a document or graph base, but we'll focus on the key/value store here). Some of the larger internet sites (Twitter, Facebook, LinkedIn, Digg, Reddit) have run into the limitations, mostly regarding scalability, of a traditional database. For instance, both Digg and Reddit moved to Cassandra, which I'll use in the examples, in 2010. The main difference is that with a NoSQL approach you have to think about how you want to access your data, what kind of queries you're likely to make, and based on that information set up your NoSQL data store because you can't make arbitrary queries such as SQL provides. Later in this chapter I'll show how I used it for the examples in this chapter.

The next layer we'll look at is the logic layer.

LOGIC LAYER

The logic layer is where the business logic of the application is stored. This layer consists of the domain objects (which contain the data and the logic) and a thin service layer, which mainly serves as a façade to the domain objects and the data layer. In this book I follow a domain-driven design (DDD) approach as much as possible. For those of you new to DDD, it means that when you create software, you follow these two core principles (from www.domaindrivendesign.org):

- For most software projects, the primary focus should be on the domain and domain logic.
- Complex domain designs should be based on a model.

For more information on DDD you should check out Eric Evans's great book, *Domain-Driven Design: Tackling Complexity in the Heart of Software*. You'll implement this layer using POJOs and glue all the various parts together using Spring.

SERVICE REMOTING

The final layer is the service remoting layer. This layer handles the communication based on a REST or a WS-* architecture. This layer delegates all calls to the logic layer I talked about in the previous section. I mentioned before that many tools and libraries provide REST and WS-* functionality. You'll use the following libraries and tools:

- *REST approach*—For the REST approach you'll use the REST provided by CXF. CXF implements the JAX-RS (JSR-311) specification. With this support you can easily create and expose REST-based resources using plain Java and annotations. For the data part of REST you'll also use JSON in some examples. You'll use the json-lib library, which gives you direct control of your JSON output.
- *WS-* approach*—For the WS-* based services, you'll also use the CXF library. CXF is one of the best Java web service libraries and also provides support for various WS-* standards that are used throughout this book. As with REST, you'll create your services using annotations and plain Java.

Now that you have an idea of what the services look like, let's start installing the various tools and applications and setting up the Eclipse environment.

2.2 Setting up the Eclipse environment

In this section we'll check out the sources for the examples in this chapter, and you'll create a Java project based on these sources. Before you do this, though, you need to make sure the environment is configured correctly. You'll install the following components:

- *Eclipse IDE*—The IDE you'll use to test your applications.
- *SVN plug-in*—The sources are located in an SVN repository; with this plug-in you can easily retrieve them.
- *Maven plug-in*—All the examples are mavenized. This makes it easier to get the projects up and running and handles the dependencies.
- *Maven*—Just installing the plug-in isn't enough; you also need to install Maven itself.

Detailed instructions on how to install Java, Eclipse, the Eclipse plug-ins, and Maven can be found in the appendix. If you don't have a recent version of these tools installed, please look at this appendix for instructions and install them.

Now that you have your IDE set up and the plug-ins installed, the next step is to check out the examples from SVN. Because you installed the SVN plug-in in Eclipse, you can do all this directly from Eclipse. First, open the SVN Repository Exploring perspective and click the New Repository Location button (shown in figure 2.3).

In the pop-up that appears, you'll see an input field labeled URL. In that field enter `http://ossoagov.googlecode.com/svn/trunk` and click Finish. Because you'll

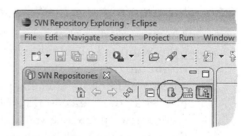

Figure 2.3   The New Repository Location button, which can be used to add a new SVN repository location

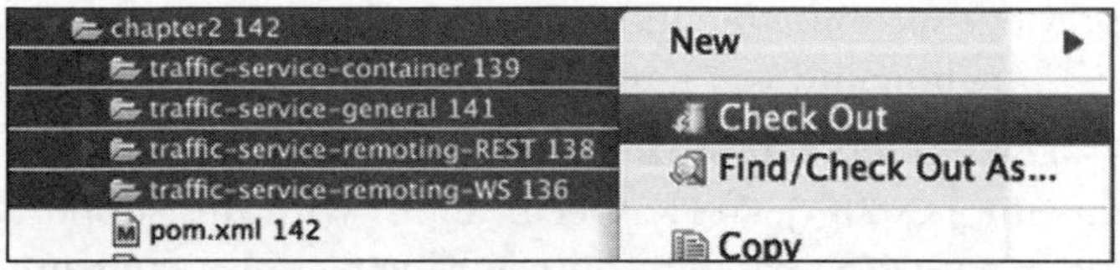

Figure 2.4
The services to check out for the examples in chapter 2

connect as anonymous, you don't need to enter any credentials. After you click Finish, you might get a question from Eclipse about whether to cut off part of the URL; select No. Eclipse will probably also ask you about whether you want to enable password recovery. If you want, you can do this, but it isn't necessary.

You'll now see the URL you've just entered in the SVN Repositories view. If you open this location by double-clicking it, you'll see a list of chapters. These folders contain all the examples from this book. Open the chapter2 folder and you'll see four projects (see figure 2.4). Select all these projects as well as the chapter2 project, right-click, and select Check Out.

This will download the code from the SVN repository and store it in your local workspace. Now open the Java perspective and you'll see these five projects in your workspace. All you need to do now is mavenize them. This will set up all the source folders and test folders and load all the required dependencies. To do this select all the five projects in the workspace, right-click them, and from the menu select Maven > Enable Dependency Management. Now wait a bit while Maven downloads all the dependencies, and when it's done you'll have four Java projects in your workspace. Sometimes Maven doesn't correctly update a project configuration after it has loaded the dependencies. If you have a project that doesn't correctly show its source folders, you can fix this by right-clicking this project and selecting Maven > Update Project Configuration.

In the following chapters I'll mention the name of the project(s) we're working with for a specific example. You can use the same process as you did here to get the sources and enable Maven for those projects.

So far we've discussed how to install Eclipse and Maven, add the SVN and the Maven (m2eclipse) plug-in to Eclipse, and retrieve and configure the projects for this chapter. In the next couple of sections we'll dive into the code and see some actual services, but before that let's look at the use case you'll implement in this chapter.

2.3 *Introducing the traffic avoidance example*

The use case describes a small fictional city with about 50,000 residents. This municipality wants to improve the way its residents can interact with the various departments within the city. I use this example, and expand on it in the later chapters, because it allows you to define a number of applications and services that you can use to show how SOA governance works and how you can implement it yourself. The goal of this section is to introduce you to the various tools, techniques, and architecture used throughout the book, which include:

- Creating a REST and a WS-* based service using a modern application architecture
- Using a NoSQL datastore in which to store your data

- Using soapUI to test the services

Now let's look at the use case.

The municipality of Seeport has decided it wants to reduce the number of traffic jams that occur on the highways during the morning and evening rush. They looked at many options but finally decided that the best approach was, not to create more roads, but to make sure fewer people were using the roads during the busiest hours of the day. To achieve this they decided to start a program that financially rewards drivers for avoiding the roads during peak driving times.

To accomplish this they'll supply all the participants with a small cell phone with custom software that sends its location and the car's license plate whenever the participant is driving. This information will be stored, and based on this information and the travel times, the participant will receive a small financial reward. There are cameras set up along the roads where traffic needs to be reduced, to prevent drivers from misusing the system by turning the device off.

Everybody who participates in this system will also receive a username and password for a web application where the routes they took since using the system can be viewed. The user information itself will be stored in a CRM system, which will periodically update the accounts in the traffic avoidance system.

Besides these functional requirements, the city has also defined a set of policies that need to be followed for building applications and services:

- *They need to be able to run in the cloud*—The city has defined that services must be scalable and should be able to run in a cloud-like environment. They don't want to invest heavily in hardware but do want to able to grow easily if the program is a success. This policy applies to this system because if the first tests with this system are successful, the city wants to expand this to more residents. Eventually all the residents should have this small gadget installed in their cars so they can be easily billed or compensated for driving at specific times and locations.
- *Machine-to-machine communications should be done using WS-**—The rationale is that a couple of key systems that they've bought for future use allow only WS-* type communication. For this scenario it means that you need to expose the account service to the CRM system using WS-*.
- *All internal services need to be registered with the SOA repository*—This policy mandates that all services be registered in the central SOA repository. This is done to avoid having duplicate services and increase the reuse of existing services. This means that you have to register the account service interface in the SOA repository.
- *They must be able to handle 5000 new GPS data points each minute*—The last policy is one you can only check at runtime. You need to be able to monitor the usage of the service to see if you fulfill this policy.

In figure 2.5 you can see a complete overview of this system and its components.

In this figure you can see that you have a basic logic and data layer. On top of the logic layer you have the two remoting technologies: REST and WS-*. You can also see

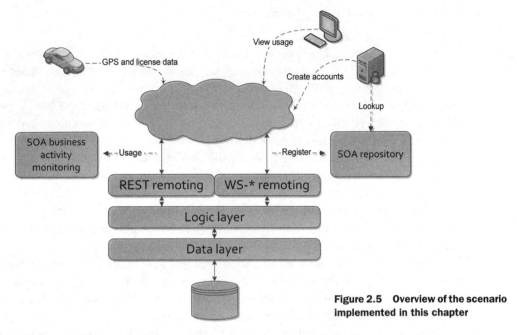

Figure 2.5 Overview of the scenario implemented in this chapter

that you've added a SOA repository where services are registered and a BAM monitoring application that will monitor specific events from your services. In the following chapters we'll look at how to implement the various parts of this scenario and connect everything together.

2.4   Configuring the general services and database

As you've seen in figure 2.5, the REST and WS-* layers are separate remoting layers on top of the logic layer. In this section we'll look at how this logic layer is set up and how the data for this example is stored and retrieved from the database. Section 2.3 explained that you want to create a service that can register and display car movements and that you want to be able to scale this service to not just this municipality but, in a later stage, even the whole country.

2.4.1   The data model used in this service

Let's start simply and look at the (simplified) domain model that you'll use for this example, shown in figure 2.6.

In figure 2.6 there are only a couple of domain objects. The main object is the Account entity. This entity contains

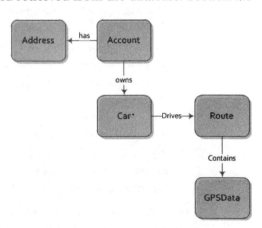

Figure 2.6 Domain model for the traffic avoidance system

all the personal data of the participants in this program. As you can see it contains the Address of this participant, and it contains a list of Cars this participant owns and has registered in this program. The Car entity itself keeps track of the Routes that have been driven with this Car. The Route itself contains information about the GPSData points that make up the Route. In code these entities are just plain old Java objects (POJOs). An example of the Car entity is shown in the following listing.

Listing 2.1   The Java code for the `Car` entity

```
public class Car {

    private String licenseplate;
    private String make;
    private String model;
    private List<Route> drivenRoutes;

     public Car(String licenseplate, String make, String model) {
        super();
        this.licenseplate = licenseplate;
        this.make = make;
        this.model = model;
    }

    {...} // getters and setters for the entity
}
```

In section 2.3, Introducing the traffic avoidance example, I mentioned a couple of policies that you need to follow. One of those particularly applies to the way you set up the data layer. You need to create an environment that can easily run in a cloud environment, and because you want to be able to scale effortlessly to a large number of users, you need to choose a data access pattern that suits those two requirements. For this example let's use a NoSQL approach using Cassandra.

2.4.2   *Setting up the data access layer*

Because this isn't a book about how to configure and design NoSQL data stores, I won't dive into those details here. For your NoSQL database you'll use Cassandra. Cassandra is a project from Apache that's used in many high-traffic websites and has features such as high scalability and fault tolerance. To be better able to understand the technologies and concepts used, I'll give you a quick overview of the basic concepts of Cassandra before showing you how it's used for your scenario. Before you start, though, you have to install Cassandra. Please look at the appendix for installation instructions. After installing Cassandra you need to set up the schema that's used by the applications in the book. This schema is provided in the src/test/resources folder of the traffic-service-general project. You can import this schema by using the cassandra-cli tool:

```
./cassandra-cli -p 9160 -h localhost -f
<PATH_TO_WORKSPACE>/traffic-service-general/src/test/resources/cassandra-
➥ schema.text
```

With this command you create the correct Cassandra configuration. An example of the commands used to create this schema is shown in the following listing.

Listing 2.2   Configuration used to create the Cassandra schema

```
create keyspace Keyspace1
    with strategy_options = [{replication_factor:1}]
    and placement_strategy = 'org.apache.cassandra.locator.SimpleStrategy';

use Keyspace1;

create column family Accounts
    with comparator = BytesType;
```

With this configuration in place, you can start Cassandra by using the shell script from the bin directory from the Cassandra installation. If you want to know more about how data is stored in Cassandra and what the differences are between a `Column`, a `SuperColumn`, a `ColumnFamily`, and a `SuperColumnFamily`, check out the excellent documentation at Cassandra's website: http://cassandra.apache.org. For now, it's enough to know the basics that are explained in table 2.1.

Table 2.1   Explanation of the various types of data you can store in Cassandra

Type	Description
`Column`	A `Column` in Cassandra is a single name/value pair. It stores the timestamp containing the last time it was modified. This is the basic `HashMap` idea. `{  Title: "Open source SOA Governance" }`

`SuperColumn`	A `SuperColumn` is also a name/value pair, but the values are an unlimited set of `Column`s.
	`{ Address:`
	`    { street: "52nd street",`
	`      city: "New York",`
	`      zip: "90210" }}`

To access and store data in Cassandra you use an open source library named *Hector*. Hector provides you with an easy-to-use API for storing and retrieving data from Cassandra. I won't go through all the different repositories created for this example, but look in the following listing at how to use these different technologies to store and retrieve the `Car` entity.

Listing 2.3   Using Hector and Cassandra to store and retrieve the `Car` entity

```
...
private static final String MODEL = "Model";                    Mutator used to ❶
private static final String MAKE = "Make";                      insert records
private static final String CARS = "Cars";

public void createCar(String licensePlate, String make, String model) {
    Mutator mutator = HFactory.createMutator(keyspace);         ◁─┘
```

```
    mutator.addInsertion(licensePlate, CARS
            ,HFactory.createStringColumn(MAKE, make));
    mutator.addInsertion(licensePlate, CARS
            ,HFactory.createStringColumn(MODEL, model));
    mutator.execute();
}

public Car getCarByLicensePlate(String licenseplate) {
    SliceQuery<String, String> query = HFactory.createSliceQuery(keyspace
            ,stringSerializer, stringSerializer);
    query.setColumnFamily(CARS)
            .setKey(licenseplate)
            .setColumnNames(MAKE, MODEL);
    QueryResult<ColumnSlice<String, String>> result = query.execute();
    Car foundCar = toCar(licenseplate, result.get());
    return foundCar;
}

private Car toCar(String licenseplate,
    ColumnSlice<String, String> result) {
    Car foundCar = new Car(licenseplate
            ,result.getColumnByName(MAKE).getValue()
            ,result.getColumnByName(MODEL).getValue());
    return foundCar;
}
```

② **Create two columns to insert**

③ **Create the Car record, keyed to the license**

④ **Create a query**

⑤ **Set the parameters and the columns to retrieve**

⑥ **Convert to the domain object**

To create a `Car` entity you define each of the fields you want to store (**❶** and **❷**). In this first line you create a `Mutator` for a specific `Keyspace`. You can compare a `Keyspace` with a schema when working with relational databases. For Cassandra it defines where you want to store the information. When you execute **❸** the `Mutator`, the corresponding columns will be stored in Cassandra. To retrieve the `Car` based on its license, you have to create a query. With a `SliceQuery` **❹** you can retrieve multiple columns **❺** at once and use the results from this query to transform **❻** the retrieved columns back to a `Car` entity again. All the repositories used in this chapter follow this same pattern.

Now that you've seen how data is stored and retrieved, the next thing to look at is the logic layer.

2.4.3 *Setting up the logic layer*

This layer consists of two parts. First are the domain objects, which you've already seen in figure 2.6. These objects, besides containing data, also contain the required business logic. Say, for instance, that when you want to register a new `Car` on a specific `Account` you'd call the `Account.registerCar(Car toRegister)` method.

The other part of this layer is a thin service façade. This façade merely delegates the calls to the correct domain object to be executed or to a repository if it's related to the lifecycle of the object. The code in the following listing shows a part of this service layer.

> **Listing 2.4 How the service façade delegates calls to the domain objects**

```
public class AccountServiceImpl implements AccountService {

    AccountRepository accountRepository;
```

```
public void registerCar(String ssn, Car car) {
   Account account = accountRepository.getAccount(ssn);
   account.registerCar(car);
   accountRepository.updateAccount(account);
}
}
```

As you can see from this listing, this simple façade doesn't do anything more than just delegate the calls to the domain objects and the repositories.

2.5 *Checking out and configuring the REST services*

Now that you've set up your data and logic layers, we can look at the service remoting layer. This layer provides the interface other parties can use to communicate with your services. If you look back at figure 2.6 you can see that you want to use this REST interface to register the route a car is traveling. In this section we'll look at how the REST remoting layer is set up, and in section 2.6, Checking out and configuring the SOAP services, you'll see what the SOAP remoting layer looks like.

2.5.1 *Overview of the REST layer*

Figure 2.7 shows the setup of the REST remoting layer.

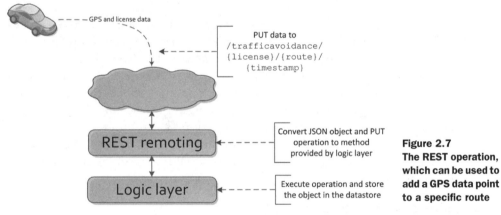

Figure 2.7
The REST operation, which can be used to add a GPS data point to a specific route

As you can see from this figure, you want to provide a URL for a PUT operation, which allows your GPS tracking device to register the current position from the car and the route identification (just a number). You need to know which car you're dealing with, so the license plate of the car is also provided in the URL. So what does such a request look like?

```
PUT http://localhost:9002/trafficavoidance/gps/qwewqe/10/12345678 HTTP/1.1
Content-Type: application/trafficavoidance.gpsdata+json
Host: localhost:9002
Content-Length: 77

{"gpsdata": {
   "x-coordinate": 54.5476328,
   "y-coordinate": 5.387484
}}
```

And the response from the server will be this:

```
HTTP/1.1 201 Created
Location: http://localhost:9002/trafficavoidance/gps/qwewqe/10/12345678
Content-Type: application/trafficavoidance.gpsdata+json
Date: Wed, 29 Dec 2010 18:09:40 GMT
Content-Length: 0
```

In this case I didn't write a complete API documentation; in the following chapters in this book, I'll also show you how to document your REST services so that they can be easily used by your service's clients. You'll also see that writing service documentation can be one of the policies that you want your services to comply with. From the previous small fragment you can see that with this PUT operation you register a GPS point. This GPS point will be added to route 20 for the car with license plate WWEERR.

PUT versus POST

When you look at the four main operations REST offers (ignoring OPTIONS, HEAD, TRACE, and CONNECT for now), it usually isn't that hard to determine which one to use for a specific operation. If you want to retrieve a specific resource you use the GET operation, which will retrieve the resource(s) identified by the specific URL and supplied parameters. DELETE is also straightforward; the resource(s) specified by the provided URL are deleted. It becomes a bit more complicated when you look at the PUT and POST operations. When you want to create or update a resource identified by a specific URL, do you use the POST operation or the PUT operation?

The answer can be found in the HTTP specifications. In these specifications the PUT, GET, DELETE, and HEAD operations are defined as being idempotent. If you execute identical requests, the responses should be the same. Note that POST isn't in the list. So when you send a number of POST requests, you have no guarantee that the responses will be the same. This feature is also the reason that when you hit the Back button after submitting a form, a pop-up is shown warning you that you're about to resubmit the data. If the form was submitted using a PUT operation, no such warning would be issued.

Now that you know the difference between these two operations, which should you use? Simply put, with the PUT operation you have to send the complete resource you want to update or create, and the result of this operation will always be the same resource, no matter how many times you send the request. With the POST operation you rely on the server to create or update a specific resource so you can send partial data and let the server figure it out. Also with POST you usually use the parent resource URI to create a new resource and not the complete URI of the resource you're going to create.

You've just seen what you want to accomplish with your REST remoting layer. In the next section we'll look at how this service is implemented.

2.5.2   *Implementation of the REST layer*

You've configured the REST services using JAX-RS annotation. JAX-RS in itself is a standard of which there are multiple implementations. For examples in this book, I'll use the CXF's JAX-RS implementation. The reason for this is that this way you can configure both your REST and SOAP-based services using the same framework, because CXF also has great support for the various WS-* standards.

Let's start with looking at your service implementation, shown in the next listing. Remember, what you want to expose is a service that can be used to register GPS data points.

Listing 2.5   Resource implementation that can be used to add GPS data

```
@Service                                    ←─ ❶ Define as service for detection by Spring
@Path("/trafficavoidance/gps/{license}/{route}/{timestamp}")  ←─┐ Location of
public class RestTrafficService {                               ❷ this resource

    @Resource                                               ←─ ❸ Service you're
    private CarService carService;                             delegating to

    @PUT                                                    ❹ PUT operation
    @Consumes("application/trafficavoidance.gpsdata+json")    and MIME
    public Response registerGPSDatra(String jsonData,         type of data
        @PathParam("license") String license,                expected
        @PathParam("route") int route,
        @PathParam("timestamp") long timestamp,
        @Context UriInfo info) {

        GPSData data = jsonToGPSData(jsonData, timestamp);    ←─ ❻ Convert JSON object
        carService.addGPSData(license, route, data);          ←─ ❼ to Java object
                                                                   Call the delegate
        URI us = info.getBaseUriBuilder().segment("trafficavoidance", "gps",
            license, Integer.toString(route),
            Long.toString(timestamp)).build(new Object[]{});
        return Response.created(us).type("application/json").build();
    }
```

Parameters from the path get injected ❺

Set up and return a 201 message ❽

Here you create a Spring service ❶ that exposes a resource on the path specified in ❷. When a PUT request with the correct MIME type is received ❹, this service will use the data from the request URI ❺ and the JSON object ❻ to create a new Java GPSData object. This object is then stored in the NoSQL store using the delegate ❼ that was injected ❸. Finally, a Response object is created ❽ and returned to the client.

Let's look at how this service is configured in Spring and how you can start it. The following listing shows the Spring configuration with the configuration of the required beans.

Listing 2.6   Spring configuration used to configure the RESTful services

```
<context:component-scan
    base-package="soa.governance.chapter2.traffic" />
```

❶ Scan packages that contain Spring components

```
<jaxrs:server address="http://localhost:9002" >
  <jaxrs:serviceBeans>
   <ref bean="restTrafficService" />
  </jaxrs:serviceBeans>
</jaxrs:server>
```

❷ Define the address resources can be accessed on

❸ Define a JAX-RS annotated Spring bean

In listing 2.6 you add the @service annotation to the class that implements your REST service. To make sure Spring sees this annotation you need to add the element shown at ❶. You also need to configure the port your REST services will be running on ❷, and finally you need to tell which annotated beans you want to make available ❸. Now that you've tied everything together, you can start the server. You can do this in two different ways. If you already have the projects imported into Eclipse, you can run the soa.governance.chapter2.traffic.CXFBasedJettyLauncher class from Eclipse. If you've only checked out the code, or you don't want to run this from Eclipse, you can also start this directly from Maven. To do this, execute the following code from the command line: mvn exec:java. You should see something like the following in your console:

```
INFO 22:47:28,027 Setting the server's publish address to be http://
    localhost:9002
INFO 22:47:28,085 jetty-7.2.0.v20101020
INFO 22:47:28,088 Started SelectChannelConnector@localhost:9002

--Press enter to terminate this service--
```

Now that you've successfully started your first REST service, let's look at how you can test this service to see if it's working. For this you'll be using soapUI, which is a tool that can be used to test REST-based services but also WS-* based services.

2.5.3 Testing the REST layer

Before you can start testing with soapUI, you first need to install it (see the appendix for the soapUI installation).

After installation, start up soapUI and you'll be presented with the following screen (figure 2.8).

At this moment there isn't much you can do with soapUI. You need to create a project and configure the services you want to test. Because this is rather cumbersome and error prone, I've provided you with a

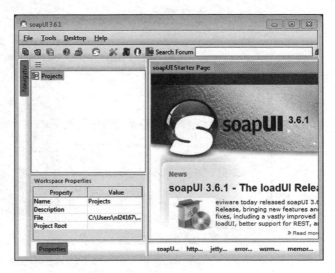

Figure 2.8 soapUI welcome screen

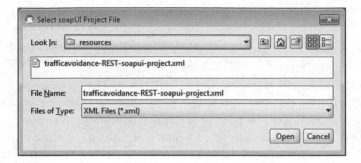

Figure 2.9
Importing the soapUI project,
which can be used for testing

project you can load so you can start testing directly. In soapUI select File > Import Project and navigate to the location where you've put your Eclipse workspace. In that workspace look for the trafficavoidance-REST-soapui-project.xml file, which is located in the traffic-service-remoting-REST project. Click Open to import this project (shown in figure 2.9).

Now that you've imported the project, open the tree and you'll see two requests there (see figure 2.10): a PUT request used to create a new GPSData entry and a GET request, which retrieves a specific GPSData point.

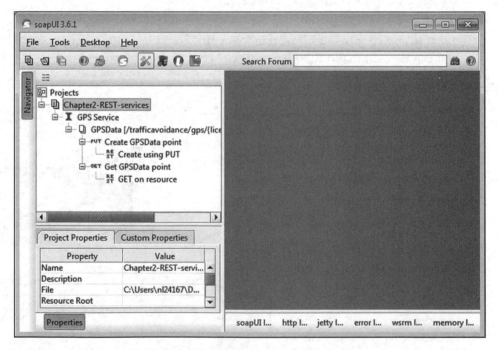

Figure 2.10   The soapUI project, which can be used to test the REST service

To test the service, open a request by double-clicking it. When it's open, you can click the green arrow in the top-left corner, which will fire the request. The best way to see what's being sent and received is to use the Raw tab on the request and the response.

Now that you've seen how the REST environment is set up, let's examine the WS-* based environment.

2.6   Checking out and configuring the SOAP services

In the previous section we looked at how you can create a REST service and expose it using the frameworks chosen. Now let's do the same for the traditional web services. If you once again look back at figure 2.9, you can see that you'll use the WS-* interface for the communication with the CRM system.

2.6.1   Overview of the WS-* layer

Figure 2.11 provides an overview of how to set up your WS-* remoting layer. If you look back at how you did this for the REST layer, you should see many similarities.

You've again created a specific remoting layer that handles the technology conversion part. Just as you did for the REST service where you had a layer that converted from a REST/JSON model to a Java model, you did the same here. In this case you converted from a WSDL/XML-based model to the same Java model.

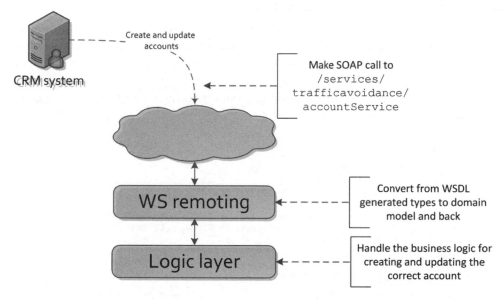

Figure 2.11   The operation exposed through the WS-* layer and how it connects to the generic logic layer

Bottom-up versus top-down contract design

When you want to create a WSDL as a contract for your WS-* based web service, you have two different approaches. You can start from scratch and define how the XML looks that you want to send over the line, and from there on work your way down to the messages, operations, and service definition. On the other hand, if you already have an implementation of a service that you want to expose, you can use various WS libraries and let those libraries create the WSDL for you. This first approach is called top-down contract design; the other approach is called bottom-up contract design. As you've probably noticed by now, a well-defined and documented contract is important if you want to create high-quality services and apply some form of governance on these services. A top-down approach lends itself better to this than a bottom-up approach, especially because in the latter you're dependent on the code generation provided by your WS library, and customizing the generation is often difficult. This, however, doesn't mean that generating a WSDL is completely without merit. What's often done is the "meet in the middle" approach. In this approach you use the tools provided by the WS library to create the initial WSDL and XSD definitions from your existing service. That way you have a lot of the tedious work done for you, and you'll change and append to this generated WSDL to create your final, policy-compliant WSDL.

Before we look at this, let's first look at the contract this service provides, so you can see the kinds of messages you need to send.

2.6.2 *The WSDL-based contract for this service*

With a WS-* based approach you have a mechanism to define a contract that exactly specifies how your service needs to be called. This document is called a *WSDL*, which stands for *Web Service Definition Language*. With a WSDL you can specify the operations your service provides, its arguments, its return types, and any fault handling. Let's look at the various parts of a WSDL (as shown in figure 2.12) and how they're filled in for the example.

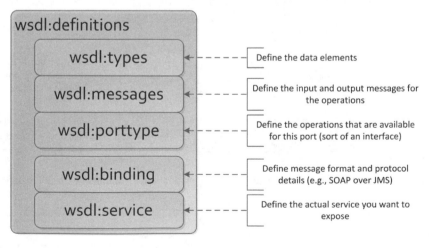

Figure 2.12
The various parts that make up a WSDL

The first thing you need to do is define the data that's sent over the line. For a WSDL you do this by specifying types using an XSD (XML Schema Definition). As you can see in figure 2.12 you need to define this in the `wsdl:types` section of the WSDL. The relevant part of the WSDL is shown here.

Listing 2.7   The `wsdl:types` section of the WSDL for the account service

```
<wsdl:types>
  <xsd:schema
    targetNamespace="urn:trafficavoidance:xsd:account:service:types-1.0">
    <xsd:import
        schemaLocation="./traffic-avoidance-types.xsd"                   ❶ Import
        namespace="urn:trafficavoidance:xsd:account:types-1.0" />           XSD type
                                                                            definitions

    <xsd:element name="createAccount">
      <xsd:complexType>
        <xsd:sequence>
          <xsd:element name="account" type="types:account" />           ❷ Define
        </xsd:sequence>                                                    parameters for
      </xsd:complexType>                                                   createAccount
    </xsd:element>


    <xsd:element name="createAccountResponse">
      <xsd:complexType>
        <xsd:sequence>                                                  ❸
          <xsd:element name="accountNumber" type="xsd:string" />          Define
        </xsd:sequence>                                                   response for
        </xsd:complexType>                                                createAccount
      </xsd:element>
          ...
  </xsd:schema>
</wsdl:types>
```

First, you import the XSD type definitions ❶. You then define the input ❷ and output ❸ elements for the `createAccount` operation. The actual XML type used here, `types:account`, isn't defined in this WSDL. It's good practice to externalize these definitions to an external file for ease of maintenance and, as you'll see in later chapters, for versioning. The next thing you need to do is define the input and output messages that are sent by your operations. For this we'll once again look at the `createAccount` operation. The definition of this operation is in the `porttype` element, as shown in the following listing.

Listing 2.8   Message definition and `porttype` for the `accountService`

```
<wsdl:message name="createAccountRequest">
  <wsdl:part element="servicetypes:createAccount"              ❶ Define the input
            name="parameters" />                                 message
</wsdl:message>
<wsdl:message name="createAccountResponse">
  <wsdl:part element="servicetypes:createAccountResponse"      ❷ Define the
            name="parameters" />                                 output
</wsdl:message>                                                   message
```

```
<wsdl:portType name="accountServicePortType">
  <wsdl:operation name="createAccount">
    <wsdl:input message="tns:createAccountRequest"/>
 <wsdl:output message="tns:createAccountResponse"/>
  </wsdl:operation>
...
</wsdl:portType>
```

❸ **These messages make up createAccount operation**

In listing 2.8, you define the input ❶ and output ❷ messages for the createAccount operation. The definition of this operation is in ❸. With the types, messages, and portType defined, you're finished with the abstract part of the WSDL. We haven't talked about SOAP yet or HTTP; you've only defined the abstract part of your contract. If you want to do something with these definitions, you need to fill in the concrete part of the WSDL: the binding and service elements. The following listing shows how you do this for the example.

Listing 2.9   Binding and service elements for the accountService

```
<wsdl:binding name="accountServiceBinding"
              type="tns:accountServicePortType">

  <soap:binding style="document"
                transport="http://schemas.xmlsoap.org/soap/http" />
...
    <wsdl:operation name="updateAccount">
      <soap:operation
          soapAction="...:account:service-1.0/updateAccount" />
      <wsdl:input><soap:body use="literal" /></wsdl:input>
      <wsdl:output><soap:body use="literal" /></wsdl:output>
    </wsdl:operation>
</wsdl:binding>

<wsdl:service name="accountService">
  <wsdl:port binding="tns:accountServiceBinding"
             name="accountServicePort">
    <soap:address
        location="http://.../trafficavoidance/accountService"/>
  </wsdl:port>
</wsdl:service>
```

❶ **Create binding for portType in listing 2.8**

❷ **Bind the operation to SOAP**

❸ **Define service and how it can be accessed**

You filled in the concrete part of the WSDL by binding the portType you created to a SOAP implementation (❶ and ❷). The final part is done by defining the service ❸. The service defines how a specific binding can be accessed.

When you specified your REST service, you needed to think about what the XML representation of your arguments looks like, how the input and return types of your operations were defined, and finally how this abstract definition could be bound to a specific technology and service. It was a lot of work. If you compare this with the REST approach where you only needed to know where the service could be found and were provided with a couple of example messages, you can probably see why many people think WSDLs are overly complex. WSDLs do provide a powerful way of defining your contract, but they're not meant for human consumption and are better for machine-to-machine communications. In the next section we'll look at how you can use this WSDL as a starting point for the WS-Remoting layer.

2.6.3 *Implementation of the WS-* layer*

In the previous section I already mentioned that a WSDL is often used for machine-to-machine communication. The reason for this is that it's easy to generate code from a WSDL that handles all the glue code such as XML parsing, SOAPAction mapping, and method invocation. In the example we'll use CXF's cxf-codegen-plugin Maven plug-in to generate code from the WSDL defined in the previous chapter. Because you've set up the m2eclipse plug-in and mavenized all the projects already, you won't have to set up this code generation manually. Every time you make a change to the WSDL, the generated code will be automatically updated. You can find this generated code in the target/generated/cxf folder in the traffic-service-remoting-WS project. One of the classes generated is an interface that matches the operations you've defined in the WSDL. For your WS-Remoting layer you'll write an implementation of that interface, shown in listing 2.10.

> **Listing 2.10 Convert from the WSDL-generated model to the common model**

```
@WebService(
  portName="accountServicePort",
  targetNamespace="urn:trafficavoidance:wsdl:account:service-1.0",
  serviceName="accountService",
  wsdlLocation="contract/accountService.wsdl"
)
public class AccountServiceImpl implements AccountServicePortType {

  @Resource
  AccountService service;

  @Override
  public Account updateAccount(Account account) {
    soa.governance.chapter2.traffic.model.Account result =
        service.updateAccount(ConvertUtil.convertFromWS(account));
    return ConvertUtil.convertToWS(result);
  }

  @Override
  public String createAccount(Account account) {
    soa.governance.chapter2.traffic.model.Account result =
        service.createAccount(ConvertUtil.convertFromWS(account));
    return result.getSsn();
  }
}
```

❶ Define web service parameters

Implementation of updateAccount operation ❷

The WS-Remoting layer is trivial; you don't need to know much about SOAP, XML, or the underlying HTTP. All you have to do is convert the objects that were generated from the WSDL to the objects your service in the logic layer expects ❷. From a Java code perspective, you're pretty much finished here; you do need to tell your WS library how this service is to be exposed and which port and service from the WSDL you're implementing. You do this using the @WebService annotation ❶. Here you specify that you want to use a specific service and port from the contract/accountService.wsdl WSDL. You can now start up your application in the same way you did for the REST example, either by running the soa.governance.chapter2.traffic.CXFBasedJettyLauncher class from Eclipse or executing the following code from the command line (in the traffic-service-container directory): mvn exec:java. You should see something like the following in your console:

```
INFO 15:45:12,756 Setting the server's publish address to be
     http://localhost:9002
INFO 15:45:12,856 jetty-7.2.0.v20101020
INFO 15:45:12,916 Started SelectChannelConnector@localhost:9002
INFO 15:45:13,026 Creating Service
     {urn:trafficavoidance:wsdl:account:service-
     1.0}accountService from WSDL: /contract/accountService.wsdl
INFO 15:45:13,866 Setting the server's publish address to be
     http://localhost:9001/accountService
INFO 15:45:13,886 jetty-7.2.0.v20101020
INFO 15:45:13,889 Started SelectChannelConnector@localhost:9001

--Press enter to terminate this service--
```

Now that you have the service running, let's test it. You'll again use soapUI as you did for the REST example.

2.6.4   *Testing the WS-* remoting layer*

Just as I did for REST, I've provided you with a soapUI-based project you can use to test this service. After you've started soapUI, select File > Import Project and browse to the workspace location. In the workspace select the traffic-service-remoting-WS project and browse to the src/test/resources folder. In this folder you'll find a file named Chapter2-WS-services-soapui-project.xml, which you can import (shown in figure 2.13).

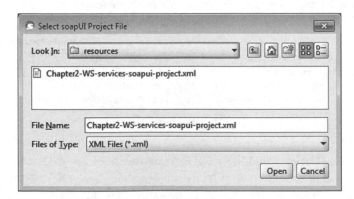

Figure 2.13   Import the project to test the WS-* services.

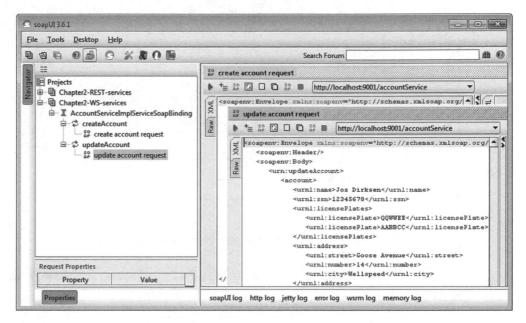

Figure 2.14   Two requests with which you can test the WS-* service you've created

After you've imported the project, you'll see the two operations from the `account-Service` and the requests with which you can test the service, as shown in figure 2.14.

To test the service, open one of the requests by double-clicking it. Now, when you hit the little green play icon at the top left of a request window, you invoke the operation and should see a response.

So now that you've seen how the services are created and how you can start and test them, let's move on to the next section and implement some of the policies that were defined in section 2.3, Introducing the traffic avoidance example.

2.7   Setting up the SOA registry

In section 2.6, Checking out and configuring the SOAP services, you created a WS-* based service. In this section we'll look at how you can store this service in a registry and query the registry. The first thing you'll do is download and install the registry from the WSO2 site. Instructions on how to install the SOA registry can be found in the appendix.

2.7.1   Running the SOA registry for the first time

Before you can do anything with the registry, you need to log in. Start the WSO2 registry from <GOV_HOME>/wso2greg-3.6.0/bin and point your browser to https://localhost:9443. This will start the application, and you'll be shown the login screen (see figure 2.15).

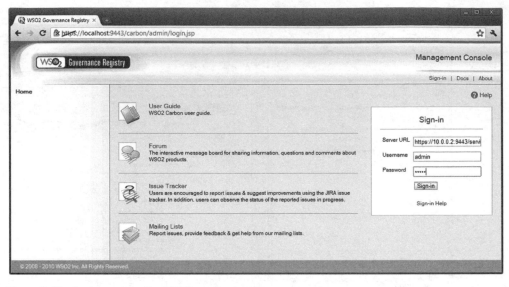

Figure 2.15   Login page for the WSO2 service registry

As username enter `admin` and as password also enter `admin` and click the Sign-in button. This will bring you to the WSO2 Governance Registry home screen (see figure 2.16). Next, you'll see how to register your service in this registry.

2.7.2   *Registering a service manually in the registry*

In section 2.6, Checking out and configuring the SOAP services, you created a WSDL that defined your contract. In this section you'll register this service into the registry so that it can be easily found and reused by others. From the home screen of the

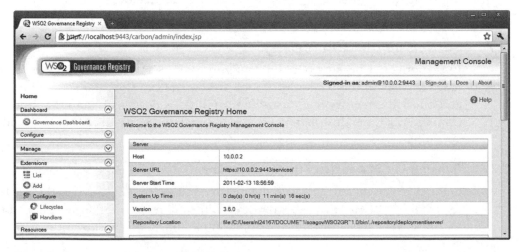

Figure 2.16   The WSO2 Governance Registry home screen

Figure 2.17 Add a WSDL to the SOA registry.

registry, select the Add WSDL option from the left side (it's under Metadata). You use the Add WSDL option instead of the Add Service option because your WSDL defines your service. So if you add the WSDL, the registry will automatically define a related service element and an XSD element. In the Add screen (see figure 2.17), choose the option Import WSDL from a url. In the WSD URL field enter the URL of the `account-Service` you created: `http://localhost:9001/accountService?wsdl`. The Name field will be automatically filled in. Now click the Add button to add the WSDL and its related resources to the registry.

You'll now have the following three items in your registry:

- *Service*—A service with the name `accountService`, the name you specified in the WSDL, is now registered under the metadata/list/services menu option.
- *WSDL*—The WSDL itself is registered. You can find this one in the metadata/list/WSDLs menu option.
- *XSD*—You created your schema separately from the WSDL. The registry has detected this from your WSDL and has created an entry for it. You can see this in the metadata/list/schemas menu option.

If this was a real work scenario, you'd now start adding documentation about this service in the registry so that other people would know what your service does, how it should be used, or, for instance, how it should be accessed for a test environment. For now, we'll keep it like this and look at how you can access this repository, besides using the provided web application.

2.7.3 *Accessing the WSO2 Governance Registry*

In this section we'll look at the simplest way you can access the information from the repository. This is done by using the client provided by WSO2 for this purpose. This client is called the `WSRegistryServiceClient`. If you look at the projects available for chapter 2 (in SVN), you'll also see a project called registry-client. In this project you'll find the code for the example discussed in this section. Before we dive into the Java code let's quickly look at the registry again. Start up the WSO2 Governance Registry and log in at https://localhost:9443. On the left side of the overview screen, you'll see a tab with the name Resources. On the Resources tab click the Browse option and you'll see a tree layout of the repository. All the data you store in the registry will be

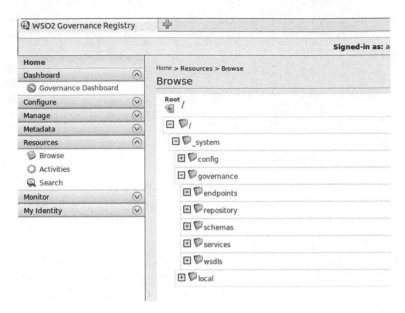

Figure 2.18
Browsing the WSO2
Governance Registry

accessible through this tree. When you open it, you won't see much except a _system folder. Open this folder and then click the governance subfolder (see figure 2.18).

In the governance folder you'll find all the resources related to WSDLs, services, schemas, and the like. Now click a bit further until you see the WSDL you uploaded. If you click this resource, you'll find its location (its path) at the top of the screen. For this WSDL this will be something like /_system/governance/trunk/wsdls/_0/ service_1/account/wsdl/trafficavoidance/accountService.wsdl. We'll use this path to look up this WSDL in the example in the following listing.

Listing 2.11 Access the WSO2 registry using the `WSRegistryServiceClient`

```
public static void main(String[] args) throws Exception {
  Registry registry;                                               ① Initialize the client
  registry = initialize();                                            before using it

  // get the governance folder
  Resource governanceFolder = client.get("/_system/governance");  ② Show the
  System.out.println("Folder description: " +                        description
                   governanceFolder.getDescription());              of a resource

  // get the WSDL folder resource (use the url we browsed to)
  String wsdlUrl = "/_system/governance/trunk/wsdls/_" +           ③ Get the WSDL
          "0/service_1/account/wsdl/trafficavoidance" +              using its path
          "/accountService.wsdl";
  Resource wsdlResource = client.get(wsdlUrl);

  // output the content of the wsdl
  System.out.println(new String((byte[])wsdlResource              ④ Print out the
                              .getContent()));                       content of
}                                                                    the WSDL
```

In this example you use the Registry ❶ to connect to a registry. If you're interested in the configuration of this client, you can find this in the examples in the chapter 2 source folders. If you want to access a resource, use the GET operation from this client. This operation takes a String, which is the path you want to access, as a parameter, and returns this as a resource. In ❷ this operation is used to print out the description of the /_system/governance folder. Then ❸ this same operation retrieves your WSDL resource and prints out its content ❹. Besides its content through the wsdlResource object you also have access to any tags, properties, and other metadata that have been added to this resource. In later chapters you'll use this client to integrate the repository with various other tools and components.

2.8 Setting up the BAM application

One of the policies specified for this example is that you want to make sure you get a certain amount of performance out of your service. You specified that you want to be able to process at least 5000 requests per minute. In this section you'll take the following steps to accomplish this:

- *Install required applications*—In chapter 1 I mentioned that there aren't any good open source BAM tools available. The few that are out there are tied to a specific product line (for example, WSO2 BAM) and are hard to customize and extend for other environments. As explained in chapter 1, you'll use various open source tools to create your own BAM application. For this, though, you need to install some tools and libraries. In this chapter I'll show you how to install the basic components, which you'll expand in later chapters.
- *Attach an event sender to the REST traffic service*—Each time a request is received on the REST traffic service, you need to send an event to your BAM application so that you can count the events.
- *Set up the statistics queries*—You want to monitor the number of requests that have been sent in the last minute. But just counting how many events were sent the last minute isn't enough, because you won't know if the issue is with the clients not sending enough requests or with your server not responding fast enough. Therefore, I'll also show how you can monitor the average processing time of an event.
- *Visualize the statistics*—The final step you need to do is to visualize the statistics. You do this by configuring two gadgets inside the WSO2 gadget server.

Let's start by installing the required software.

2.8.1 Installing BAM tools and checking out the code from SVN

Before you can install your BAM tools, you first need to install the gadget server in which your gadgets will run. Installations instructions for the gadget server can be found in the appendix. If you haven't done so, install the WSO2 gadget server before continuing with the next part.

With the gadget server installed, the visualization part of your BAM solution, let's now get the code from SVN, which provides you with functionality to store, process, and query for events. This is done in the same manner as shown in section 2.2. In Eclipse open the SVN Repository Exploring perspective, navigate to the Bamos folder, and, just as you did before, check out all the bamos-* projects and mavenize them. This will download all the dependencies and set up the Eclipse projects correctly. When you've finished doing this, you can run the `org.bamos.core.launcher` `.BamosLauncher` class from Eclipse to start the Bamos server.

Now run the Bamos server; after it's started you'll see the following output in the console:

```
INFO 11:53:33,742 Started SocketConnector@0.0.0.0:9003
INFO 11:53:33,789 --BAMOS Server started--
INFO 11:53:33,789

--Press enter to terminate this service-
```

Now that you've installed the required software, you need to connect the service you created in section 2.5, Checking out and configuring the REST services, to the Bamos application.

2.8.2   *Attaching an event sender to the service*

Let's first take a step back and look at the bigger picture. Figure 2.19 shows what you're trying to accomplish here.

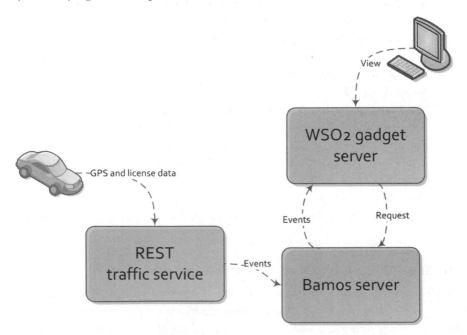

Figure 2.19   Overview of how you'll connect the REST service to the Bamos tooling

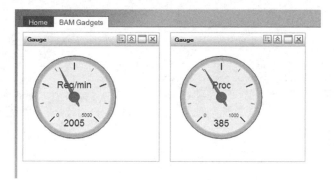

Figure 2.20   Two gauges showing the runtime information in real time

In figure 2.19 you can see that the REST traffic service sends events to the Bamos server. This server will store these events (in Cassandra), and it also provides a REST interface (as you'll see in more detail later on) that other applications can use to find and retrieve events. In this case you'll create a gadget that will request events from the Bamos server and show them in a gauge to the user. In the next couple of paragraphs we'll look at how you can send events from the REST traffic service to the Bamos server. What you're aiming for is shown in figure 2.20.

What you need for this is a filter that gets invoked each time a request is received by your REST service. All REST frameworks provide features for this, because you use CXF together with JAX-RS. You'll see an example here of how to do this with that framework. Creating a filter consists of two steps. You have to implement this filter class, and you have to configure your application context in such a way that this filter gets invoked for each request. First, we'll look at your filter implementation. In the following listing, the most important parts of this class (`...chapter2.traffic .services.rest.util.StatisticsRequestHandler`) are shown.

Listing 2.12   Filter implementation that sends events to the Bamos service

```
public Response handleRequest(Message m,
                ClassResourceInfo resourceClass) {
  long receivedAt = System.nanoTime();
  m.getExchange().put(RECEIVED_AT, receivedAt);
  return null;
}

public Response handleResponse(Message m,
      OperationResourceInfo ori, Response response) {
  if (m.getExchange() != null &&
        m.getExchange().get(RECEIVED_AT) != null) {
    if (ori != null) {
      Method methodToInvoke = ori.getMethodToInvoke();
      if (methodToInvoke.getName().contains(method)) {
        long processedAt = System.nanoTime();
        long receivedAt = (Long) m.getExchange()
                  .get(RECEIVED_AT);
```

❶ **Get start time of request**

❷ **Check if you're interested in this method**

```
        String serviceName = methodToInvoke
                .getDeclaringClass().getName();
        String jsonData = createJSON(server, serviceName
                , classifier
                , Integer.toString(response.getStatus())
                , Long.toString(processedAt - receivedAt));
        sendRequestAsynchronously(jsonData);
      }
    }
  }

  return response;
}
```

❸ Create a JSON object to send

❹ Send request asynchronously

Listing 2.12 shows a simple class that implements the `ResponseHandler` and `Request-Handler` interfaces provided by CXF. During the request phase you look at the current time and store it in the message context ❶. When the response comes back, the `handleResponse` operation is invoked. In this operation you check to see whether it's the operation you're interested in ❷ and create your JSON object ❸ that will be sent to the Bamos service ❹. The final thing you need to do now is attach this handler to the REST service you defined in section 2.5.2, Implementation of the REST layer. This is done by extending the applicationcontext.xml from the traffic-service-container project. This is shown in the following listing.

Listing 2.13 Add configuration for the filter that sends events to the Bamos service

```
<jaxrs:server address="http://localhost:9002" >
<jaxrs:serviceBeans>
  <ref bean="restTrafficService" />
</jaxrs:serviceBeans>
<jaxrs:providers>
   <bean id="requestTimeFilter"
     class="...traffic.services.rest.StatisticsRequestHandler" >
     <property name="server" value="TrafficServer"/>
     <property name="method" value="registerGPSData"/>
     <property name="classifier" value="CAR_DATA"/>
     <property name="url"
             value="http://localhost:9003/services/event"/>
   </bean>
  </jaxrs:providers>
</jaxrs:server>
```

❶ Register filter as a jaxrs:provider

❷ URL the event needs to be sent to

Here you add a `jaxrs:providers` element ❶ to the `jaxrs:server` configuration you defined earlier. In this element you can configure beans, which are then called when requests are processed by the REST services you've exposed in this `jaxrs:server`. Here you also tell your filter where the requests need to be sent ❷.

That's it. If you now repeat the tests you did in section 2.5.3, Testing the REST layer, and make sure the Bamos service is running, every time a request is received by your service an event is sent to the Bamos service. Now that you have your Bamos

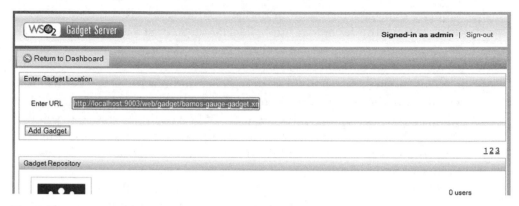

Figure 2.21   Add a gadget from a URL for the WSO2 gadget server.

service running and the traffic avoidance service connected to it, you only have to add your gadget to the gadget service and you can visualize and monitor your events.

2.8.3   *Setting up the widget to visualize the statistics*

In section 2.8.1, Installing BAM tools and checking out the code from SVN, you installed the WSO2 gadget server. Now you'll configure a gadget in it to monitor the number of events and the average event processing time. So start up the gadget server and point your browser to http://localhost:8080/portal. You'll be greeted with the standard page from the gadget server. On this page click the Sign-in link in the upper-right corner. As username enter admin and as password also enter admin. Now you'll be presented with a portal that you can easily customize for yourself. You'll start by creating a new tab where you'll put your gadgets. Click the Add New Tab button and enter BAM Gadgets as the name of the new tab. Then click Select Tab Layout, and select the layout with three vertical columns. You are now presented with an empty tab where you'll add your gadgets. Click the Add Gadgets button, and you'll be presented with the screen shown in figure 2.21.

In this screen you can enter the URL of the gadget you want to add. For this example enter http://localhost:9003/web/gadget/bamos-gauge-gadget.xml and click the Add Gadget button. This will return you to the tab you just created and show you a simple gauge. You now need to configure this gauge to show the type of events you want. For this click the Settings icon (the leftmost icon in the menu bar), and you'll be presented with a list of properties, as shown in figure 2.22.

In later chapters in this book we'll dive deeper into the different configuration options. For now you'll create the gauge that measures the number of

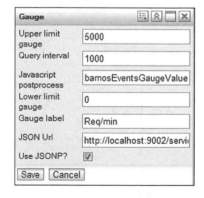

Figure 2.22   Configuration options for the gauge

requests that have been sent in the last minute. For this you only need to alter the JSON URL to the following: http://localhost:9003/services/event/list?server=Traffic-Service&service=soa.governance.chapter2.traffic.services.rest.RestTrafficService&count=5000&reverse=false&lastms=60000.

This will make a call to the Bamos service and receive all the events for the last 60 seconds for the server with the name TrafficService and the service with the name soa.governance.chapter2.traffic.services.rest.RestTrafficService, and you'll retrieve a maximum of 5000 events. If you click the Save button, the gadget will start making calls to the Bamos service and retrieving events. The number of events will then be shown in the gadget.

For the other gadget, the one that you want to show the average processing time, you need to add a gadget in the same manner as you just did. And once again change the JSON URL to the value shown previously. If you want to, you can also change the label that's shown on the gauge (for instance, set this to Proc. time). If you stop here, you'll have a gauge that's exactly the same as the previous one (but with a different label). What you need to alter here is the JavaScript postprocess value. Without going into too much detail here, this is the place where you can put custom JavaScript code that defines what's shown in the gauge. For now, put the following line of JavaScript in there:

```
function average(data) { var av = 0;  var len = data.length;  for (var i = 0;
    i < len; i++) {    av += parseInt(data[i]);''} return av/len;}
bamosEventsGaugeValue =
  Math.round(average(JSONQuery("..processingTime",data)));
```

This will calculate an average of the `processingTime` of an event. Click Save, and when you start adding new data points, you'll see the gauges moving, as shown in figure 2.23.

If you look at the source code for the Bamos service, you'll find a couple of unit tests there that make it easy to add some test events if you want to test various configurations and parameters.

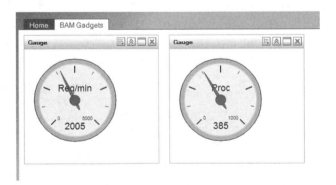

Figure 2.23   Gauges showing the average processing time and number of processed requests

2.9   Summary

- You've installed Eclipse, which you'll use as your IDE, and you can run the examples directly from the IDE or run them from Maven.

- All the code and examples are stored in SVN. You can check out the examples and play around with them to get a good feel for the environment.

- You can easily test WS-* and REST using soapUI. soapUI projects are available in the various projects in the src/test/resources directories. In these projects example requests are already provided.

- You should use a clean separation between your remoting technology and your business logic.

- The WS-* service is designed contract first; this same contract can be used directly in the WSO2 Governance Registry.

- The gauges in the monitoring environment can be customized by using the settings in the menu bar. If you play around with the JavaScript postprocess property, you can use Firebug to help find those nasty JavaScript bugs.

- You can customize the data sent to the Bamos service by adding extra `userdata` elements.

3

Using a case study to understand SOA governance

This chapter covers

- A case study used to explain SOA governance
- The stakeholders and how they define policies
- The services used to demonstrate how to apply policies
- An overview of the policies defined by the stakeholders

In this chapter we'll look at a fictional company named OpenGov. This company, like most companies, has many different departments, each with its own goals and requirements. I'll use this company, its products and services, and the different stakeholders to explain why you need SOA governance and how you can apply it.

The following sections will each show a specific part of the OpenGov organization. We'll start by looking at how the company is organized. This will help you understand the different goals the stakeholders within this company have and will explain why certain policies were chosen. To demonstrate how to apply SOA governance you need a set of products and services on which you can apply these policies. In sections 3.3 and 3.4 I'll show you the product and service portfolio of the

OpenGov organization. All the products, services, and policies you see in this chapter will show up again in the examples in parts 2 and 3 of this book.

Let's start by looking at what this organization does and how it's organized.

3.1 Getting to know OpenGov

The fictional company, OpenGov, is an organization that began providing services for municipalities in 2000. It started out small by offering a simple standard website to municipalities, which they could use to provide their residents with contact information and some news about what was happening in their city. Since then, it's grown from a simple content provider to an organization that provides many different products and services to over 50 municipalities, ranging from mobile applications used to register complaints and get localized news to web forms people can use to request building permits. OpenGov provides support for its products and offers other services such as process optimization and trend watching. All the products are offered in a cloud environment. Customers don't need to host the applications and services; they use the centrally hosted applications on the infrastructure of OpenGov.

3.1.1 The organizational chart of OpenGov

Before we look at the set of products OpenGov offers, let's look at an organizational chart so you can get a good overview of the various departments within this company. This is interesting because each department has its own specific goals and requirements. For instance, the Legal department follows all new legislation. Based on new laws, it may define new policies that have to be applied to various products and services OpenGov provides. The organizational chart is shown in figure 3.1.

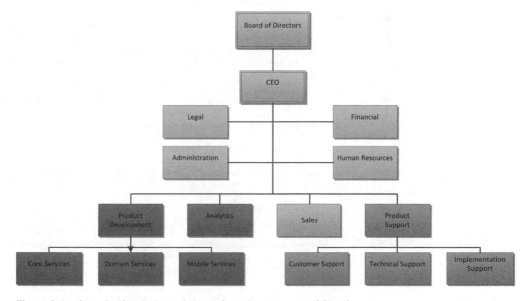

Figure 3.1 Organizational chart of the various departments of OpenGov

As you can see in figure 3.1, OpenGov is a fairly standard organization. It has a board of directors and a CEO who direct the company and a couple of support departments: Legal, Financial, Administration, and Human Resources. The interesting departments, at least for the scope of this book, are Product Development, Analytics, and Product Support. As you'll see later in this chapter, each of these departments has its own requirements and goals that will lead to a set of policies. For a good overview of what these departments do, look at table 3.1. This table will help you understand why a specific policy is defined in section 3.4.

Before I show you the various products and services OpenGov provides, let's look a bit closer at these departments. More specifically, we'll look at the managers of these departments and their different goals and requirements for the services and products.

Table 3.1   The role of the various departments of the OpenGov organization

Department name	Description
Product Development	The OpenGov organization does its own product development. All product development is centralized in the Product Development department, which has three subdepartments. Each of these subdepartments focuses on a specific area.
Analytics	The Analytics department analyzes how the services and products are used. It watches for trends and helps the customers optimize how they use the provided services and products.
Sales	The role of the Sales department is to find new customers and improve the number of municipalities OpenGov provides services to.
Product Support	The Product Support department provides support in the following areas: customer support, technical support, and implementation support.
Core Services	Core Services is a subdepartment of Product Development. This department focuses on developing and extending the core services provided by OpenGov. These services include providing statistics, returning information on residents, and delivering information about the municipality itself (e.g., GIS information for buildings).
Domain Services	Domain Services handles the development of specific products and services. For instance, the traffic jam reduction system you saw in chapter 2 was developed and is maintained by this department.
Mobile Services	Mobile Services does all the mobile apps development.
Customer Support	Customer Support handles questions regarding the use of the products and services.
Technical Support	Technical Support deals with connection issues, technical integration, and security-related issues.
Implementation Support	Implementation Support helps the customers of OpenGov get connected.

3.1.2 *The stakeholders of OpenGov*

These managers and the CEO are the main stakeholders. Because the stakeholders ultimately define the policies for this company, it's good to know a bit more about them. In table 3.2 I name these stakeholders and let them explain their primary goals.

Table 3.2 The stakeholders and their primary goals

Stakeholder	Primary goal
CEO	"I want this company to grow. We now have 50 municipalities as customers; I want to grow to 100 customers in the coming two years. We do need to keep the IT expenses in line, because they have been steadily rising the last couple of years."
Sales manager	"Our customers are asking for different deployment options. Some already have their own private cloud and don't want to run in ours. Besides this, they want easier access to the data so that they can incorporate it in their own applications."
Development manager	"We need to consolidate service development. Services use different types of models. We've also noticed that some services provide pretty much the same functionality, and we want to refactor a number of services to remove this duplication."
Product Support manager	"We have too many different versions running in production, which are hard to support, and we don't have good monitoring in place. We want a single version that all the customers use. We also get many questions about how to use the services, which should be documented somewhere."
Lead analyst	"We need to be able to create customized reports to better help our customers. I want to see which services are used when and by whom and how long the permit request process runs."

As you can see, it isn't such a complex organization, but even in this small organization different departments have different goals. The business end wants to minimize development costs, get as many customers using their existing services as possible, and be able to quickly introduce new products and services. The IT organization, on the other hand, wants to improve the quality of the services, and the Sales department wants to help customers who already have a private cloud.

Understanding the types of cloud computing

Cloud computing is a broad subject that's been getting a lot of attention these last couple of years. But what is cloud computing? Is it really that revolutionary and new? With cloud computing you don't host your application or service yourself; you run it on infrastructure provided by a third party. Amazon, for instance, provides computing resources, Google provides an application platform through its App Engine, and Microsoft is on board with its Azure platform. You can roughly divide cloud computing into three main areas: software as a service (SAAS), platform as a service (PAAS),

(continued)

and infrastructure as a service (IAAS). Software as a service is where you use applications and services provided online by a third party. Google, with its application stack, is a good example of this. But Producteev, Salesforce, and Microsoft Office 365 are also examples of SAAS. With PAAS you use complete platforms that are provided in the cloud. Google's App Engine and Amazon's S3 platform are examples of PAAS. Finally, there's IAAS, which focuses on providing infrastructure in the cloud such as network storage and CPU resources. Microsoft has a nice offering with its Azure platform.

Besides these types of cloud computing, there's also the difference between a private cloud and a public cloud. A public cloud is hosted outside your own company and is shared by all the users of the cloud. If you want to develop on Google's App Engine you share the infrastructure and resources with all the other users. A private cloud is a cloud environment that's hosted in your company's own infrastructure. In the introduction of this chapter I mentioned that OpenGov provides a hosted environment, a cloud, which all the customers use. If it deployed all its applications on an environment hosted by a single municipality, that municipality would have its own private cloud.

Throughout this book, you'll see how SOA governance can help you formalize the goals and requirements of the various stakeholders and comply with them. Before we start looking at policies, though, let's look at the main products OpenGov provides.

3.2   *Explaining SOA governance using OpenGov products*

As you've seen, OpenGov has a couple of different development departments. In this section we'll look at the main products that OpenGov offers. In the following chapters I'll use these applications as examples of how you can create your services and products to comply with a set of policies.

We'll look at the following applications:

- *GovForms*—An application to apply for permits and track the state of your permit application.
- *GovTraffic*—This system rewards users driving outside the busiest hours of the day. It does this by tracking when they use their car and the route they take. We've already looked at this system in the previous chapter.
- *GovMobile*—The GovMobile platform provides citizens with the ability to register complaints instantly from their mobile phones. It also provides some general information, such as the opening times of public buildings.
- *GovPortal*—With the GovPortal application residents can get information on the products the city offers, learn which permits are available, ask questions, view frequently asked questions, and so on.

- *GovData*—The GovData service provides all kinds of information regarding the city that residents can use in their own applications.

In the following sections we'll look at what each application does and how you'll use it throughout the rest of the book. Let's start with the GovForms application.

3.2.1 GovForms: permit registration

GovForms is one of OpenGov's oldest products. With this product residents of a specific city can use online forms to apply for specific permits. Permit applications are then stored in a specific permits database where the city's civil workers can process them. Any updates on a permit application are communicated to the applicant using email, and the status of the application can also be viewed online using a simple website. I'll use this system to show how you can work with canonical models and service repositories. This system and its dependencies are shown in figure 3.2.

In figure 3.2 you can see that a citizen can use the GovForms system to apply for a permit. When a form is being filled in, information is retrieved from other systems. The civil registration system provides information on citizens and companies, and the reference information system provides reference information such as types of buildings when you want to apply for a building permit. When the form is filled in, it's sent to a central permit system, where a civil worker can process the permit. Any updates on the status of the application are communicated with the applicant through the simple permit-tracking website. The next application we'll look at is GovTraffic.

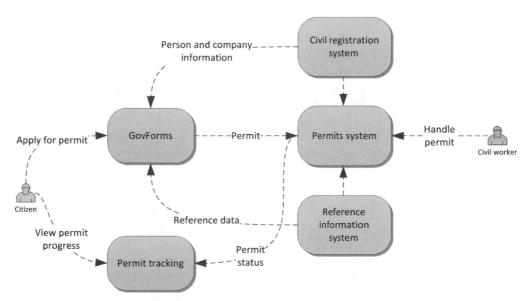

Figure 3.2   The GovForms system and its dependencies

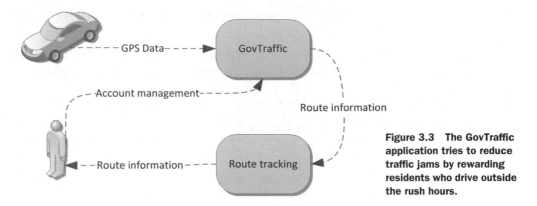

Figure 3.3 **The GovTraffic application tries to reduce traffic jams by rewarding residents who drive outside the rush hours.**

3.2.2 GovTraffic: the traffic avoidance system

I've already introduced this application in the previous chapter, so for details on how this application works, look at the first couple of sections in chapter 2. I'll use this product and its services to demonstrate how to measure runtime policies. In figure 3.3 a high-level overview of how this application works is given.

Cars that use this system transmit their GPS coordinates and time to a central system. This system registers this information and, based on the routes driven and the time of day, rewards participants. Participants also have the option of checking which routes they've driven and how much money they were rewarded for each route.

3.2.3 GovMobile: registering your complaint using mobile devices

When you're walking through a park, you might notice someone has dumped their trash there or sprayed graffiti on some monument. When you see this, you remind yourself that you have to mention this to the city board to have it cleaned up. When you get home, though, you've forgotten the exact location and decide to just forget about it. What if you had an application on your smartphone with which you could register this complaint directly? OpenGov provides a mobile app for this scenario. When people download this application, they can submit complaints directly from their phone. This is shown in figure 3.4.

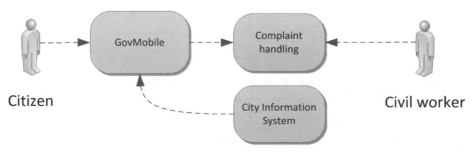

Figure 3.4 **The GovMobile application is an app for the Android and iPhone platforms that residents can use to register complaints and access city information.**

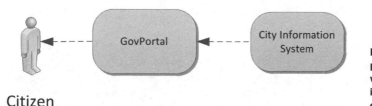

Figure 3.5 GovPortal provides a simple website where all relevant information regarding a city can be found.

If, for instance, someone sees a pothole in the road, with this application they can take a photo and directly send this to the complaint department of their city, where a civil worker can assess the complaint and send out workers to fix the pothole. This application also provides some general information about the city, such as opening times of public buildings, contact information for the various departments, phone numbers of police and fire stations, and the like. This general information isn't just available on mobile phones; it's also available through the GovPortal website.

3.2.4 GovPortal: information about city services

The GovPortal website serves as a general portal, as shown in figure 3.5, to all the information the city has to offer, such as garbage pickup times, contact information, things to do, and so on.

This information is pretty much the same as what's available through the Gov-Mobile application, but this time it's available on a website. I'll use this application to show you how you can work with multiple versions of the same services and how you can maintain backward compatibility.

3.2.5 GovData: OpenGov's open data portal

The GovData service provides a WS-* and REST interface to all public information in the various systems provided by OpenGov. This includes geographic information, supplied permits, crime rates, average housing prices, demographic information, and traffic info. A high-level overview of this application is shown in figure 3.6.

In later chapters you'll see how this information is provided to the customers, how performance can be monitored, and more.

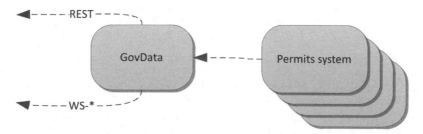

Figure 3.6 The GovData service aggregates information from the various other systems provided by OpenGov and provides a simple-to-use interface to access this data.

Open data initiatives

We're getting used to having information available to us. We can access information regarding books using Amazon's APIs; we have a wealth of movie, actor, and series information available through sites such as IMDB and thetvdb.com. There are many other sources of freely available public data (just look at the http://www .programmableweb.com website for a list of open APIs). One source of data has been missing until the last couple of years: government-related data. In recent years lots of governments have started an open data initiative where they are opening up public data. The United States had launched the http://data.gov website, the UK has http://data.gov.uk, and many other countries such as Canada and The Netherlands also provide portals where residents can access data ranging from government spending to birth rates and from traffic information to crime rates.

Now that you've seen the product portfolio of OpenGov, let's look at the services the various systems provide. These are the services that are used in the examples in the later chapters. Note that we won't be looking at the actual web or mobile applications in this or future chapters. Designing web and mobile applications is out of the scope of this book.

3.3   *Overview of the available services*

Before we look at the policies that have been defined by the OpenGov organization, it's important to know which services are available within the OpenGov organization. In the following chapter these services are used to demonstrate how to apply the defined policies and how to monitor these policies at runtime. Table 3.3 gives a short overview of what these services do.

Table 3.3   Overview of all the services OpenGov applications use

Service name	Description
PeopleRegistration-Service	This service provides information on residents of a specific city. It contains data such as address, relatives, marital state, birth dates, and anything else related to who a person is.
PublicSpace-RegistrationService	A public space can be anything from a park to a street to a lake. This service deals with public spaces that are located within the city limits. With this service you can request information regarding a specific public space such as name, registration date, GIS information, and so on.
CompanyRegistration-Service	Just as the PeopleRegistrationService handles the registration of persons, the CompanyRegistrationService does the same for companies. It allows access to when a company was founded, how many employees it has, and various registration numbers.
PermitService	The PermitService handles everything that deals with the registration and processing of permit requests. For example, this service provides functionality for changing the status of a permit.

Table 3.3   Overview of all the services OpenGov applications use *(continued)*

Service name	Description
ReportService	Through different channels residents can register complaints. They can use the mobile app as well as the website. This service is used to register these complaints and provides functionality to process the complaints.
QAService	Besides complaining to the city, it's also possible to ask questions or perhaps inform the issuing authority about the status of your permit. Every contact that's made with the city is registered in the QAService.
ReferenceDataService	When you fill in the various forms, some data is required that isn't handled by any of the other services. For instance, when you want to request a permit to cut down an old tree in your garden, you need to specify the type of tree. That kind of information is stored in the ReferenceDataService.
TrafficAccountService	For the GovTraffic application you need to store specific account information; as you've seen in the previous chapter, this account information is handled by this service.
TrafficDataService	This service handles the storing of GPS data and provides information on the routes traveled.
ProductsService	The ProductsService provides information on all the products and services that are offered by the city.
NewsService	This simple service provides a news feed of interesting events that have happened in the city.
ContactInformation-Service	All the contact information from the various public offices in a city is provided through this service. This contains the contact information for the public library, the public swimming pool, and so on.
OpenDataService	This service combines data from various sources to provide data to the residents in an easy-to-process format. It also allows residents to create their own applications using data provided by the city.
ParkingPermitService	This service allows residents to get an overview of the parking permits that have been issued by the city and allows city officials view all the parking permits.

So far you've seen how the OpenGov organization is organized, the products it offers to its customers, and the underlying services that handle the data.

3.4   *Defining policies for the OpenGov organization*

In this section we'll look at the policies that have been defined by this organization. The policies are divided into the same categories as shown in chapter 1. These policies use the following properties (based on a template from TOGAF, an enterprise architecture framework):

- *Name*—The name of the policy should represent the essence of the policy. It should be as unambiguous as possible.

- *Statement*—This describes the policy in a couple of sentences.
- *Rationale*—This section describes why this policy is in place. It should list the benefits to be gained from adhering to this policy.
- *Implications*—This describes how this policy affects those who must comply to it.

The headings of the following sections are quotes from a specific stakeholder that summarize the policy. In parts 2 and 3 of this book you'll see how to implement and comply with these policies. For ease of reference I've numbered each of these policies. In the following section, when we talk about a policy I'll reference this number, so you can easily refer back to the various policies. I'll use the following shortcuts as reference for the policies:

- SSD_POL_# for the service design and documentation policies
- SEC_POL_# for references to security-related policies
- PER_POL_# for the performance and testing polices

Let's look at the service design and documentation policies that OpenGov has defined.

3.4.1   Service design and documentation policies

The first policies we'll look at are those dealing with service design and documentation.

"OUR SERVICES MUST BE SELF-DOCUMENTING."
The OpenGov organization has grown a lot the last couple of years. It started with one application and one service, but it has now grown to four applications, multiple platforms, and a large number of services. With the GovData platform the organization is now at a point where it has multiple consumers of its services. The Support manager has complained a lot that they have to answer many basic questions about how customers can use their APIs. To remedy this, the SOA governance board has decided that the following policy should be followed for all services.

Policy: SSD_POL_1	Create self-documenting services.
Statement	All services, REST and WS-* alike, must be self-documenting. There shouldn't be the need for extensive manuals on how to use the services we provide.
Rationale	We want our customers to be able to use our services without the help of online documentation or calling the help desk. Creating self-documenting services will help us keep the available documentation succinct and up to date. If our services are self-explanatory, consumers will have less need to call the help desk, and we can focus on creating new services and functionality.
Implications	For all the WS-* based services the WSDL will serve as the base for the documentation. When registering a service in the repository, from this WSDL human-readable documentation must be created and linked to this service. The REST services should use relations and links to show intent regarding how these services should be used. For REST services a text document must be created and stored in the repository together with the REST service definition. This document explains, in a human-readable manner, how the service is to be used.

"WE MUST USE THE GENERALLY ACCEPTED DATA MODELS."

OpenGov isn't the only player in the public sector that offers these kinds of systems. Other companies offer pretty much the same functionality. A number of big players offer extensive web applications that help the customer apply for permits. The Sales manager noted that they lose business because they can't integrate easily with the applications from these other companies. Luckily there are some national standards that define what such an electronic form should look like and that could ease the integration effort. The SOA governance board has decided on the following policy to address this issue.

Policy: SSD_POL_2	Reuse existing message standards.
Statement	If there are (inter)national standards defined for the entities we exchange, we should at least offer an interface that can work with these entities. We must also make sure that before we start defining our own internal model, we look at the existing models to see whether we can use or extend an existing one.
Rationale	If we follow these standards, integration with other parties will be quicker and more cost efficient. We can more easily go to market with these other parties and get more reuse out of the services we define based on these models.
Implications	<ul><li>Before specific models are defined, we need to look at the standards that are available. If a standard that matches our requirements is already available, we should follow that standard.</li><li>If no standard is available, or the standard doesn't match, we'll define our own model.</li><li>If our model is a superset of a standard that's available, we'll still provide an interface to our systems based on that standard.</li></ul>

"WE HAVE MULTIPLE SERVICES THAT HANDLE ACCOUNTS."

The Development manager has analyzed which services are currently available and is detecting duplication. When he mentioned this issue to the SOA governance board, the Sales manager and Support manager recognized the problem. When they were dealing with customers they had to search for customers in multiple systems. This duplication introduced a lot of extra effort and errors. To make sure that in the future this wouldn't happen again, the SOA governance board defined the following policy.

Policy: SSD_POL_3	Design for reusability.
Statement	All services with their descriptions must be registered centrally. Before a new service is developed, this registry must be checked to see whether there's already a service offering this functionality or whether this functionality should be added to an existing service instead of introducing a new service.
Rationale	We want to avoid creating new services when the functionality is already available in one of the existing services. By introducing a central repository where all the services are stored in a uniform way, we make it easier to reuse existing services and avoid unnecessary duplication. This will allow us to more quickly roll out new functionality to our consumers.

(continued)

Policy: SSD_POL_3	Design for reusability.
Implications	<ul><li>Before a service is created, business analysts and developers must search through the repository to see if a similar service is already available.</li><li>The centralized repository must be available during design time so that it can be used for service discovery.</li><li>Services must be specified and registered in such a way that they can be easily discovered by searching in the repository.</li></ul>

"OUR CUSTOMERS DEMAND SUPPORT FOR MULTIPLE VERSIONS."

The Sales manager noted that since the first release of the GovData platform there have been many releases, and the customers struggle to keep up. They write their custom applications to a specific version of the service, and before they're up and running, a new version is released, which causes customers to rewrite their own applications. On the other hand, the Sales manager noted, this isn't something that should prevent adding functionality quickly that allows response to the market. During a SOA governance board session, the following is decided.

Policy: SSD_POL_4	Support multiple versions of services.
Statement	We must be able to support two versions at a time. Our customers are allowed to run one version behind. When we bring out a new version, we also need to check whether it's a breaking change, which introduces a new version number, or a backward-compatible change, which doesn't warrant a new version.
Rationale	The reason for the policy is that we can't expect consumers of our services to immediately update to a new version of a service they're using. A breaking change will also require changes on the client side. To allow our consumers to smoothly move to a new version of a service, we allow them to run one major version behind.
Implications	<ul><li>WSDLs and schemas must be set up in such a way that they can be easily versioned. This means that we have to make sure the namespaces used reflect the correct version of a service or message.</li><li>REST services will also have to be versioned. This means that in their content-type description a version number must be present.</li><li>A service lifecycle must be in place that informs the consumer of the state the service is in.</li><li>The repository must be able to support multiple versions of the same service, and users of the repository must be able to easily discern the version of the service they're looking at.</li></ul>

3.4.2   *Security policies*

The next policies we'll look at are the security-related policies.

"WE NEED TO COMPLY WITH NEW LEGISLATION, AND OUR DATA CHANNEL MUST BE SECURED."

Some of the applications provided by OpenGov deal with sensitive information. The central government has created new legislation that states that any data handled by a local authority (for example, a municipality) needs to be encrypted. The Legal department of the OpenGov organization wants to make sure its applications comply with these new laws. The SOA governance board decided on the following policy.

Policy: SEC_POL_1	Encrypt a communications channel for sensitive data.
Statement	All sensitive data regarding persons and permits needs to be encrypted before being sent to the customer. This not only goes for the websites we provide but also must be applied on the service level.
Rationale	We can't afford to have our consumers lose trust in the services we provide. If sensitive information is leaked, the negative press will cause consumers to run away to other service providers. By providing encrypted access to our services, we ensure our customers that no third parties can eavesdrop on the data.
Implications	<ul><li>When a service is developed that deals with sensitive information, this service must be exposed through HTTPS.</li><li>A process needs to be set up to deal with the server certificates lifecycle.</li><li>If client certificates are used, a process must be set up that deals with the administration and registration of these certificates.</li></ul>

Identity theft and public data

Most people have a good idea what identity theft is. It's a form of fraud where someone pretends to be someone else. The thief can empty bank accounts, take out loans, and much, much worse. With internet and social media sites such as Facebook, MySpace, and Twitter, it's becoming easy to obtain information about other persons and take over their identity, especially on the internet, where you can still be fairly anonymous. Many organizations and sites have acknowledged that this is a serious problem and are taking measures to prevent such access. Logins are only possible over secured channels, people are warned about the personal information they make available, and they're warned about the risks of accepting every friend request. Many governments have also acknowledged this as a serious problem and are restricting access to personal data or requiring strict audit logs.

The main problem, though, is with people themselves. In recent research it was shown that if you ask people in a random survey for their passwords, many people will hand them out. So, even though a lot of information (some say too much) can be easily retrieved from social networking sites, the biggest issue is still with people themselves.

"THERE HAVE BEEN ATTEMPTS TO FALSIFY GPS DATA; WE NEED AN ANSWER TO THIS."
The lead analyst mentioned that the Analysis department had been seeing some strange behavior the last couple of weeks. The GovTraffic application had been receiving some strange GPS data that didn't seem completely legit. It looks like some users of the traffic avoidance system have been falsifying their GPS data to get a higher reward. The CEO wants this stopped, because if bad press on this program could mean

losing a lot of customers. The SOA governance board has defined the following policy to handle the CEO's request.

Policy: SEC_POL_2	Validate message integrity and non-repudiation.
Statement	We need to be sure that all messages that create or update information in our systems can be checked for message integrity and non-repudiation.
Rationale	With our GPS data service clients are paid based on whether they have avoided traveling at specific times or over specific routes. If customers are able to send falsified data, the calculations will be incorrect and the company will lose money.
Implications	▪ We need to define a way our message can be signed for both our WS-* and REST architectures. This must allow us to identify whether the message has been tampered with. ▪ Our clients need to add a signature to each message they send. ▪ We need to alter our services so that each message is validated before it's processed.

"OUR CUSTOMERS WANT SIMPLER AUTHENTICATION AND AUTHORIZATIONS MECHANISMS."

All the applications OpenGov currently has have been more or less been developed in isolation. They all have implemented their own authentication and authorization mechanisms. Customers have been complaining that they need several different kinds of usernames and need to log in multiple times when switching applications. The Support manager recognized this problem and added that the same problem occurs in the authorization area. The more applications they need to support, the more authorization mechanisms they need to support. The Support manager and the Development manager decide on the following two security policies that apply to services and applications.

Policy: SEC_POL_3	Use a centralized identity system for authentication.
Statement	All applications and services will use a central single sign-on mechanism for authentication.
Rationale	Having multiple authentication systems forces our customers to remember multiple usernames and passwords. With a single system for authentication we can more easily track which clients are using the various services. A single system will also bring down development costs because not every service needs to implement its own schemes.
Implications	▪ A federated identity system for authentication needs to be set up and made available to the various services. ▪ All services that require authentication need to be changed to make use of this new federated system. ▪ Processes need to be in place for creating and administering users stored in this federated system.

Policy: SEC_POL_4	Use a centralized identity system for authorization.
Statement	All applications and services will use a central system that determines the roles and rights users of our systems and applications have.
Rationale	Implementing authorization is often done in a very application-specific manner. Each service and application invents its own authorization schemes that have to be developed and administrated separately. With a single authorization system we standardize the way applications deal with authorization and we can centralize the administration of the roles, rights and users.
Implications	■ A federated identity system for authorizations needs to be set up and made available to the various services. ■ All services that require authorization need to be changed to make use of this new federated system. ■ Processes need to be in place for creating and administering the rights and roles stored in this federated system.

3.4.3 Performance and testing-related policies

The final policies we'll look at are the performance and testing-related policies.

"WE MUST PROCESS GPS DATA WITHIN 10 MS."

The traffic avoidance system has been successful the last six months. The Sales manager has gotten a request from one of their biggest customers that they also want to start using this system. This customer, however, wants guarantees that the system can cope with the high demand that will be placed on it. For this the Sales manager has defined a service-level agreement (SLA) with this customer. One of the items from this SLA is that the average processing time of the GPS data will be less than 10 milliseconds.

Policy: PER_POL_1	Process messages within 10 ms.
Statement	The average processing time of the GPS data messages must be less than 10 milliseconds.
Rationale	To be able to cope with the increasing load, the service that deals with GPS data needs to be able to process messages within 10 ms.
Implications	■ We need to monitor the environment to see the average processing time. ■ We need to execute stress tests to see how the system performs under increasing load.

"WE WANT TO MEASURE THE PERFORMANCE OF OUR SERVICES IN REAL TIME."

The Product Support manager has complained that they can't proactively monitor the services available. They only detect problems when a service is already down. The Service manager would like to see performance monitoring in real time on all the services that OpenGov provides. During a SOA governance board session, this is defined in the following policy.

Policy: PER_POL_2	Monitor services in real time.
Statement	All services need to be monitored in real time.
Rationale	If we want to be able to monitor our services effectively and respond to any problems as quickly as possible, we need to monitor our services in real time.
Implications	■ All our services need to be changed so that they send out events. ■ Events need to be processed by a BAM solution in real time. ■ A dashboard is required, which business analysts and the Product Support department can use to monitor the usage of the services.

"I WANT TO SEE AN OVERVIEW OF THE DIFFERENT PERMIT APPLICATIONS FROM THE LAST DAY."

The lead analyst doesn't have an easy way to access information on how the services are being used. She requires this information to determine which new services to develop and whether new products might be required. The Sales manager also believes he can serve his customers better if he has better statistical information regarding the use of the services and applications. They defined the following policy for this.

Policy: PER_POL_3	Provide a flexible view for how services are used.
Statement	The services need to offer a customizable view of specific events.
Rationale	If we can see how the clients use our services, we can better help them. If downtime is required, we can do this while the least number of consumers are using our services. If we see many errors in a specific service, we can focus our attention on that problem. This allows us to better focus our effort where it has the most effect.
Implications	■ Set up dashboards that monitor specific functionality of our services. ■ Allow complex processing of events to create the view the business analysts require.

"WE NEED TO BE ABLE TO HORIZONTALLY SCALE OUR SERVICES."

The CEO and Sales manager expect a lot of growth in the coming years. In a SOA governance board meeting they discussed this with the other members. Everybody agreed that if they want to grow, without spending too much money, they need to make their services able to scale horizontally. They defined this requirement in the following policy.

Policy: PER_POL_4	Run services in the cloud.
Statement	All our services should be able to scale horizontally. To keep costs down it should be possible to run our services in a cloud-like environment.
Rationale	The usage of the services is expected to grow greatly. But investing at this time in hardware resources isn't possible. To keep costs low and to be able to easily increase computing resources, our services must be able to run in the cloud.

(continued)

Policy: PER_POL_4	Run services in the cloud.
Implications	<ul><li>There are many cloud providers available. A cloud provider must be selected that provides the functionality our services require.</li><li>A new reference implementation of our services must be created that makes use of the functionality offered by the cloud platform.</li><li>The monitoring environment will need to be appended so that it can monitor services that run in the cloud, instead of just those running in our own environment.</li></ul>

"OUR USERS FIND TOO MANY BUGS IN OUR SERVICES."

The Development manager had been getting a lot of requests and bug reports from the Product Support manager, because the Product Support manager had received a number of complaints from their customers about various bugs in the services they use. Because of these bugs a number of customers had to put their own development on hold, and they were looking around for a different service provider. The Development manager decided it was time to take the quality of their code more seriously. As a first step he defined the following policy.

Policy: TST_POL_1	Enforce code quality and test coverage.
Statement	All of our services must be tested before being shipped. These services must be tested on all the different layers. Besides these tests an automatic check must be used to determine the code quality and the test coverage for a specific service.
Rationale	If we don't test the various layers, it will be very hard to quickly find problems with the code. By testing each layer we can be sure that the code does what it has to do and that we quickly spot bugs. To make it easier to check the quality and the test coverage of the code, an automatic tool should be used. With this tool we can get a quick overview of the quality of the code and see whether we tested enough.
Implications	<ul><li>Each layer of each service needs to be tested. For this we need to decide how we can do this the most effectively.</li><li>We must decide what test coverage we want to achieve.</li><li>There are many metrics that can be used to determine code quality. We need to select the metrics we want to measure.</li></ul>

In this section we explored a lot of policies this company wants to comply with. In part 2 of the book we'll start by looking at how to implement these policies.

3.5 *Summary*

- The applications and services provided by OpenGov form the basis of the examples in the rest of the book.
- OpenGov is a fairly standard organization, where there are many stakeholders with different goals.

- OpenGov supports five applications: GovForms, GovTraffic, GovMobile, GovPortal, and GovData.
- GovForms is an application that residents can use to request various types of permits.
- GovTraffic is an application that rewards residents for traveling outside the rush hours by using GPS information.
- GovMobile is a mobile app for the iOS and Android platforms by which complaints, for instance, about trash in a public space, can be made.
- GovPortal is a simple web application that provides information on the products and services that are offered by the city.
- GovData is a central service that can be used to access all kinds of different public data, which residents themselves can use in their own mockups.
- OpenGov currently has a large number of services but no policies.
- The stakeholders have come together and, based on their various views, have defined a set of policies that need to be followed.

In the following chapters I'll use these applications and services as examples when I talk about policies and how to implement and comply with them.

Part 2

Design-time policies

In this second part of the book we'll look at three different categories of policies that can be applied during design time. We'll start by looking at policies that deal with service design and documentation. In this category we'll examine the following policies:

- SSD_POL_1: Create self-documenting services.
- SSD_POL_2: Reuse existing message standards.
- SSD_POL_3: Design for reusability.
- SSD_POL_4: Support multiple versions of services.

Besides documentation policies that can be applied during design time, there are also a number of security-related policies that can be applied during this phase. In this part we'll look at the set of security policies, as shown in the following list:

- SEC_POL_1: Encrypt a communications channel for sensitive data.
- SEC_POL_2: Validate message integrity and non-repudiation.
- SEC_POL_3: Use a centralized identity system for authentication.
- SEC_POL_4: Use a centralized identity system for authorization.
- The last chapter in this part of the book looks at how you can effectively test your service and use metrics to define the quality of your code, as well as how you can design and implement a service that can run in a cloud:
- PER_POL_4: Run services in the cloud.
- TST_POL_1: Enforce code quality and test coverage.

Service design and documentation policies

4

This chapter covers

- Making your services self-documenting
- Reusing existing standards and definitions
- Increasing service reusability
- Versioning your services

If you want to create services that can be easily used by your consumers, you need to provide good documentation and versioning strategies. If you don't have these in place, you'll either not get anybody to use your service or, with the first upgrade, scare your existing consumers away with breaking changes. When you keep good documentation, versioning, and reuse in mind during the development phase of your service, you make it a lot easier on your consumers; they have a clear set of documentation on how your service should be used and also know the consequences of a version change.

In this chapter we'll discuss a number of design-time-related policies that can help you in this area. I'll start by quickly introducing the policies we'll be discussing in this chapter, and after that we'll discuss each of these policies in detail, using the case study from chapter 3. A quick overview and short explanation of these policies is shown in table 4.1.

Table 4.1 Service design and documentation policies

Policy name	Description
Create self-documenting services.	It's important for your consumers to have good documentation for the services they want to use. Often this documentation is in a separate document they need to read before the service interface makes sense. With this policy I'll show you that most of the functionality a service provides can be described by the service itself, without the need for extensive external documentation.
Reuse existing message standards.	An often-seen antipattern is the "Not invented here" pattern. Instead of using standards (or de facto standards), organizations, especially IT groups, have the tendency to reinvent the wheel. In this policy implementation you'll see how easy it is to reuse existing standards in REST and WS-* environments.
Design for reusability.	When you design a service, it would be nice if this service could be reused by other services and consumers. In the section dealing with this policy, I'll present a set of common guidelines and practices that can help you in creating a service that can be more easily reused.
Support multiple versions of services.	The final policy we'll discuss in this chapter deals with versioning. A service isn't static. During its lifetime, bugs will be fixed and functionality will be added or removed. The contract of a service will change. Having a good versioning strategy will help you minimize the impact these changes have on your consumers.

In the next section you'll see how to comply with the self-documenting service policy and how to create self-documenting services.

4.1 *Complying with the self-documenting service policy*

During the last couple of years we've been moving from an application-oriented way of software development to a more service-oriented approach. More and more functionality is offered through third-party services that you can include into your own applications. This also means that instead of customers receiving a large user manual for the application they just bought, they now need to know how to use a specific service. Because people usually don't want to read through hundreds of pages of documentation, make sure your services are self-documenting and require minimal additional documentation. In the ideal situation the consumer of your service should know how to use this service by just looking at its contract. For WS-* based services this usually means examining the WSDL, and for REST-based services, the messages used should explain how to use the service.

In this section I'll first show you how to design a REST-based service in such a way that a user can determine how to use the service just by looking at the response messages. After that you'll learn how you can create a well-documented WS-* service by using the standard WSDL constructs. Because it's also always nice to have a simple description of the API you provide (for instance, on your website), I'll also show you how to write/create some basic HTML API documentation for your REST- and WS-* based services. First, we'll look at the REST service.

4.1.1 Documenting a REST-based service

Chapter 3 showed you the product portfolio for the OpenGov organization. One of the products it provides is a mobile application that can be used to instantly register a complaint when a user spots some graffiti or sees trash scattered around the park. This complaint is instantly sent to the correct department of their municipality, and they can send out the cleaning crews. In the next couple of paragraphs we'll look at the REST/JSON–based service that this app uses to register the complaints. A simplified scenario of how this app works is shown in figure 4.1.

In figure 4.1 the GovMobile app uses the REST/JSON–based `ReportService` to register these complaints. Each complaint will be registered as a report for further processing. Besides the mobile application that creates these reports, there's also a civil worker shown, who can delete reports, update their status, and mark the reports as invalid or duplicate.

What does this service look like? How should it be called? What data should be sent to create a report? We're describing a REST-based service here, so it's important to start by looking at the resource we're dealing with. Before we start with the resource description, though, we'll quickly look at the functionality this service should provide.

This service needs to

- Provide functionality to add new reports from the GovMobile application
- Allow a citizen to add URLs of photos of the complaint/report
- Offer search functionality so that users can search for reports in a specific vicinity
- Let the user add comments to a specific report
- Give the civil worker the option to relate a report to other reports
- Provide the civil worker basic CRUD functionality to manage the various reports

As you'll see further on in this section, when you use REST a lot of this functionality doesn't need specific documentation, because it can be mapped to the standard

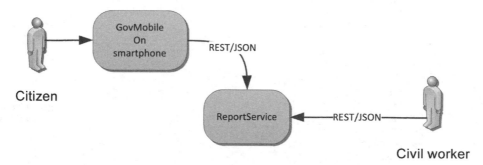

Figure 4.1 A citizen uses a mobile app to access a service provided by OpenGov.

HTTP verbs. The most important part when creating REST services is the resource, so we'll start with that.

ANALYZING THE REPORT RESOURCE

With REST you don't focus on operations and remote procedures. Instead you look at a resource and use the standard HTTP operation to modify this resource. For this service you're working with a `report` resource. This means that if you know the location of a resource—its uniform resource identifier (URI)—you don't need documentation for the basic functionality. With REST you can be sure that when you know the location of a resource, you can use the following:

- HTTP GET method to retrieve a resource
- HTTP PUT method to add a resource
- HTTP DELETE method to delete a resource
- HTTP POST method to update a resource

If you start the `ReportService` from the chapter 3 examples you can retrieve a resource by executing a HTTP GET method on the following URL: http://local host:9002/opengov/reports/{report-id}. If you open this URL and replace {report-id} with report-1, you'll be shown the report identified by that id. This report resource is shown in listing 4.1, which also includes the HTTP headers. In one of these headers, this resource's `Content-Type` is defined as `application/vnd.opengov.org.report +json`. This tells the consumer that the resource they're looking at is of a custom type `vnd.opengov.org.report` and the format used is `json`.

Listing 4.1 Report-1 in JSON format

```
HTTP/1.1 200 Ok
Date: Wed, 12 Feb 2011 17:18:11 GMT
Content-Type: application/vnd.opengov.org.report+json;charset=UTF-8

{"report": {
    "self": "report-1",                                          Which report you're
    "status": "New",                                          ❶ dealing with
    "location": "Corner of ninth street",
    "x-coordinate": 52.34,
    "y-coordinate":  4.34,
    "description": "There is ugly graffiti
                sprayed on the mailbox at the corner
                on ninth street",
    "date": "25-11-2010",
    "time": "15:46"
    "images": [
     {"href": "images/image1.png"},                            ❷ Images related
     {"href": "images/image2.png"}                                to this report
    ],
    "related":[
      {"href": "../report-4"},
      {"href": "../report-7"},                                 ❸ Reports related
      {"href": "../report-9"}                                     to this report
    ]
```

```
    "links": [
      {"relation": "invalidation",
       "href": "http://localhost:9002/opengov/invalidations/"},        ❹
      {"relation": "duplication",                                       Operations
       "href": "http://localhost:9002/opengov/duplications/"}          that can be
      {"relation": "relation",                                         executed on
       "href": "http://localhost:9002/opengov/relations/"}            this report

    ]
    "comments": []                                                      Comments added
                                                                     ❺ to this report
  }
}
```

We're talking about self-documenting services in this section, so before we continue, take a good look at listing 4.1 and see if you can understand what's shown there. You can probably determine how to add and remove new image locations to/from this report and how to add and remove report relations. By looking a bit closer at this example, you'll see how easy it is to make REST/JSON services self-documenting. If you look at the first annotation in the code ❶, you'll see a key with the name `self`. The value of this key is used to uniquely identify this resource. If you get a list of reports from a search query, you can use this id to directly access or modify a report. If you look at ❷, you'll see a list of image `hrefs`. With REST you're working with resources. If you wanted to access such an image, you could do so by following its relative URL: http://localhost:9002/opengov/reports/report-1/images/image-1 for the first image in the list and http://localhost:9002/opengov/reports/report-1/images/image-2 for the second image in the list. Because these images are also resources, you can modify them the same way as you can with this report. You can use the basic HTTP verbs to retrieve, add, delete and update this image.

LOOKING AT REFERENCED RESOURCES
What else can you learn from the resource shown in listing 4.1? The ❸ annotation in the code shows reports that are related to this report. For example, another piece of graffiti may be found across the street from the piece that has already been reported. This can be useful when the city hires a cleaning crew to remove the graffiti. It can tell them to clean not only the graffiti from this specific report but also from those related to it. For the related reports you follow the same principle as you did for the images. If you want to access the resource, follow the relative URL and you'll find the related report. So far we've only looked at basic REST functionality where you have resources that you can modify by using the HTTP GET, PUT, DELETE, and POST verbs, but how do you tell your service consumer which other actions can be executed on this resource?

USING LINKS TO SHOW WHICH OPERATIONS CAN BE EXECUTED ON THIS RESOURCE
Listing 4.1 specified a number of links ❹. These links are basic URLs that point to a specific resource. In this example they point to a `relation`, `duplication`, and `invalidation` resource. This resource can be accessed in the same manner as other REST resources; this time, though, you don't create or update the resource but execute a specific action. In this example you can mark a specific report as invalid by

submitting a PUT request, with the report as its content, to the URL specified by the invalidation relation (`http://localhost:9002/opengov/invalidations/`). This same principle can be applied to the `relation` and `duplication` links.

More on links: Atom and RDF

The use of links isn't something new. The `<link>` tag is specified in the HTML 4 standard and is used to link a specific web resource to another resource. Generally, though, you won't see it used much in standard web pages. It was used a lot by some feed protocols. One of the best known is Atom. The Atom Syndication Format is a simple XML-based format that can be used to define web feeds. One of the interesting features of this format is the use of the `<link>` tag. The `self` link we used in this documentation example is defined as a standard relation in the Atom specification. Besides the `self` type, Atom also specifies relations such as `edit`, `alternative`, and more. If you need to publish data in a specific format, Atom would be a good choice. More information on Atom can be found in the relevant RFCs: http://tools.ietf.org/html/rfc4287 and http://tools.ietf.org/html/rfc5023.

Besides the relations defined in the Atom specification, there's a different standard that focuses exclusively on describing the semantics of resources. This is called the Resource Description Framework (RDF). With RDF you describe all kinds of information regarding a resource. You have a standard way of describing who the author is, when the resource was published, and so on. If you have a strict set of relations between various resources, you can use RDF to describe this information in a standard way. RDF is a W3C standard, so a lot of information on RDF can be found on the W3C pages at http://www.w3.org/RDF/.

So far the REST service is pretty much self-explanatory. What is missing, though, and where additional documentation is required, is a description of the resources themselves. What does a report look like, which fields are required, what does a comment look like? In this example, if you wanted to add a comment ❺, you could determine from the listing that you need to PUT a `comment` message to the `/reports/report-1/comments/` URL. But what does this message look like? If you'd used XML instead of JSON, you could have used an XML schema to define what the resources look like. With JSON, however, there isn't a standard way (not including WADL, because it isn't used in practice), to describe what the JSON messages look like. What you usually see is that with a JSON-based REST service, a simple HTML or plain-text description for the different resources is provided in a human-readable format.

CREATING HUMAN-READABLE DOCUMENTATION

As you've seen before you don't need to document everything. What you should describe are the following items:

- URLs used to access or search for a report
- Links relations that describe how various resources are linked together
- Media types that are used by this service

Let's make such a description for this service. The first thing you describe is the URL on which this service can be accessed:

```
URLs:
http://localhost:9002/opengov/reports?location=xPos,yPos&radius=r
Submit a GET request to this URL to search for reports. You can optionally
    specify a location and a radius to only return reports for a specific
    area. If no location and radius are specified, the first 100 reports,
    sorted by date (newest first), are returned. The reports that are
    returned have the application/vnd.opengov.org.report+json  media type.
xPos: x-coordinate of the location. Accepts GPS coordinates.
yPos: y-coordinate of the location. Accepts GPS coordinates.
r: radius to search for in meters.
```

You can see that you've provided a search function with which reports for a specific location can be retrieved. You also specify the media type of the report you're returning. A media type should specify exactly what type of resource you're dealing with. In the previous example you defined a media type of `application/vnd.opengov.org.report+json`. The first part of this media type, `application`, defines the category the media type belongs to. There are a couple of commonly used categories such as application, audio, image, message, text, and video. You can use these categories to indicate the general type of the resource. `application` is a rather general category that's used for multipurpose resources. The second part of this media type starts with vnd. This indicates that you're using a vendor-specific resource. There isn't a standard for the resource you're defined, so it's good practice to indicate this with the vnd prefix, which means that you created your own custom media type. The next part of the media type, `opengov.org.report`, indicates that you're working with a report resource. This identifier uniquely indicates the type of resource this is. Finally you have the postfix `+json`. This postfix tells your consumers that the format in which the resource is sent is JSON.

This makes it easier for the consumers to work with your responses, because they know exactly what the service returns.

The next item in your list is to describe the links:

```
Links:
self: identifies the current resource. This (relative) URL can be used to
    directly access or modify a report.

http://localhost:9002/opengov/invalidations/: This URL can be used to
    invalidate this resource. Use an HTTP PUT operation on this URL with
    media type application/vnd.opengov.org.invalidation+json.

http://localhost:9002/opengov/duplications/: This URL can be used to mark a
    report as a duplicate. Use an HTTP PUT operation on this URL with media
    type application/vnd.opengov.org.duplication+json.

http://localhost:9002/opengov/relations/: This URL can be used to relate two
    reports to each other. Use an HTTP PUT operation on this URL with media
    type application/vnd.opengov.org.invalidation+json.
```

The last thing you need to do is describe the resources themselves. If you'd used XML you would have mentioned where the schema could be found that describes a specific media type. In this case you just describe the properties of the media types. If some elements should be sent in a specific format (for example, a date) or elements are required, this is the place to describe it:

```
Media types:
application/vnd.opengov.org.report+json
- status: The status of this report
- location: Readable description of the location of this report
- etc.
```

With these items described you have enough documentation for your consumers to use your service. As you've seen, a REST service by itself doesn't need much documentation. Because you're using REST, the consumers already have a good idea how your resources can be accessed, modified, and deleted. It's important, though, if you want a good, self-describing service that requires a minimal amount of additional documentation, to keep the following items in mind:

- Follow the basic REST principles for the HTTP PUT, GET, DELETE, and POST operations.
- Use href/links when linking to other resources. It doesn't matter if you use relative links or absolute links for this, although relative links are more flexible should you relocate your resource.
- Use media types to inform your consumers of the type of resource they're dealing with.
- Use links with a specific relation property to tell your consumers what they can do with this resource.
- Add a simple description of the URLs, media types, and links that are supported by your service.

A complete description of this service can be found in the source code for chapter 4. Look in the Self-Documenting-Service-REST project supplied with the book. In the next section you'll again create a self-documenting service, but this time you'll document a WS-* based service.

4.1.2   *Documenting a WS-* based service*

Documenting a WS-* based service is easier than describing a REST-based service. For a WS-* based service there's a standard format in which contracts are defined. This contract, a standard WSDL, already provides a good technical description of what operations the service offers and how the service can be accessed, all from a technical point of view. What you need to do is add human-readable documentation that explains how your service should be used, what the operations do, and any special information regarding the request and response messages.

For this example you'll take a use case from the GovForms application. In chapter 3 I showed you that this application, among other functionality, allows citizens to apply for specific permits (building permits, commercial permits, and the like). The GovForms application uses a WS-* based service to communicate with the permits system, as shown in figure 4.2.

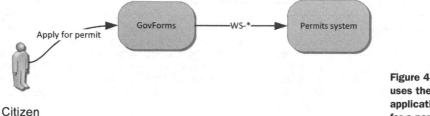

Figure 4.2 A citizen uses the GovForms application to apply for a permit.

Describing WS-* based services can quickly get verbose because of all the XML, so for this example we'll focus on a single operation that's provided by this permit system: the addPermit operation.

THE WSDL FOR THE PERMITSERVICE

In this section we'll look the various parts of a WSDL and how you can document these parts. Before diving into the details, a quick sidestep on how to add documentation to a WSDL is in order. If you look at the XML of a WSDL file you'll see lots of different elements: definitions, types, bindings, ports, services, messages, and so on. These are all elements in the http://schemas.xmlsoap.org/wsdl/ namespace. For all these elements you can add documentation like this:

```
<wsdl:documentation>
  ..
</wsdl:documentation>
```

Anything entered between the wsdl:documentation tag is treated as documentation. The only restriction is that the content needs to be valid XML. Besides elements from this namespace, in a WSDL you'll also find type definitions, either using an inline schema or included from an external XSD file. If you have complex types in your schemas, it's good practice to document these. For schemas this is done like this:

```
<xsd:annotation>
   <xsd:documentation>
   ...
   </xsd:documentation>
</xsd:annotation>
```

With these two elements you can describe all the elements from a WSDL. Table 4.2 shows the different parts of the WSDL you should document.

Table 4.2 Parts of a WSDL that should be documented

WSDL section	How to describe
wsdl:definitions	This is the main element of a WSDL. Here you should describe in a human-readable way what the service does and the functionality it provides. If your service requires special authentication or other requirements, this is the place to put it.

Table 4.2   Parts of a WSDL that should be documented *(continued)*

WSDL section	How to describe
wsdl:types	In this section all the XSD types used throughout the WSDL are defined. When you include many different schemas, it's important to give an overview here of the various included schemas and the types they provide. In this element you often have simple wrapper elements for compliance to the document/literal/wrapped messaging style.
xsd:*	In a WSDL you use an XML schema to define the XML messages that are sent and received by your service. When you start documenting these types in your WSDL, you should also add XSD-specific information for the complex types. If you have a type definition where it isn't clear from the name or the definition how it can be used, you should add documentation. Most often, though, an XSD provides enough information without the need for extra documentation.
wsdl:porttype	This is the interface of the service you provide. You should document this service as you would an interface when you're programming.
wsdl:operation	For each operation you should describe what the operation does, because from the WSDL definition the user can determine how the operation can be accessed but not how it should be used.

Let's look at a couple of the points mentioned in table 4.2 using the PermitService, part of the PermitSystem from figure 4.2, as an example. I'll show you an example for a wsdl:porttype and for a wsdl:operation, because those are the most important items to document in a WSDL. You shouldn't write technical documentation; rather, you should describe how the service works from a functional perspective, because the standard elements from a WSDL already describe the technical part of how the service should be called. See the following listing.

Listing 4.2   Example of how to describe a wsdl:porttype and a wsdl:operation

```
<wsdl:portType name="PermitService">
<wsdl:documentation>
<p>The PermitService porttype defines the operations provided by the
PermitService. This portType defines the following operations that
can be used to interact with the PermitService:</p>
<ul>
  <li>getPermit: returns a permit based on a permitID</li>
  <li>submitPermit: add a new permit. When the permit is added a unique
     permit ID is returned.</li>
</ul>
</wsdl:documentation>
<wsdl:operation name="getPermit">
  <wsdl:documentation>
    <p>With the getPermit you can retrieve stored permits. This operation
       is called with a permitID and if the permitID is found, the
       corresponding Permit is returned. If no permit can be found for the
       id, or the permitID is in the incorrect format, a fault message
```

```
            will be returned. This fault message will contain the details of
            why the error occurred.</p>
      </wsdl:documentation>
      <wsdl:input message="tns:getPermitRequest"/>
      <wsdl:output message="tns:getPermitResponse"/>
      <wsdl:fault name="fault" message="tns:getPermitFault">
      </wsdl:operation>
</wsdl:portType>
```

Using WADL and JSON schema for describing resources

In this section we talked about WSDL and XML schemas. You might wonder why there isn't something like that for the REST/JSON space. Actually, there is something similar for REST. For describing a REST contract there's a standard called WADL, and for describing JSON messages there's something called JSON.

Neither has been widely adopted by the REST and JSON communities. Why is that? If you look at WADL (http://www.w3.org/Submission/wadl/), you'll see the similarity between a WADL and a WSDL. This is also something a lot of people in the REST space aren't happy with. With a WADL you describe an RPC-based style of interacting with a resource. This doesn't match well with the resource-oriented style REST promotes. Besides that, WSDLs are often used as a base for generating the plumbing code needed to interact with WS-* based services. With REST an easy-to-use interface is already provided, and with a couple of easy GET and POST calls you can already explore a service. The JSON schema was also not that well received within the JSON community. The JSON community wants to avoid the heavyweight specifications that define the WS-* stacks. They want to keep it simple and to the point.

The idea is that JSON requests and responses should be self-documenting, and the way you use a REST service to access or modify resources should follow the basic RESTful principles.

With this functional and technical description, you have a good self-describing service. For the REST example I provided a simple text-based version of this documentation. By adding the documentation to the WSDL itself, you don't have such a simple readable document that can be used as documentation. Users of this service will have to dive into the WSDL and find the information from there, which isn't practical. Luckily, though, there are some tools that can help in generating readable documentation from a WSDL.

GENERATING DOCUMENTATION FROM THIS WSDL

A WSDL is an XML file, so you can use XSLT to transform your WSDL to a simple text or HTML file that can be used as documentation. You aren't the first with these requirements, so you don't have to write this XSLT from scratch. The XSLT you use can be downloaded from http://code.google.com/p/wsdl-viewer/.

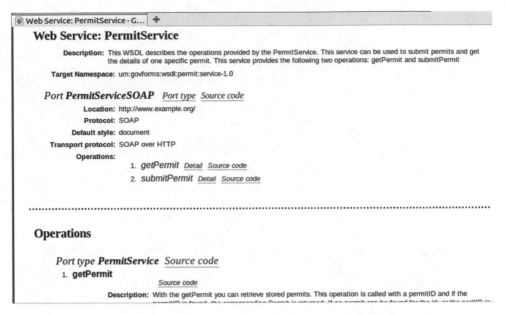

Figure 4.3   WSDL as shown in the browser after the wsdl-viewer.xsl XSLT has been applied

Using this XSLT you can generate an HTML overview of this service. An example of this is shown in figure 4.3.

There are different ways to apply an XSLT to an XML document. For this example you'll use the standard functionality browsers support. If you put an XSLT declaration at the top of an XML file and open it in a browser, the browser will apply this XSLT and show you the results. To see this in action you need to add this to the top of the WSDL:

```
<?xml-stylesheet type="text/xsl" href="wsdl-viewer.xsl"?>
```

The href attribute points to the relative location of the XSLT to apply. In this case you need to download the wsdl-viewer.xsl file from the previously mentioned site and put it in the directory where your WSDL is located. After you've downloaded the XSLT and added the code fragment, you can open the WSDL in your browser and see the WSDL documentation, as shown in figure 4.3. From your browser save this file as HTML; in the next section you'll add this document to your repository for easy reference.

4.1.3 *Adding documentation to the service repository*

Now that you have the documentation, what should you do with it? Send it along when you get a new consumer of your service? Store it on a shared drive? What you need is some way to register this document so that you can reference it from your service and also be able to access it programmatically if you want to automatically publish the latest version to a website. If you store this documentation in your service repository, you can do all this. The steps to do this are simple. Start up the SOA Service

Figure 4.4   Service List shows the two services you just added

registry and go to the address https://localhost:9443. This will redirect you to the login page, where you can log in using admin/admin. The first thing you'll do is register the two services you've worked with in this section. Click the Add Service button, and you'll be shown a large form where you can fill in all kinds of information. For now fill in the name of the service and its namespace. For the WS-* based service use PermitService as the name and urn:govforms:wsdl:permit:service-1.0 for the namespace. Scroll down and click the Save button to store this service. You could have also uploaded the WSDL for the WS-* based service, which would have created this service automatically. We'll show you how to do this later on, but for now having a service is enough.

For the REST-based service you'll use ReportService as the name and http://localhost:9002/opengov/reports as the namespace. You use the URL as the namespace because in REST a resource's URL should uniquely identify the location of a resource. This means you won't run into any naming conflicts, and REST services can be registered in a consistent manner. After you've added both services, click the List Services button, and you'll be shown an overview like the one in figure 4.4.

You have your services in the repository (we'll dive deeper into the specific configuration for services later on in this chapter), and the next step is to add the documentation for these services. As you've probably noticed, there isn't an Add Document button. You can, however, add arbitrary content to the repository. Click the Browse button in the Resources menu. This will show you a tree-based view of all the resources in the repository. In this tree navigate to the /_system/governance resource and click the Governance link. This will show the details of the Governance resource. The governance resource is the parent resource under which all the services, policies, WSDLs, and schemas are stored. Here you'll create a new collection, where you'll store the documentation.

On the /_system/governance screen click the Add Collection button. You'll be shown a small form. As name enter Documentation, and set Media Type to Not Specified. Then click the Add button. In figure 4.5 you can see what this folder looks like after you've added the Documentation resource.

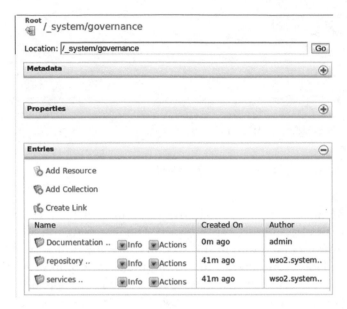

Figure 4.5   The _system/ governance resource after adding the Documentation collection

This Documentation resource is where you'll add your service documentation. Open the Documentation resource and click the Add Resource button. Here you're shown a form with different methods you can use to add content to the repository. As the method use Upload Content From File. Click Choose File and browse to where you stored the HTML from the WS-* documentation example. Click Add and the resource will be added. If you open this resource, you can now download it, edit it, add metadata, and do all the things you can do to other resources in the registry. There's one more thing to do: make sure you know which documentation belongs to which service. For this you need to relate the PermitService resource and this Documentation resource to each other.

Open the Documentation resource you just created, and on the right side you'll see an Associations tab, as shown in figure 4.6. In this tab click the Add Association button.

As Type enter Documents, because this resource *documents* the service. For the Path click the browse button and navigate to the PermitService you added earlier. Click the Add button to create the association. Now you'll see a direct link to the PermitService resource from this resource. To finish adding the documentation, use this same method to also create an association back from the service to the Documentation resource, and repeat this exercise for the REST service and its documentation. You now have two centrally registered services with associated documentation.

Figure 4.6   Add an association to the PermitService

Before we move on to the next policy, let's quickly recap why you created this documentation in this manner. In chapter 3 we defined a number of policies. The one we discussed in this section, SSD_POL_1, has the following statement:

"All services, REST and WS-* alike, must be self-documenting. There shouldn't be the need for extensive manuals on how to use the services we provide."

With the approach outline in this section, you can comply with this policy. In the next section we'll look at the policy that specifies that we should follow existing standards if they're available.

4.2   Following existing standards and definitions

There are many standards that you can use to make your work easier. If you follow existing standards and definitions, other people will better understand how to use your service, and it will be easier to integrate various services. Note that when I say *standards* here, I mean standards in the broadest sense of the word. They can be anything from internal standards and industry standards to specific W3C or OASIS standards.

In this section we'll look at how you can comply with policy in two different ways. We'll first look at how you can use an XSD in a WS-* service and in a REST service. After that we'll look at a different kind of standard: a standard way you can define a search interface by following the OpenSearch specification.

4.2.1   Including an existing XML schema in a WSDL

When your service is used in a domain where standards are available, it's a good idea to follow those standards. This will make it easier for your consumers to understand what your service does and will increase its interoperability. For instance, if your service has to deal with electronic invoices and purchase orders, you can decide to define a format yourself or use the Universal Business Language (UBL) standard. UBL (http://www.oasis-open.org/committees/ubl) was created to serve as a standard way to do business electronically. It defines a set of XML schemas and processes that you can freely use in your own applications. In this section I'll show you how easy it is to reuse existing message definitions in your services. I'll first show you how to do this in a WS-* based service where you can directly import the message definitions in the WSDL. After that I'll show you how you can return an XML response from a REST service that's defined by an existing message definition. In chapter 3 I described the OpenDataService. With the OpenDataService consumers can retrieve all different kinds of information from the various systems offered by OpenGov. One of the information sources this service returns describes specific road events such as road works, traffic light failures, and traffic jams. You could define your own model for these messages, but a little research shows that, at least in the UK, there's already a standard defined for these kinds of messages. This message definition describes the various types of road events that can occur and how they should be reported. You can find this message definition at the following URL: http://interim.cabinetoffice.gov.uk/govtalk/schemasstandards.aspx. I've also included them in the source folder for chapter 4.

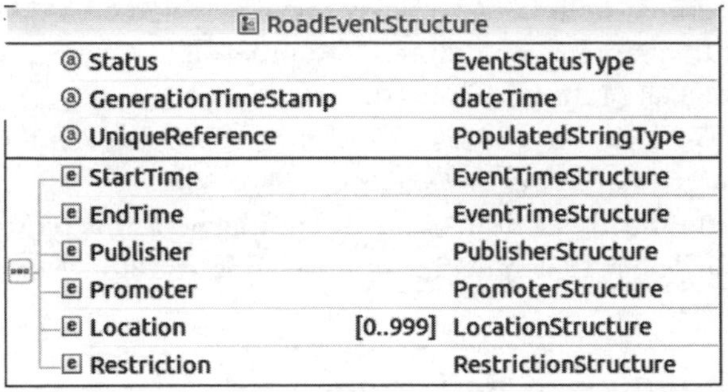

🗄 RoadEventStructure	
ⓐ Status	EventStatusType
ⓐ GenerationTimeStamp	dateTime
ⓐ UniqueReference	PopulatedStringType
🄴 StartTime	EventTimeStructure
🄴 EndTime	EventTimeStructure
🄴 Publisher	PublisherStructure
🄴 Promoter	PromoterStructure
🄴 Location [0..999]	LocationStructure
🄴 Restriction	RestrictionStructure

Figure 4.7   The RoadEvent message that you'll reuse in your services

In the RoadEventMessage-v1.0.xsd schema you can find the RoadEventStructure complex type. I'll show you how to use this specific type in your services. Figure 4.7 shows some more detail about this type.

For a WS-* based service all messages and operations are defined in a WSDL. In the following couple of paragraphs I'll show you how to reuse this schema in your own service. To test this you'll create a simple FindRoadWorks operation in a new service called RoadWorksService. The WSLD elements required for this operation are shown in the following listing.

Listing 4.3   The WSDL that includes the external schema

```
<wsdl:types>
  <xsd:schema targetNamespace="urn:opengov:wsdl:roadworks:types-1.0"
  <xsd:import
     namespace="http://www.govtalk.gov.uk/LocalGovernment/RoadEventMessage"
  schemaLocation="../xsd/RoadEventMessage-v1.0.xsd"/>

<xsd:element name="FindRoadWorks">
    <xsd:complexType>
      <xsd:sequence>
      <xsd:element name="status" type="xsd:string"/>
      </xsd:sequence>
    </xsd:complexType>
</xsd:element>

<xsd:element name="FindRoadWorksResponse">
    <xsd:complexType>
      <xsd:sequence>
        <xsd:element name="roadEvents"
                   type="rw:RoadEventStructure"
                   minOccurs="0" maxOccurs="unbounded"/>
      </xsd:sequence>
    </xsd:complexType>
 </xsd:element>
  </xsd:schema>
</wsdl:types>

<wsdl:message name="FindRoadWorks">
  <wsdl:part element="tns:FindRoadWorks" name="parameters"/>
</wsdl:message>
```

Import the ❶ external schema

Define the ❷ input message

Define the ❸ response

Use external ❹ type

```
<wsdl:message name="FindRoadWorksResponse">
  <wsdl:part element="tns:FindRoadWorksResponse" name="parameters"/>
</wsdl:message>

<wsdl:portType name="ServiceWhichIncludes">
  <wsdl:operation name="FindRoadWorks">
    <wsdl:input message="tns:FindRoadWorksRequest"/>
 <wsdl:output message="tns:FindRoadWorksResponse"/>
  </wsdl:operation>
</wsdl:portType>
```

5 **Define the operation**

Listing 4.3 shows the important parts of this WSDL. The first step is to import the external schema **1** and refer to the namespace in which the types in that schema are defined. This namespace is defined in the root element of your own WSDL (not shown) so that you can easily refer to it from your message definitions. Now that you have access to the types defined in this external schema, you can use them in your service. You do this by referencing this external type **4** in the response message **3**. This response message and the request message **2** are then used to define the messages that serve as input for your operation **5**. This is all that is needed to reuse an existing schema in a WSDL.

If you generate code based on this WSDL, you can directly use the elements from this external schema in your service implementation. As an example of what you can generate, a Java interface for this service is shown in the following listing.

Listing 4.4   Generated interface showing the externally defined type

```
@WebService(targetNamespace = "urn:opengov:wsdl:roadworks:types-1.0",
                    name = "RoadWorksService")
@XmlSeeAlso({uk.gov.govtalk.people.addressandpersonaldetails.ObjectFactory.
class, uk.gov.govtalk.people.persondescriptives.ObjectFactory.class,
uk.gov.govtalk.people.bs7666.ObjectFactory.class, ObjectFactory.class,
uk.gov.govtalk.core.ObjectFactory.class,
uk.gov.govtalk.localgovernment.roadeventmessage.ObjectFactory.class})
public interface ServiceWhichIncludes {

    @WebResult(name = "roadEvents", targetNamespace = "")
    @RequestWrapper(localName = "FindRoadWorks", targetNamespace =
"http://www.example.org/ServiceWhichIncludes/", className =
"org.example.servicewhichincludes.FindRoadWorks")
    @WebMethod(operationName = "FindRoadWorks", action =
"http://www.example.org/ServiceWhichIncludes/FindRoadWorks")
    @ResponseWrapper(localName = "FindRoadWorksResponse", targetNamespace =
"http://www.example.org/ServiceWhichIncludes/", className =
"org.example.servicewhichincludes.FindRoadWorksResponse")
    public java.util.List<uk.gov.govtalk.localgovernment.roadeventmessage.
    ➥ RoadEventStructure> findRoadWorks(
        @WebParam(name = "status", targetNamespace = "")
        java.lang.String status
    );
}
```

If you create an implementation of this service and call it from soapUI (using the provided soapUI project you can find in the chapter 4 sources), you'll get the following result from a simple status query (namespaces removed for clarity), which uses the information from the external referenced schema:

```
<soap:Envelope
      xmlns:soap="http://schemas.xmlsoap.org/soap/envelope/">
   <soap:Body>
      <ns2:FindRoadWorksResponse>
         <roadEvents
             Status="Active" UniqueReference="REF-1303239979330">
            <ns3:StartTime Estimated="no">
               <ns3:Date>2011-04-19+02:00</ns3:Date>
               <ns3:Time>21:06:19.328+02:00</ns3:Time>
            </ns3:StartTime>
            <ns3:EndTime Estimated="no">
               <ns3:Date>2011-04-19+02:00</ns3:Date>
               <ns3:Time>21:06:19.330+02:00</ns3:Time>
            </ns3:EndTime>
            <ns3:Publisher>
               <ns3:OrganisationName>OpenGov</ns3:OrganisationName>
               <ns3:OrganisationSectionName>Traffic
                   department</ns3:OrganisationSectionName>
               <ns3:SystemName>GovTraffic</ns3:SystemName>
            </ns3:Publisher>
            <ns3:Promoter>
               <ns3:OrganisationName>OpenGov</ns3:OrganisationName>
               <ns3:OrganisationId>OP-1</ns3:OrganisationId>
            </ns3:Promoter>
            <ns3:Restriction
                TrafficManagementCode="RoadClosure"
                Type="TrafficLightFaults">
               <ns3:Description>Road closed
                 because of traffic
                 lights failure</ns3:Description>
            </ns3:Restriction>
         </roadEvents>
      </ns2:FindRoadWorksResponse>
   </soap:Body>
</soap:Envelope>
```

Reusing existing XML schemas in a WS-* based service isn't that difficult. If you've included the schemas correctly in your WSDL, you can reference them for your messages and use those messages in your service. Even though for a REST service there isn't a WSDL you can use to include external schemas, you can use the same schemas to generate code that you can use directly in your REST service implementation.

4.2.2   *Using an existing XML schema in a REST resource*

As you've seen earlier in this chapter with REST, you don't (usually) have a contract that defines what the operations look like. This isn't a big issue. In the previous example we used Maven to generate Java code from the WSDL definition. If you want to know how that's done, look at the pom.xml file for that example. What are also generated are JAXB classes for all the different types defined by this schema. In this section we'll look at how you can use these JAXB classes as a response message for a REST call.

For this example you'll create a REST service that returns a list of road works. If a GET request is made to the /opengov/roadworks/{status} URL, you want to receive an XML result that looks like the result you got from your SOAP service in the previous section.

Doing this is easy. The following listing shows all the code that's required to implement this service.

Listing 4.5 REST service that returns road events

```
@Service
@Path("/opengov/roadworks/{status}")
public class RoadWorksService {

    @GET
    @Produces("application/govtalk.localgovernment.roadeventmessage+xml")
    public RoadEventMessage findRoadWorks(@PathParam("status")
                                          String status) {
        RoadEventMessage result = new RoadEventMessage();
          result.getRoadEvent().
                  addAll(RoadWorksUtil.findRoadEvents(status));
        return result;
    }
}
```

In this listing you don't do anything special to return this message as XML. The REST implementation you use for these examples (JAX-RS using CXF) will automatically marshal the RoadEventMessage you return to XML. You can use SOAP-UI to test this service with the test project I've provided. You can also open your browser and navigate to http://localhost:9001/opengov/roadworks/new, and the result will be returned in your browser.

In the last two sections we looked at how to reuse existing message definitions. This is something you often see when working in the WS-* space. In the REST world, however, WSDLs and schemas aren't used that much. What you do see more and more in the REST space is a more loosely based definition. In the next section, we'll look at how you can create a REST-based search engine using one of the available standards in that domain: the OpenSearch.org standard. You'll use this specification to offer a standard-based search engine to search through the road works registered in the RoadWorksService.

4.2.3 *Using a REST-based search definition*

A common requirement for websites and applications is that they need to provide an interface that can be used to search through the resources provided by this interface. eBay offers functionality to search through auctions; Amazon allows you to search through their catalog of books, music, movies, and much more. It would be nice if this search functionality could be offered in a standard manner that would integrate with your browser. If you follow the OpenSearch specification, you can easily accomplish this.

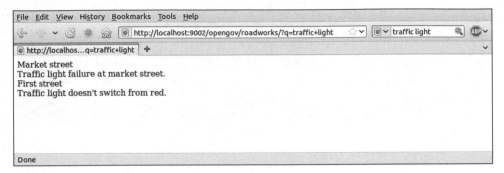

Figure 4.8   Integrating OpenSearch in the web browser and searching your service from there

The OpenSearch specification describes a number of simple formats you can use to describe a search engine. This specification, which can be found at http://www.opensearch.org, defines a standard way to expose your search functionality and describe what the search results should look like. This is all defined in a standard format so that clients (such as browsers) can read this file and provide custom search functionality based on this information. In section 4.2.1 we looked at reusing existing XML schemas and showed a service that could be used to manage road works. In this section you'll create an OpenSearch-based search definition that can be used to search information directly from the browser.

You want to create a service that allows you to search based on the type of road-work so that, for instance, you can query for all the traffic light failures. The result should look like figure 4.8.

To get all this to work, take the following steps:

1 Provide an OpenSearch-based description file. This file describes the interface clients can use to query your service.
2 Create a service that can process the search requests and return these results in the format specified by the OpenSearch specification.
3 Install this OpenSearch search engine in your client (in this case you'll use Firefox) and test to see if you can search.

An OpenSearch-based description file is an XML file that describes how your service should be queried. The following listing shows the description of your search engine.

Listing 4.6   OpenSearch-based description of a custom search engine

```
<?xml version="1.0" encoding="UTF-8"?>
<OpenSearchDescription
    xmlns="http://a9.com/-/spec/opensearch/1.1/"
    xmlns:moz="http://www.mozilla.org/2006/browser/search/">
    <ShortName>RoadWorks</ShortName>
    <Description>A simple search engine that returns a
            list of roadworks</Description>
    <InputEncoding>utf-8</InputEncoding>
    <Url type="text/html"
```

❶ The name of the search engine

❷ Human-readable description

❸ The type of content you'll be returning

```
template="http://localhost:9002/opengov/roadworks/?q={searchTerms}" />
</OpenSearchDescription>
```
The URL to send
the query to ❹

In listing 4.6 you specify the name of your search engine ❶; this is the name you'll see in the drop-down box in your browser. You can also specify a human-readable description for your service ❷ that can be used by OpenSearch clients to show to the user. If you want to use this in a browser, you need to provide a query URL the browser can use. A browser requires a URL of the type `text/html` ❸. If you used this from an RSS reader, you could have a specific URL that would return the results in Atom or RSS format. For the `text/html` URL you also need to specify how this service should be called. In ❹ you specify the URL on which your service needs to listen. In ❹ you can also see the `{searchTerms}` parameter. This parameter will be replaced with the content from the search box. If you want to search anything, you need a service that can be queried. For this you'll create a simple JAX-RS–based service, as shown in the following listing.

Listing 4.7   The service that handles the search request

```
@Service
@Path("/opengov/roadworks/")
public class RoadWorksSearchService {

    @GET
    @Produces("text/html")
    public Response searchRoadWorks(
            @QueryParam("q") String query) {

        ...
        return Response.ok().entity(resultAsString).build();
    }
}
```

The URL this service
❶ is listening on

❷ Map the q parameter
of the URL to the
query String

Listing 4.7 shows the implementation of your search service. This is a simple REST service ❶ that maps the GET method to the `searchRoadWorks` operation. In this operation you use the query parameter q ❷ as input for your search. After the search you make a `text/html` String and return the result.

The final step is registering this search engine in your browser. For this example I've used Firefox, but the scenarios for other browsers are pretty much the same. The OpenSearch specification provides a standard way in which browsers can discover new search engines. If you put a specific link in the top of a webpage, browsers will see this and allow you to add a search engine. For this example I've created a simple HTML page with the following content.

Listing 4.8   The web page that registers this OpenSearch provider

```
<html>
  <head>
    <link rel="search"
        type="application/opensearchdescription+xml"
```

Define this link
as a search link

Media type
of this line

```
        title="RoadWorks"                      ⟵——— Name of the search engine
        href="./opensearch-specification.xml">  ⟵———┐
<meta http-equiv="Content-Type" content="text/html; charset=UTF-8">
<title>Roadworks search</title>                    Location of this
</head>                                             search engine
<body>
    Use the roadworks search from your browser's search screen
</body>
</html>
```

If you open the web page from listing 4.8 in your browser (you can launch the web server from the sources in this chapter), you'll see the screen shown in figure 4.9.

Figure 4.9 **The web page is rendered as a normal web page in your browser.**

Because of the link in this webpage, Firefox has detected that this website provides a search engine following the OpenSearch standards. To use this search engine, click the downward-pointing arrow next to the search box. This will give you the option to add a RoadWorks search engine. If you click this option, as shown in figure 4.10, the search engine will be added to the list of search engines your browser supports.

Now you can search directly from your browser in the RoadWorksSearchService, and you'll be presented with results like those shown in figure 4.8.

Not all big parties provide an OpenSearch–based description of their services, but there's an open source project at https://github.com/graudeejs/opensearch that

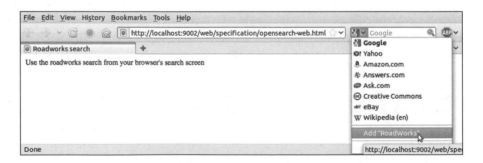

Figure 4.10 **Add your custom search engine to the list of browser-supported search engines.**

provides OpenSearch-based descriptions of over 50 services such as eBay, Duck-DuckGo, and Yahoo!.

Having a standard-based search engine as an access point to your service is a good way to improve the reusability of your service. In the following section I'll present you with a couple of guidelines that can help you in making your service more reusable.

4.3 Creating a reusable service

Our next policy states that we should create services that are reusable. In the previous chapter we have many services that could be reused. For instance, we could centralize the storage of information in a reusable service. Many books have been written on how you can create services that can be reused by other services or applications. In this section I won't go into specific details of how you can design and implement a reusable service, but I'll give you a set of guidelines and best practices that can help in creating services that are reusable.

4.3.1 Define the correct level of granularity

If you look at a set of services you'll probably notice that services provide different levels of granularity. You can have anything from services that allow you to modify a single property of an entity in your system to services that allow you to apply for a mortgage. Now why is this granularity important? The granularity of a service defines how easily it can be reused. Fine-grained services can often be more easily reused than coarse-grained services. Let's look at the different types of services you can define:

- *Process services*—Process services are the coarsest-grained services. These kinds of services most often offer services or products to their consumers. For instance, you can have a process service that handles the sale of a house. In this scenario the tax system needs to be updated, the homeowner's system needs to be updated, and a lot more systems are involved in this transaction. A process service will call other process services and business services to accomplish its task. When you're thinking about orchestration, you're probably talking about a process service.
- *Business services*—A business service provides a single, specific business function for a system. In the previous example, a business service would be a service that you can use to update information in a tax system.
- *Technical services*—The finest-grained services are the technical services. A technical service provides a small piece of functionality to other services. An example of this could be a service that allows you to update a `Person` entity in the database, send an email, or call a legacy backend.

If you want to improve the reusability of your services, you can get some quick wins by looking at the technical services. These are often services that can be easily reused by the business services or by other technical services and that are often duplicated throughout the organization. If you set up a SOA registry (like the WSO2 registry) and get all the services registered, you can quickly track any duplication in your service portfolio and perhaps remove the duplication.

4.3.2   *Decoupling the transport layer from the logical layer*

One of the best ways to make sure your services can be reused is to decouple the technical transport layer from the implementation of the business logic. Figure 4.11 shows a logic layer that can be accessed by multiple remoting technologies.

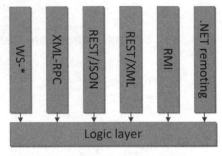

If you keep the business logic of your service separated from the technical communication details, you can create additional remoting interfaces if needed and reuse your existing business logic.

Figure 4.11   Decouple the remoting implementations from the logic of a service.

In figure 4.12 you can see the responsibilities of these two layers. The remoting layer takes care of any protocol negotiations and message transformation and then connects to the business logic using the internally provided interface.

4.3.3   *Service discovery*

When you want other consumers to use your service, it's important that they can easily find your service. This can be done in many different ways. You can give your consumers access to your repository and let them browse through the services registered there. That way they can quickly find what they're looking for and manually configure their clients. There are also other options. The WSO2 service registry provides a simple-to-use client that your consumers can use to access the repository programmatically. In section 4.1.2 you created documentation for the `PermitService` and added this along with the service to the repository. In the next few pages I'll show you how you can search for this resource using two different methods:

- *Searching for specific tags*—When you have a lot of services and resources and you're interested in a specific kind of resource, it's useful to search based on

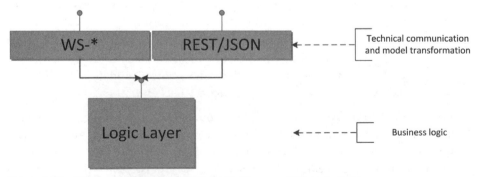

Figure 4.12   The responsibilities of the remoting layer and the logic layer

tags. For this example you'll tag the `PermitService` and its documentation and we'll show you how you can locate these resources.

- *Finding services that are linked*—In section 4.1.2 you also linked the documentation to the `PermitService`. In this example I'll show you how you can follow this link through the WSO2 client.

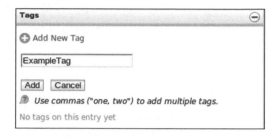

Before you can start searching on specific tags, you first need to add a tag to the service and the documentation. To do this, open the WSO2 registry console (https://localhost:9443) and use the Resources > Browse functionality to navigate to the HTML documentation. On the lower right-hand side you have the option to add tags. For this example add a tag with the name `Example-Tag`. This is shown in figure 4.13.

Figure 4.13   Add a tag with the name `ExampleTag` to a resource.

After you've added this tag, browse to the `PermitService` (or follow the association) and also tag the service with this tag. You now have two resources in your repository with the tag `ExampleTag`. Using the WSO2 client you can now locate these resources. The interesting part of this example is shown in the following listing.

Listing 4.9   Use the WSO2 client to search for tagged resources

```
WSRegistryServiceClient client = initialize();                      ❶ Get the client

TaggedResourcePath[] resources =                                    ❷ Search for tag
      client.getResourcePathsWithTag("ExampleTag");
   for (int i = 0; i < resources.length; i++) {                     ❸ Get the found
      String resourcePath = resources[i].getResourcePath();            resource path
      Resource foundResource = client.get(resourcePath);           ❹ Get the resource
      // Do stuff with your resource
   }
```

In listing 4.9 you search for a specific resource based on tags. To do this you need to get a reference to a client ❶, and with that client you can use the `getResource-PathWithTag` method to search, case insensitive, for resources with a certain tag. With the full `resourcePath` ❸ you can retrieve the resource ❹ and, for instance, automatically create a client or show the documentation.

Another nice feature of the WSO2 registry is that it's easy to follow any associations made from one resource to another. In a previous example you created an association between a service and its documentation. The code in the next listing shows how you can follow this association.

Listing 4.10   Use the WSO2 client to follow a resource association

```
Association[] associations = client.getAllAssociations           ❶ Get associations
      ("/_system/governance/Documentation/PermitService.wsdl.html");
```

```
for (Association association : associations) {                    ◄─┐
  System.out.println("Type: " + association.getAssociationType());  │
  System.out.println("To: " + association.getDestinationPath());    │  ❷ Show
  System.out.println("From: " + association.getSourcePath());       │     associations
}                                                                  ◄─┘
```

You use the getAllAssociations operation ❶ to retrieve all the associations for a specific resource. You can now easily iterate over these associations to show them ❷. If you run the previous example you'll see output similar to this:

```
Type: Documents
To: /...services/urn:govforms:wsdl:permit:service-1/0/PermitService
From: /...governance/Documentation/PermitService.wsdl.html
```

These are two of the large number of operations provided by this client. An overview of the available operations can be found in the Javadocs for this client, which you can find at http://wso2.org/project/registry/3.5.0/docs/apidocs/org/wso2/registry/app/RemoteRegistry.html.

4.3.4 *Versioning, documentation, and using standards*

If you want to create a reusable service, the other policies we've talked about in this chapter already help you with this. Let's look a bit closer at these policies and how they help with reusability:

- *Create self-documenting services*—When you want your service to be reused, people need to be able to find this service and easily understand what it does. For this, good documentation is important. If you combine this documentation with a central SOA repository, it will be easy for consumers to find out what your service does.
- *Support multiple versions of services*—It's not just important to get new consumers to use your service. It's also important to keep these consumers using your service. If you change too much in your service and break the service of your existing consumers, there's a good chance—especially after this happens a couple of times—that they'll try to find another service or workaround. If you apply good versioning practices, you can minimize the impact on your consumers and inform them beforehand if a chance of breaking is coming.
- *Reuse existing message standards*—When consumers start looking for a service to use, there's a much better chance they'll use your service if that service follows the standards models used in your organization. This avoids the need for specific model transformations and minimizes the integration effort.

Before we look at how to version services, here's a final note on service reusability. As you've seen in this section, you can make your service more reusable by applying a set of simple practices. One thing we skipped here is that besides these technical efforts, service reusability is affected by how your organization is organized. If other departments use your service, you'll need to be able to bill them accordingly; they might expect specific uptimes for which you might need to buy additional hardware. If your organization doesn't have processes in place for these kinds of requirements, service reusability is hard to set up. In the third part of this book we'll look a bit closer at how you can gain insight into the usage of your service. This can help you get support for reusing services within your organization.

4.4 How to version services

One of the policies we discussed in chapter 3 deals with versioning. Services evolve, new functionality gets added, and old functionality is removed. Suppose you want to change your services, but you have many different clients. In that case you need to be careful that you don't break their applications through a change in your service. In this section we'll look at how you can apply versioning to services. We'll start with a WS-* based service where versioning can be applied on the contract level, and after that we'll look at how you can apply versioning to a REST service, while still following the core REST principles.

4.4.1 Versioning a WS-* based service

When you want to version a WS-* based service you need to look at the contract provided by this service. Luckily for WS-* based services, all contract information is defined in a WSDL. In this section we'll look at what kind of changes you can expect, whether they're breaking or nonbreaking changes, and how you can change your version numbering accordingly. We'll start with the nonbreaking API changes. These are shown in table 4.3.

Table 4.3   Nonbreaking API changes for a WSDL-based service

Type of change	Description
Adding new operations	When you add a new operation to a WSDL, your current consumers don't need to change anything. The messages and operations they currently use aren't changed.
Adding new XML schema types	When you add new operations, you often also need to add new XML schema types. As long as you don't change existing or referenced XML schema types, this won't break backward compatibility.

There are also a number of changes you can't make without breaking backward compatibility. These types of changes are listed in table 4.4.

Table 4.4   Breaking API changes for a WSDL-based service

Type of change	Description
Removing an operation	When you remove an operation, you break backward compatibility. Consumers expect the operation to be there.
Renaming an operation	Renaming an operation is nothing more than removing an existing operation and adding a new one. This is also a breaking operation.

Table 4.4 Breaking API changes for a WSDL-based service *(continued)*

Type of change	Description
Changing the parameters	If you change the parameters of your service, in WSDL terms this would mean changing the `input` and `output` elements of your operations. Your consumer won't be able to invoke these operations without changing their client code.
Changing an XML schema type	When you change an XML schema type, you could break backward compatibility. This depends on how strictly the client and the server check the XML they receive. Generally speaking, adding optional elements to existing `sequence` elements is allowed and is also often used. Other changes should be avoided to maintain backward compatibility.

Now that I've defined what breaking and nonbreaking changes are, let's see what the implications are for versioning. The simplest way to version a WS-* based service is by adding a version number to the relevant parts of the WSDL. You'll use two different levels of versioning: major versioning and minor versioning. You'll use the following format for this: `<servicename>.<major>.<minor>`. The major number will be increased if you make a change that isn't backward compatible, and you'll increase the minor number when you have a backward-compatible change. This means that consumers know when they need to rewrite their client and when they can keep using their existing client. In the next section we'll look at how to apply this to a WSDL.

As an example for this policy we'll use the GovPortal application from chapter 3. Through this application OpenGov offers all kind of information to its citizens (see figure 4.14).

Through this portal OpenGov also offers information on the garbage pickup schedule. For this, the City Information System retrieves information from a dedicated garbage collection service. In the rest of this section we'll look at how this service can be versioned.

WS-* BASED VERSION NUMBERING GUIDELINES AND BEST PRACTICES
A WSDL contains a number of constructs on which you can apply versioning, including XSD definitions, service definitions, various namespaces, and interface definitions. On which element do you define your versions? Let's look at a number of best practices for this:

- *Put the major and minor version numbers in the WSDL filename:* The first thing to do is make sure the filename of the WSDL reflects the correct version number.

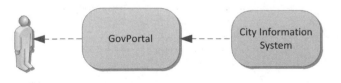

Citizen

Figure 4.14 GovPortal provides a website where all relevant information regarding a city can be found.

You should use both the major and the minor version numbers for this. The WSDL is the contract you have with your consumer, and there should be no ambiguity about which version the client is using. This means that a WSDL for the garbage collection service should have the following name: `garbage-collection-service-v3.2.wsdl`.

- *Use only major version numbering for WSDL target namespace:* The major version number changes only when there's an incompatible, breaking change. The minor version number can change when there's a nonbreaking change; for instance, when you add an operation. If you embed the minor version number in the WSDL target namespace, you'll get into trouble with your consumers. If you change the namespace, the XML messages that are sent across the line will have a changed namespace. This also means that any schema that's used by these messages shouldn't change its namespace in case of a compatible change. In such cases your consumers will have to update their clients even though the actual data sent over the line hasn't changed, only their namespace.

  So you should do this

```
<wsdl:definitions name="garbage-collection-service-v3"
targetNamespace="urn:govforms:wsdl:garbage-collection:service-v3">
```

  and not this

```
<wsdl:definitions name="garbage-collection-service-v3.2"
targetNamespace="urn:govforms:wsdl:garbage-collection:service-v3.2">
```

  It's also good practice to have the name of the service reflect the major version number. This once again indicates to the consumer that as long as the major version stays the same, they don't have to change anything on the client side.

  Another approach, which is often used for schemas, is using a year/month combination for versioning. In this way, you can always directly see which version you're using, the date it's released, and which other services belonged to this same release. But this introduces a big issue with backward-compatible changes because even in the event of a compatible change, namespaces and service names change, and this will cause clients to fail.

- *Apply version numbers when adding a new operation:* In table 4.3 I mentioned that adding an operation is a nonbreaking change. For nonbreaking changes you only have to increase the minor version number. If you add an operation to a WSDL, you usually need to add the following: wrapper types for the standard document/literal/wrapped style, messages referring to the added wrapper types, and the operation definition itself. For traceability it's good to apply major and minor version numbering to the wrapper types and to the operation. For the messages themselves you don't do this, because this will then conflict with the document/literal/wrapped guidelines. The following paragraphs will show you the changes that need to be made. The next listing shows the wrapper elements that are needed when you add a new operation. This operation allows you to get a garbage collection schedule based on a specific ID.

Listing 4.11   Major and minor versioning on wrapper elements for a new operation

```xsd
<xsd:schema
   targetNamespace=
"urn:govforms:xsd:garbage-collection:service:types-3.3"          ◄── ❶ Namespace with new version
  xmlns:types="urn:govforms:xsd:garbage-collection:types-1.0"


>

<xsd:import schemaLocation="./garbage-collection-service-types.xsd"
        namespace="urn:govforms:xsd:garbage-collection:types-1.0" />

<xsd:element name="getGarbageCollectionSchedule">          ◄── ❷ New request wrapper
    <xsd:complexType>
        <xsd:sequence>
        <xsd:element name="in" type="types:sheduleID">
        </xsd:element>
        </xsd:sequence>
    </xsd:complexType>
</xsd:element>
<xsd:element name="getGarbageCollectionScheduleResponse">   ◄── ❸ New response wrapper
    <xsd:complexType>
        <xsd:sequence>
            <xsd:element name="out" type="types:shedule" />
        </xsd:sequence>
    </xsd:complexType>
</xsd:element>
...
</xsd:schema>
```

In listing 4.11 you add a version number to this specific schema ❶. This allows you to see in the WSDL which version introduced these specific types (❷ and ❸). When you add an operation you also need to change the interface, or portType, of your service. You create a new portType, which contains the old operations and the newly added one. This portType will reflect the version of this service in its name. An example of this is shown in the following listing.

Listing 4.12   Create a new portType when adding an operation

```wsdl
<wsdl:portType name="GarbageCollectionService_v3_3">  ◄──❶ New version of portType
  <wsdl:operation name="getAllSchedules">
    <wsdl:input message="tns:getAllSchedulesRequest" />      ◄──❷ Old operation
    <wsdl:output message="tns:getAllSchedulesResponse" />   ◄──
  </wsdl:operation>                                           ❸ New operation
  <wsdl:operation name="getGarbageCollectionSchedule">
    <wsdl:input message="tns:getGarbageCollectionScheduleRequest"/>
    <wsdl:output message="tns:getGarbageCollectionScheduleResponse"/>
  </wsdl:operation>
</wsdl:portType>
```

In listing 4.12 you define a new `portType` ❶. In the name of the `portType` you explicitly define the major and minor version numbers. In this `portType` you add the old operation ❷ and the new operation ❸. When generating code you'll get different services for different versions, while still maintaining backward compatibility.

- *Reflect version information in the service and endpoint:* The final part where you need to show the version information is in the service definition in the WSDL and in the URL that's used to call the service. For the service you'll follow the same principle as you did for the `portType` definition. You create a new service and binding for each version of the service. The name of the binding should reflect the specific `portType` this binding is defined for, and the name of the service should also contain both the major and minor version numbers. You also want to show the version of a service in the URL used to access that service. This means you can have multiple major versions running next to each other and gradually phase out older major versions. An example how to do this is shown in the next listing.

Listing 4.13 Create a new service for each `portType`

```
<wsdl:service name="GarbageCollectionService_v3_2">        ◀─❶ Old service
  <wsdl:port binding="tns:GarbageCollectionService_v3_2"    ◀─
      name="GarbageCollectionServiceSOAP">
                                                              ❷ Old portType
    <soap:address location=
      "http://localhost:9001/garbageservice/v3" />  ◀─❺ Show major version in URL
    </wsdl:port>
</wsdl:service>
<wsdl:service name="GarbageCollectionService_v3_3">        ◀─❸ New service
    <wsdl:port binding="tns:GarbageCollectionService_v3_3"  ◀─❹ New portType
      name="GarbageCollectionServiceSOAP">
    <soap:address location=
      "http://localhost:9001/garbageservice/v3" />  ◀─❺ Show major version in URL
    </wsdl:port>
</wsdl:service>
```

Listing 4.13 shows two service definitions. The 3.2 version ❶ points to the old `portType` ❷. The new service ❸ points to the new `portType` ❹. In this listing you can also see that you don't change the URL where the service is running ❺ because it's only a minor change. If you were to make a breaking change, you'd also increase the version number used in the URL.

If you follow these steps, you get a service that can be easily versioned, allows you to add operations, and can provide backward compatibility.

4.4.2 Versioning a REST service

For the REST service, for which you use JSON as the message format, we'll start once again by looking at breaking and nonbreaking API changes. After that I'll show you a set of best practices that can help you in versioning REST-based services. The non-breaking API changes for a REST-based service are shown in table 4.5.

Table 4.5 Nonbreaking API changes for a REST-based service

Type of change	Description
Adding new link relations	If you want to add new links to specific resources, you won't break your API. The current clients of your service will ignore these new links.
Adding new properties	If you add new, nonmandatory properties to your resource, nothing changes for the clients. They will ignore these new properties and continue working in the same manner. If you add a property that's mandatory, you'll have to create a new version of the resource.

Adding extra information to your REST resource doesn't break anything. The problems start when you remove items from your resource. The most common changes that result in API breaking changes are shown in table 4.6.

Table 4.6 Breaking API changes for a REST-based service

Type of change	Description
Removing properties	If you remove a property from your resource, you can break existing clients. These clients might depend on this property.
Changing properties	When you change an existing property, for example, rename it or change its child properties, you might break some clients.
Removing link relations	If you remove links to other resources, you change your resource. This is an incompatible change.
Changing link relations	Renaming or altering link relations can also break clients. They might depend on a specific name for a relation.

If you look back at the WS-* based services, you can see that we applied a versioning scheme there based on minor and major version numbers. A minor version number increase indicated a nonbreaking API change, and a major version number increase indicated a breaking API change. This minor version number increment was possible because of the way a WSDL is organized. You can define multiple `services` and `port-Types` all listening to the same (major address versioned) endpoint. For a REST-based service, however, this is different. A resource is identified by a specific URI, and you can use the basic HTTP verbs to modify this resource. But you can't have two versions of the same PUT operation or have the same resource identified by two different URIs. So having a separate version number for minor nonbreaking changes won't work. For REST-based services you need to follow these two rules:

- For a breaking change, increase the version number.
- For a nonbreaking change, keep the same version number and just change the resource.

Let's look at a set of best practices that can help you in versioning your REST-based resources.

REST-BASED VERSION NUMBERING GUIDELINES AND BEST PRACTICES

One of the big differences between REST and WS-* is that for WS-* you have a contract you can use to define specific versions and associated operations and types. For REST you have no such thing. That, and the fact that for REST you use a resource-centric way of communication instead of a remote procedure–oriented one, makes it hard to define a single place to store the versioning information. For REST there are three generally accepted approaches to handling versioning. In this section I'll discuss these three options and show you my personal favorite:

- *Use media types to indicate the version of the resource you're working with:* In section 4.1.1 we looked at how to make a self-documenting REST service. In that section I explained that with the media type you can indicate what type of resource you're dealing with. Let's assume you have a REST service where you can query a specific URL to retrieve the times your garbage is picked up. Let's look at the request and the response for this resource.

```
Request:
GET /opengov/garbageschedule?location=Main%20Street HTTP/1.1
Accept: application/vnd.opengov.org.garbageschedule+json

Response:
HTTP/1.1 200 OK
Content-Type: application/vnd.opengov.org.garbageschedule+json

{"schedule"
      "self": "schedule-2423",
        "dayOfWeek": "Monday",
     "oddOrEvenWeeks": "Odd"}
```

In both the request and the response you can see that you specify your own custom media type. As I explained in section 4.1.1, you use this to identify the resource you're interested in and the type of resource that's returned. If you have backward-compatible changes, you can keep this media type the same. In the example of garbage pickup times, we're still talking about a specific schedule, even if you add extra information about the route the garbage truck takes. This is a change that doesn't break your clients, so there's no need to change your media type. If you have a breaking change—for instance, if you don't specify the dayOfWeek as a text value anymore but as an integer in the range of 1 to 7—you have a change that can possibly break your clients. In this case you should indicate that a different version of the same resource is returned. Media types provide the perfect mechanism for this. To indicate that you return a different version, you just add a version number to the media type. So your original media-type will become

```
application/vnd.opengov.org.garbageschedule-v1+json
```

and the new one will have its version increased to

```
application/vnd.opengov.org.garbageschedule-V2+json
```

With the addition of this version number, your clients can now request resources for a specific version by using the `Accept` header. If your client wants to receive version v2, they can put the following in the `Accept` HTTP header:

```
Accept: application/vnd.opengov.org.garbageschedule-v2+json
```

This will return the v2 version of the resource. Consumers can now decide when to change to a new version by increasing this header in their client applications. If you want to remove support for an older version of a service, you could return the following HTTP code, 303 (See other), to indicate how and where the new resource can be accessed.

- *Add a qualifier to indicate the required version:* An alternative way to look at REST resource versioning is to use a specific qualifier, which is a short name/value pair you add to the `Accept` and `Content-Type` fields. This qualifier can be used to indicate the version of the resource you want to receive. Let's look at the request and response from the previous example, but this time with a qualifier:

```
Request:
GET /opengov/garbageschedule?location=Main%20Street HTTP/1.1
Accept: application/vnd.opengov.org.garbageschedule+json;v=1

Response:
HTTP/1.1 200 OK
Content-Type: application/vnd.opengov.org.garbageschedule+json;v=1

{"schedule"
    "self": "schedule-2423",
      "dayOfWeek": "Monday",
    "oddOrEvenWeeks": "Odd"}
```

As you can see, this example added a v=1 qualifier. This qualifier indicates the version of the resource you're expecting. This can be used in the same manner as the media-type approach you saw in the previous section.

- *Add the version in the URL:* The final option you have, which is one discouraged by the REST community, is adding the version information in the URL. So instead of requesting this schedule at http://localhost:9001/opengov/garbage schedule/schedules/schedule-2423, you request this resource at a URL that already contains the version you're interested in: http://localhost:9001/opengov/v1/garbageschedule/schedule-2423.

    Looking at the same example again gives us this:

```
Request:
GET /opengov/v1/garbageschedule?location=Main%20Street HTTP/1.1
Accept: application/vnd.opengov.org.garbageschedule+json
```

```
Response:
HTTP/1.1 200 OK
Content-Type: application/vnd.opengov.org.garbageschedule+json

{"schedule"
     "self": "schedule-2423",
       "dayOfWeek": "Monday",
   "oddOrEvenWeeks": "Odd"}
```

The advantage of this approach is that it's easy to understand and to use. Each version has its own unique URL, and changing from one version to the other can be done by incrementing the version number in the URL.

The main problem with this versioning scheme is that it goes against the core REST principles. A resource should be uniquely identified by its URL. When using this approach you have two instances of the same resources, `schedule-2423`, that can be identified by different URLs, a specific URL for each version of the resource you support.

I personally think the media-type approach is the most clean and RESTful way to handle versioning. All information about the current resource is transferred using its media type, as it should be. This approach also forces you to use custom media types for your resources, which make it clearer to the clients what kind of resource they're dealing with. If you're working in an environment where custom media types can't be supported, the next-best thing is using a qualifier. This keeps the basic tenant of REST intact and allows you to apply versioning without custom media types. I personally wouldn't use the URL-based approach, even though it's probably the easiest one to apply.

4.5   *Summary*

- Creating a self-documenting service is different for REST- and WS-* based services.
- REST is self-documenting through the use of links and relations.
- WS-* based services are documented through a WSDL.
- For both types of services, HTML or text documentation is a welcome addition.
- It's easy to reuse existing XML schemas in REST and WS-* based services when you use Java code generation.
- With the OpenSearch.org standard you can create search engines in a standard-based manner.
- Reusability of a service is difficult to accomplish.
- With a couple of guidelines and the policies discussed in this chapter, you can improve the reusability of your service.
- Versioning is an important part of service design.
- The most important part of versioning and service evolution is to keep backward compatibility in mind.

Security policies 5

This chapter covers

- Providing HTTPS-based access to your services
- Validating message integrity using signatures
- Using federated authentication and authorization using OpenAM
- Implementing an OAuth-based scenario

Policies that deal with security are important for any organization. If you don't have strict rules that determine how security is implemented within your services, you run a big risk of exposing confidential information. Your customers need to be sure that their credentials are handled correctly and the integrity of the information they send and receive from your service can be guaranteed. Imagine that your company provides sensitive information to its consumers. For instance, your company provides a service where authorized users can access their tax returns for the last couple of years, or your municipality provides a service where you can get an overview of all the information they have gathered on you. For these types of services, you want to ensure that this information is accessed in a secure manner where no one can eavesdrop on this information or pretend to be someone else.

If you follow the basic set of security policies from chapter 3 you can create such secure and trusted services with little effort. In this chapter we'll look at those

116

security policies and show how you can comply with them. An overview and short explanation of the security policies is shown in table 5.1. You can find more information on these policies in chapter 3. You'll start simple by adding HTTPS to your services, and from there we'll move on to more complex topics such as federated authentication, OAuth, and message integrity.

Table 5.1   Table 5.1 Service design and documentation policies

Policy name	Description
SEC_POL_1 Encrypt a communications channel for sensitive data.	When a consumer accesses a service that contains or requires sensitive information (for example, credit card information or personal details), this service should handle communication securely. This policy is a good one to start with. By using it you can make sure that you encrypt the communication on the transport level..
SEC_POL_2 Validate message integrity and non-repudiation.	It's important to be able to detect if there's something wrong with a message. It could be altered during transit, or someone could be impersonating someone else. If you make sure your services comply with this policy, you can guarantee that you process only messages that you know are valid.
SEC_POL_3 Use a centralized identity system for authentication.	Authenticating your consumers (or your internal users) is something that almost all services require. Often this is reinvented for each service. By using a centralized identity system, you can make sure every service follows the same strict policies set with regard to identification.
SEC_POL_4 Use a centralized identity system for authorization	The same rules apply to authorization. This is often something that's added in hindsight to applications and that's often difficult to maintain. By centralizing authorization you can make sure all services follow the same authorization guidelines that are defined within the organization.

Let's start with the first policy from this list and show you how to secure the communication channel.

5.1   *Encrypting a communications channel for sensitive data*

One of the policies that's often required deals with securing the communications channel. If you can guarantee that no one can intercept and read the messages that are sent between your consumer and service, you can avoid a lot of security issues. This is a simple policy to comply with on the technical level and one that immediately increases the security level of your service.

When you offer services over HTTP (as you do for REST and WS-* services), you can comply with this policy by changing the transport to HTTPS instead of HTTP. When you use HTTPS, all data sent between the consumer and the provider is encrypted. In this section we'll look at two different forms of HTTPS and show how you can configure REST and WS-* to use HTTPS. If you're not using Jetty in your environment, you can apply the concepts used with Jetty to other web servers such as Apache HTTPD, Microsoft IIS, or Apache Tomcat.

The first scenario we'll look at is the one where the client doesn't need to provide a client-side certificate to identify itself. This is the most common way of using HTTPS.

5.1.1 *Using HTTPS with Jetty*

Before we look at the configuration of HTTPS let's take a small step back and look at the services and products offered by OpenGov. In the previous discussions of the policies, we examined a specific use case based on the information from chapter 3. For this policy we won't select a single service, but we'll apply this to all the services, REST and WS-*, that are provided by the OpenGov organization.

If you run a production site or service, you want to use a certificate signed by a trusted certificate authority (CA). With a certificate from a trusted CA, users of your service can be certain that you are who you say you are. For testing purposes you'll be using a self-signed certificate. This works in the same manner as a certificate from a trusted CA, but this certificate won't be automatically trusted by your users. Creating a self-signed certificate is easy. You can use the Java `keytool` to create all the required components. First you need to create a key pair. This key pair consists of a secret key used by your server, which should never be distributed, and a public key that can be shared with your clients. To create a key pair, use the following `keytool` command:

```
keytool -genkey -alias server-key -keystore server.keystore
What is your first and last name?
  [Unknown]:  Jos Dirksen
What is the name of your organizational unit?
  [Unknown]:  OpenGov IM
What is the name of your organization?
  [Unknown]:  OpenGov
What is the name of your City or Locality?
  [Unknown]:  Waalwijk
What is the name of your State or Province?
  [Unknown]:  NB
What is the two-letter country code for this unit?
  [Unknown]:  NL
```

This will create a key store with the name `server.keystore` that holds a key pair with the name `server-key`. If you're asked for a password, enter `secret`. In a production environment you should create a key store and private key with a more difficult password. You'll be using this password throughout the rest of the example to access the key store and the private key. The next step is to configure CXF, shown in the following listing, to use this key and key store to provide the services over HTTPS instead of over HTTP.

Listing 5.1   CXF configuration to enable HTTPS

```
<httpj:engine-factory bus="cxf">                         ❶ Port to run
  <httpj:engine port="9001">                                 with HTTPS
    <httpj:tlsServerParameters>                          ❷ Define TLS parameters
      <sec:keyManagers keyPassword="secret">             ❸ Password needed
                                                             to access key
```

```
            <sec:keyStore type="JKS" password="secret"
                  file="src/main/resources/server/server.keystore"/>
        </sec:keyManagers>
      </httpj:tlsServerParameters>
    </httpj:engine>
```

❹

**Key store location and
password for key store**

In some of the previous WS-* and REST examples, you've seen that you can configure the Jetty runtime that CXF uses by specifying an `engine-factory` element in the Spring applicationcontext.xml file. To configure HTTPS you add the `engine-factory` element and specify that this engine will use port 9001 ❶. The next step is to enable HTTPS on this engine. You can do this by adding the `tlsServerParameters` element ❷. On this element you configure the password for the key ❸ and the location (`file`) and password for the key store that the key is located in ❹. This should point to the key store created in the previous section. In ❹ you also define the type of key store you have. Because you created this key store yourself, its type is JKS (Java KeyStore). If you already have a different kind of key store (for instance PKCS#12) where your key pair is stored, you can specify that type here. You can find the various key stores and configurations shown in this section in the Message Integrity project, which you can find in the sources for this chapter.

In this form of using HTTPS, only the server has to provide a certificate to identify itself. The information from this certificate is used to encrypt and protect the connection. It's also possible to set up an HTTPS connection where both sides of the connection are required to identify themselves with certificates. This is called client-side SSL. You can use this to allow connections only from clients you trust. These clients provide you with a certificate that you can trust. Only clients whose certificates you trust can use your service.

5.1.2   *Using HTTPS and client-side SSL with Jetty*

Once you've set up server-side SSL, it's not that hard to add client-side SSL (also called two-way SSL). For client-side SSL you need an extra key store where you store the certificates you can trust. Run the following two commands to create a new key store and, because you can't directly create an empty key store, delete the generated key pair:

```
keytool -genkey -alias foo -keystore trust.keystore
keytool -delete -alias foo -keystore trust.keystore
```

The `trust.keystore` key store can now be used to store certificates you've received from your clients. To import a certificate into the key store, you can use the following `keytool` command:

```
keytool -import -alias <aliasname> -file <certificate.crt> -keystore ./
    truststore.jks
```

With the trusted certificates in the key store, you can now alter the configuration from listing 5.1 to add support for client-side SSL. This is shown in the following listing.

Listing 5.2   HTTPS with client-side SSL

```
<httpj:engine port="9001">
  <httpj:tlsServerParameters>
    <sec:keyManagers keyPassword="secret">
      <sec:keyStore type="JKS" password="secret"
           file="src/main/resources/server/server.keystore"/>
      </sec:keyManagers>

      <sec:trustManagers>
         <sec:keyStore type="JKS" password="secret"
              file="src/main/resources/server/trust.keystore"/>
      </sec:trustManagers>
    <sec:clientAuthentication want="true" required="true"/>
  </httpj:tlsServerParameters>
</httpj:engine>
```

❶ The certificates you trust

❷ Always require client certificates

In listing 5.2 you add two elements: a trustManagers element ❶, which defines where the key store is with your trusted certificates, and the clientAuthentication element, which with this configuration forces your server to accept only clients that support client SSL. With this configuration all clients that want to use the services provided on port 9001 need to provide you with a client certificate ❷. You'll store this certificate in the key store identified in ❶. In the source code for this example, you can find an example HTTP client that shows how to set up client-side SSL from a client point of view.

Securing the message channel is a good and simple step to increase security and comply with the security policy you defined. But using client-side SSL is a big hassle and forces you to keep track of trusted certificates and handle the complete lifecycle of certificates. There are other options to at least ensure the authenticity of the messages you receive. In the following section we'll look at two of these options.

5.2   *Validating message integrity and non-repudiation*

When you provide a service that handles financial requests or other types of transactions, it's important that you can determine the validity of the messages you receive. You need to be sure, especially with sensitive requests, that the request wasn't altered in transit and that you can determine that the consumers are who they say they are. The PermitService, mentioned in chapter 3, allows residents to request different kinds of permits. To obtain these permits residents usually will need to enter all kinds of personal information. You want to make sure that these messages aren't intercepted or modified in any way. This could cause permits to be issued to incorrect addresses or in other residents' names.

In this section we'll look at two different ways to do this:

- *WS-Security*—For WS-* based services we'll look at how you can use WS-Security to sign (and encrypt) your messages.
- *REST*—With REST, which doesn't have a standard way of dealing with these issues, we'll look at how you can create such an integrity mechanism yourself.

We'll start with the WS-Security–based approach.

5.2.1 Applying WS-Security to SOAP messages

When you want to apply this policy to WS-* based services, you can use the WS-Security standard. This standard, which can be found at http://www.oasis-open.org/committees/tc_home.php?wg_abbrev=wss, defines how to apply message-based security to SOAP messages. The functionality that's covered by this standard is shown in table 5.2.

Table 5.2   The functionality defined by the WS-Security standard

Functionality	Description
Encryption	WS-Security defines how you can encrypt SOAP messages. It specifies where and how the encryption information is stored, how the content needs to be canonized before encryption, and how to communicate the encrypted message.
Signing	This standard also specifies how to sign a message (or part of a message). Information on how the signature was created and the algorithm used is stored inside the message.
User identification	The WS-Security standard also specifies how to transfer information regarding the user who made the call. This can be anything from X.509 certificates to a Kerberos token. Also, something as simple as a username and (plain text) password is supported by this standard.

In this section I'll show you how you can sign your message so that you can comply with the message integrity and non-repudiation policy. We won't implement this completely from scratch, because setting up the correct headers, canonizing the message, and then signing it is a complex and error-prone process. Luckily though, CXF—and most other WS libraries—provide support for WS-Security.

Before we dive into the configuration of WS-Security, let's look a bit closer at signing and encryption. With WS-Security, signing and encryption are done through the use of public and private keys. A user has a private key, which is only known to that person, and a public key, which is available to everyone. A message encrypted with a public key can only be decrypted by the corresponding private key and vice versa. Figure 5.1 shows how this can be applied to encrypt a message between two parties.

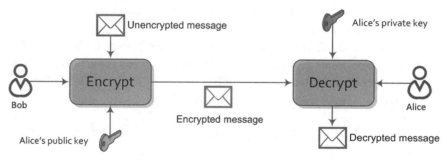

Figure 5.1   Encrypting and decrypting a message

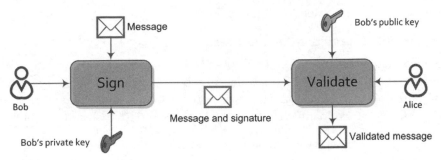

Figure 5.2   Signing and validating a message

In figure 5.1, Bob wants to send an encrypted message to Alice. To do this, he needs to make sure only Alice can decrypt this message. Bob uses the public key he received from Alice (for example, through an X.509 certificate) to encrypt the message. This encrypted message can now be sent without anyone being able to decrypt the message without the private key. When Alice receives the message, she can use her own private key to decrypt and read Bob's message.

Signing a message, shown in figure 5.2, works in pretty much the same manner. This time, the goal isn't to hide the message's content but to guarantee that the message hasn't been changed in transit. For this Bob will have to sign the message using his own private key. He does this by first creating a hash of the message body (for example, an RSA SHA1 hash) and then encrypting this hash with his own private key to create a signature. This signature is added to the message that's sent to Alice. Alice can now decrypt this signature using Bob's public key and can view the hash that was created by Bob. Because Alice also has the message that Bob sent, she can use the same mechanism to create a hash of the message herself. If both hashes are equal, she knows the message hasn't been altered in transit and was indeed sent by Bob. If the hash isn't equal, it means either someone is impersonating Bob or the message was altered during transit.

SETTING UP A SERVICE PROTECTED BY WS-SECURITY

Before we look at the source code and configuration, you need to exchange private and public keys between the client and the server. Just as I've shown for Bob and Alice, your client and server need to know one another's public keys. For this example I've already created two key stores, available in the source code for this chapter. In the server key store (named `serviceKeystore.jks`) you can find the private key for the server and the public key for the client. In the key store for the client (named `client-Keystore.jks`) you can find the private key for the client and the public key for the server (using `keytool -list -keystore <keystorename>`):

```
serviceKeystore:
myservicekey, May 5, 2011, PrivateKeyEntry,
Certificate fingerprint (MD5):
AB:CE:82:AB:10:70:CA:EB:7C:77:C7:DC:5A:8C:D5:5C
```

```
myclientkey, May 5, 2011, trustedCertEntry,
Certificate fingerprint (MD5):
D3:3B:37:17:05:39:F9:72:83:AE:3E:CE:E0:C7:44:2A
```

clientKeystore:
```
myservicekey, May 5, 2011, trustedCertEntry,
Certificate fingerprint (MD5):
AB:CE:82:AB:10:70:CA:EB:7C:77:C7:DC:5A:8C:D5:5C

myclientkey, May 5, 2011, PrivateKeyEntry,
Certificate fingerprint (MD5):
D3:3B:37:17:05:39:F9:72:83:AE:3E:CE:E0:C7:44:2A
```

If you want to add more keys to these key stores, you can use the keytool provided by the JRE. With these two key stores in place, you can configure your service for WS-Security. With CXF this is done in the Spring applicationcontext.xml file. The following listing shows the required WS-Security configuration for the ReportService example from chapter 4.

Listing 5.3 Configuring WS-Security on the server side

```
<jaxws:endpoint id="reportService"
     implementor="soa.govern...ReportServiceImpl"
     address="http://localhost:9001/reportService">
     <jaxws:outInterceptors>
       <ref bean="TimestampSignEncryptOutInterceptor"/>      ❶ Define interceptor for
     </jaxws:outInterceptors>                                   incoming messages
     <jaxws:inInterceptors>
       <ref bean="TimestampSignEncryptInInterceptor"/>       ❷ Define interceptor for
     </jaxws:inInterceptors>                                    outgoing messages
</jaxws:endpoint>

<bean id="TimestampSignEncryptInInterceptor"
     class="org.apache.cxf.ws.security.wss4j.               ❸ Define WS-Security
          ➥ WSS4JInInterceptor">                              In interceptor
  <constructor-arg>
    <map>
      <entry key="action" value="Timestamp Signature Encrypt"/>
      <entry key="signaturePropFile" value="servicekeystore.properties"/>
      <entry key="decryptionPropFile" value="servicekeystore.properties"/>
      <entry key="passwordCallbackClass"
             value="soa.govern...ServiceKeystorePasswordCallback"/>
    </map>
  </constructor-arg>
</bean>

<bean id="TimestampSignEncryptOutInterceptor"
     class="org.apache.cxf.ws.security.wss4j.               ❹ Define WS-Security
          ➥ WSS4JOutInterceptor">                            Out interceptor
  <constructor-arg>
     <map>
       <entry key="action" value="Timestamp Signature Encrypt"/>
       <entry key="user" value="myservicekey"/>
       <entry key="signaturePropFile" value="servicekeystore.properties"/>
```

```
        <entry key="encryptionPropFile" value="servicekeystore.properties"/>
        <entry key="encryptionUser" value="useReqSigCert"/>
        <entry key="passwordCallbackClass"
               value="soa...ServiceKeystorePasswordCallback"/>
    </map>
  </constructor-arg>
</bean>
```

What you add in listing 5.3 are two interceptors: one that acts on incoming messages ❶ and one that acts on outgoing messages ❷. These interceptors handle everything related to WS-Security. On the incoming interceptor ❸ you add specific WSS4J (which is an open source implementation of the WS-Security specification) properties, and on the outgoing interceptor you do the same ❹. These properties define how these interceptors process WS-Security headers. Let's look a bit closer at these properties, starting with those on the incoming interceptor in table 5.3.

Table 5.3 Incoming interceptor properties

Property	Description
action	The action property specifies what you want to do with the incoming message. In this case you tell the interceptor to check whether the timestamp is valid, check whether the signature of the message is correct, and finally decrypt the message.
signaturePropFile	When you want to validate a signature, you need information from the certificate in your key store. The information on how to access this key store is stored in this property file.
decryptionPropFile	To decrypt the message you also need information from the key store. This time you need the private key. The information on how to access the key store where your private key is stored is defined in this property file.
passwordCallbackClass	Your private key is protected by a password. This password is provided by this callback class.

The properties for the outgoing interceptor are shown in table 5.4.

Table 5.4 Outgoing interceptor properties

Property	Description
action	The action property specifies what you want to do with the outgoing message. In this case you tell the interceptor to add a timestamp, sign the message, and encrypt the message.
user	When you sign the message you need to indicate which key is used to sign it. This property points to the private key you'll use.
signaturePropFile	This property specifies how to access the key store where the private key is stored for signing.

Table 5.4   Outgoing interceptor properties *(continued)*

Property	Description
encryptionPropFile	This specifies how to access the key store where the public key is stored for encryption.
encryptionUser	This specifies the certificate you'll use for encryption. The value specified here indicates that you'll use the certificate that was used to sign your incoming request.
passwordCallbackClass	Your private key is protected by a password. This password is provided by this callback class.

To wrap up the server side of WS-Security, let's quickly look at a property file used to configure a key store (the signaturePropFile, encryptionPropFile and decryptionPropFile properties from table 5.3 and table 5.4):

```
org.apache.ws.security.crypto.provider=org...nts.crypto.Merlin
org.apache.ws.security.crypto.merlin.keystore.type=jks
org.apache.ws.security.crypto.merlin.keystore.password=storesecret
org.apache.ws.security.crypto.merlin.keystore.alias=myservicekey
org.apache.ws.security.crypto.merlin.file=serviceKeystore.jks
```

These properties define how to access the key store and define the default alias (the name the certificate or key is stored with) to use when signing a message. Note that in these property files the password is written in plain text. Make sure that these files are stored at a safe location. The callback handler is used to provide passwords based on the alias of a key. This callback handler provides the password to access a key in the key store. For this you need to implement the handle method, as shown in the following listing.

Listing 5.4   Callback that provides a password to access the key store

```
public void handle(Callback[] callbacks)
      throws IOException, UnsupportedCallbackException {
for (int i = 0; i < callbacks.length; i++) {
   WSPasswordCallback pc = (WSPasswordCallback)callbacks[i];
    String pass = passwords.get(pc.getIdentifier());      ◁─┐  Get password
    if (pass != null) {                                     ❶  from the map
       pc.setPassword(pass);
       return;
    }
 }
}
```

For this implementation in listing 5.4, you create a map (named passwords) that returns the password ❶ if it's in the map. In production environments you should do this in a more secure manner. You might notice that you iterate through an array of Callbacks. The reason is that it's possible, in some implementations, to get multiple Callbacks in one call. One Callback might be used to retrieve a user id based on a certificate, and in the same call a callback could be provided to retrieve a stored private key.

Because testing a service that support WS-Security from soapUI is rather complex, I've created a simple Java-based SOAP client that you can run from Eclipse. You can find this client in the test packages of the chapter6-message-integrity project. When you run this client, a SOAP call will be made to the service defined in listing 5.3. This call will be signed and encrypted using the keys in the key store. The service will decrypt the SOAP message and validate the signature. If all is correct, the call will proceed and a result will be returned. If there's a problem with decrypting the message or the signature doesn't validate, the server will return a SOAP fault to the client. With this configuration you comply with the policy. Your messages are secured, and you can guarantee that the messages aren't modified in transit.

Next, you'll learn how you can comply with this policy for a REST-based service. You'll do that by creating your own message integrity mechanism.

5.2.2   *Using HMAC for message integrity and non-repudiation*

What you often see with REST services is that HTTPS is seen as secure enough, and there's no need for any additional checks. But an additional check on message integrity is still necessary in those situations where HTTPS isn't an option or an additional level of security is required. There is, however, no REST Security standard you can use. To comply with the message integrity policy you have to roll out your own implementation. Luckily, though, you aren't the first to run into this problem. Cloud services, for instance, that provide a REST-based API (Azure, Amazon, Google, and Yahoo!, to name a few) have also run into this same issue. Even though all these parties haven't defined a standard yet for this problem, they all tackle this issue in pretty much the same manner.

They create a signature of the request based on a shared secret between the client and the service. This signature is called a Hash-based Message Authentication Code (HMAC). With an HMAC you create a message authentication code (MAC) for a message based on a specific secret key. If you wanted to use HMAC for your services, you'd use the following scenario:

1 Before you start, the client should have received a shared secret from the service. Usually you get this shared secret in an email message from the service, or the service provides a website where you can look up your shared secret. Note that this secret is only shared between you and the service; it's not shared like the public part of a certificate.

2 The client creates a String representation of the request. This is in a normalized format that's defined by the service.

3 The client next creates a HMAC for this String representation using the secret it received from the service.

4 The client adds this HMAC and its username to the headers.

5 The service retrieves the HMAC and the username from the headers.

6　With this username the service retrieves the corresponding secret from a data-store.

7　Based on the same headers and normalized format, the service generates the HMAC for the request it has received.

8　The HMAC value calculated by the service is compared to the HMAC value sent by the client. If they're the same, the message's integrity is guaranteed; if not, the message is invalid and should be ignored.

How do you implement HMAC? In the following sections I'll show you how using these steps:

1　Determine which fields you'll use as input for the HMAC.

2　Create client code that can create this HMAC and add the corresponding headers.

3　Create server code that can create an HMAC based on an incoming request and compare both HMAC values.

We'll start by looking at the input fields you'll be using.

WHICH FIELDS TO USE AS INPUT FOR HMAC CALCULATION

If you want to create an HMAC as a mechanism to check a message's integrity, first you need to determine which parts of the request to use as input. The first thing that comes to mind is to base this HMAC on the request body, because that's the message. But if you do only that, what do you do with GET methods? These don't have a request body. A good example that shows the parts you should use is shown in the API provided by Amazon for its Amazon Web Services (AWS). AWS defines a set of request headers that should be part of the information that's used to create the HMAC. Table 5.5, which is based on this API, shows the fields that you'll use and explains why each specific field should be included.

Table 5.5　Fields used to calculate the HMAC

Field	Description
HTTP method	With REST the kind of HTTP method you execute defines the behavior on the server side. A DELETE to a specific URL is handled differently than a GET to that URL.
Content-MD5 header	This HTTP header is a standard HTTP header. This is an MD5 hash of the body of the request. If you include this header in the HMAC code generation, you get an HMAC value that changes as the request body changes.
Content-Type header	As you've already seen in the previous chapters, the Content-Type header is an important header when making REST calls. Depending on the media type, the server can respond differently to a request; therefore it should be included in the HMAC.
Date header	You also include the date the request was created to calculate the HMAC. On the server side you can make sure the date wasn't changed in transit. Besides this you can add message expiration functionality on the server.
HTTP method path	The path part of the URL that was invoked is also used in HMAC calculation, because a URI identifies a resource within REST.

Before we look at how to implement this on the client side, let's look at an example request that could be used as input for your HMAC calculation:

```
PUT /opengov/accounts/1
Content-Md5: uf+Fg2jkrCZgzDcznsdwLg==
Content-Type: text/plain; charset=UTF-8
Date: Tue, 26 Apr 2011 19:59:03 CEST
```

This request shows all the fields from table 5.5 and contains the information you need to generate an HMAC value.

CLIENT CODE FOR HMAC-BASED MESSAGE INTEGRITY

Your client needs to be able to do two things. It has to be able to generate an HMAC value based on the fields mentioned in table 5.5, and it must then create an HTTP request that contains enough information for the server to validate this HMAC value. Before we look at how to create an HMAC based on the information from a request, we'll have a quick look at how to generate an HMAC based on some arbitrary data and a secret. The following listing shows how to do this using standard Java functionality and the Base64 encoder from the Apache Commons project.

Listing 5.5   Generating HMAC code based on an input string and a secret key

```java
private static final String HMAC_SHA1_ALGORITHM = "HmacSHA1";        ◄── ❶ Define name
                                                                            of algorithm
public static String calculateHMAC(String secret, String data) {
  try {
    SecretKeySpec signingKey = new SecretKeySpec(secret.getBytes(),
                                    HMAC_SHA1_ALGORITHM);
    Mac mac = Mac.getInstance(HMAC_SHA1_ALGORITHM);                      ❷ Create
    mac.init(signingKey);                                                  a MAC
                                                                           instance
    byte[] rawHmac = mac.doFinal(data.getBytes());          Generate ❸
    String result = new String(Base64.encodeBase64(rawHmac));   ◄── ❹ Encode to
    return result;                                                      Base64
  } catch (GeneralSecurityException e) {
    LOG.warn("Unexpected error while creating hash: " + e.getMessage(),e);
    throw new IllegalArgumentException();
  }
}
```

You first create an instance of a `Mac`, based on the supplied algorithm ❶, and initialize this `Mac` with your secret ❷. Remember, this secret is provided to you by the service. Using this secret you create an HMAC value based on your data ❸. Finally, you encode this HMAC value using a Base64 encoder ❹. You do so because this is the standard way of transmitting binary data in an HTTP header.

So far we've still left one part out. We haven't specified how create an HMAC based on data from the request and how to transmit your generated HMAC to the service. To transmit the HMAC you add a custom HTTP header:

```
opengov_hmac: <username>:<hmacValue>
```

This header contains your username or something else the server can use to retrieve the secret key from a datastore, and you add the generated HMAC value. With these two values the service has all the information it needs to generate an HMAC value itself. The following listing shows the client code that can be used to generate the HMAC value and add your custom header to an HTTP request.

Listing 5.6   Client code that generates an HMAC and adds correct HTTP headers

```
private final static String DATE_FORMAT                      ❶ Standard format
            = "EEE, d MMM yyyy HH:mm:ss z";                      for date

public void makeHTTPCallUsingHMAC() throws HttpException,
                                    IOException {
  String contentToEncode = "<body to encode>";
  String contentType = "text/plain";                         ❷ Set up content
  String currentDate = new SimpleDateFormat(DATE_FORMAT)        for HMAC
            .format(new Date());

  PostMethod method = new
          PostMethod("http://localhost:9002/opengov/accounts/ ");
  StringRequestEntity content = new
          StringRequestEntity(contentToEncode,contentType,"UTF-8");
  method.setRequestEntity(content);
                                                             ❸ Get method
  String verb = method.getName();                               verb
  String contentMd5 = HMACUtil.calculateMD5(contentToEncode);  ❹ Create MD5 hash
  String toSign = verb + "\n"+contentMd5
            + "\n"+content.getContentType()                  ❺ Create String
            + "\n" + currentDate                                to sign
            + "\n" + method.getPath();
  String hmac = HMACUtil.calculateHMAC("secretsecret", toSign);  ❻ Generate
                                                                    HMAC
  method.addRequestHeader("opengov_hmac"
                  , username + ":" + hmac);                  ❼ Add headers
  method.addRequestHeader("Date",currentDate);
  method.addRequestHeader("Content-Md5",contentMd5);

  HttpClient client = new HttpClient();
  client.executeMethod(method);                              ❽ Send the request
}
```

In listing 5.6 you first create the basic HTTP headers ❷, using the standard date format ❶, the verb ❸, and the Content-MD5 header ❹ used in HMAC calculation. The next step is to build up the String to sign ❺ and calculate the HMAC value ❻. You add the calculated HMAC value and all the other HTTP headers to the method ❼ and send the request ❽. If you want to test this code, look at the sources for chapter 5. In the Message Integrity example I added a test class named HMACTest that you can use as a simple client to set up the correct headers.

The next step is to look at how your service can use the HMAC value to validate this request. You do this by specifying a filter on the service that's called. To do this you need to modify the applicationcontext.xml file, as shown in the following listing, and add a `<jaxrs:provider>` element.

Listing 5.7   Adding an interceptor for the service you want to protect

```
<jaxrs:server address="http://localhost:9002">
    <jaxrs:serviceBeans>
        <ref bean="serviceToProtect"/>
    </jaxrs:serviceBeans>
    <jaxrs:providers>
        <ref bean="integrityFilter" />
    </jaxrs:providers>
</jaxrs:server>
```

The `handleRequest` operation of the bean specified in this element (`integrity-Filter` in this example) gets called for each request received by this JAX-RS server. If you look at the implementation of this filter in the following listing, you can see how the supplied HMAC value is validated.

Listing 5.8   Adding an interceptor for the service you want to protect

```
public Response handleRequest(Message msg, ClassResourceInfo rClass) {

    Map headers = (Map) msg.get(Message.PROTOCOL_HEADERS);
    String verb = (String) msg.get("org.apache.cxf.request.method");
    String path = (String) msg
                    .get("org.apache.cxf.message.Message.PATH_INFO");        ❶ Get values
                                                                                for HMAC
    String contentType = getHeaderValue(headers, "content-type");            calculation
    String date = getHeaderValue(headers, "Date");
    String secret = getHeaderValue(headers, "opengov_hmac");

    String md5 = calculateMd5(msg)                      ❷ Get MD5 hash based on msg body

    String toSign = verb+"\n"+md5+"\n"+contentType+"\n"                       ❸ Create string
                        + date + "\n" + path;                                   to sign

    String calculatedHMAC = HMACUtil.calculateHMAC(getSecret                  ❹ Calculate
                    (StringUtils.substringBefore(secret, ":"))                  HMAC
                    , toSign);

    if (calculatedHMAC.equals(StringUtils        ❺ Compare HMAC values
                        .substringAfter(secret, ":"))) {
        if (StringUtils.isEmpty(date)) {                        ❻ No date value
            return Response.status(401)                           find, return 401
                .entity("HMAC validation failed, no date entity present").build();
        } else {
            SimpleDateFormat format = new SimpleDateFormat(DATE_FORMAT);
            Date receivedDate = format.parse(date);

            if (new Date().getTime() - receivedDate.getTime() > 15 * 60000) {
                return Response.status(401)                    ❼ Request has expired, return 401
                    .entity("HMAC validation failed, request expired").build();
        } else {
```

```
            return null;
      }
    }
  } else {
    return Response.status(401)
          .entity("HMAC signature incorrect.").build();
  }
}
```

⟵ ❽ HMAC and date both valid, continue

⟵ ❾ HMAC values don't match, return 401

Listing 5.8 is a large one but shouldn't be too difficult to understand, because it repeats some elements you've already seen. The first thing you do is gather all the information from the request you need ❶ to calculate the HMAC value. You can't get all the information from just the headers; you also need to create a new MD5 hash from the content of the message ❷ to make sure the message wasn't altered in transit. Then you take the same steps as you did for the client from listing 5.5. You create the String to sign ❸ and then use that String to calculate the HMAC ❹. The only difference here is that you use the getSecret() operation on the first part of the opengov_hmac header (the username part) to retrieve the secret (from a specific datastore for this user) which is used in the HMAC calculation.

If your request hasn't been altered during transit, the HMAC values supplied in the request and the one calculated by the service should be the same ❺. If this isn't the case, a 401 is sent as response ❾. If these two HMAC values are the same, you don't immediately accept the request. You do an additional check on the age of the request to make sure requests don't get replayed at a later time. If the Date header is missing, you immediately return with a 401 ❻. If the header is present, you check the time difference between the received date and the current time. If this is larger than 15 minutes, you return with a 401 ❼ indicating that the request has expired; if everything is okay, you return null ❽, which tells CXF to continue processing the request.

You've seen that by implementing an HMAC-based integrity check you can validate the integrity of REST-based service requests and comply with the message integrity policy. Remember that because there's no standard for this in the REST space, you have to document the details of how you expect your clients to provide the HMAC value.

So far, we've only looked at protecting the message from prying eyes and making sure your message isn't altered during transit. We haven't looked at how you can identify your consumers using a centralized approach. This is something I'll show you in the next section.

5.3 Using a centralized identity system

Chapter 3 defined a policy that explained why you should have a federated authentication solution that's used by your services. This section describes how you can set up such an environment and design your services to use it. There are many tools that can help you in setting up an environment where your consumers only need to authenticate once. Once a consumer is authenticated, he can use that authentication for all the different services he wants to access. This is often called single sign-on (SSO). What all these solutions have in common is that they offer token-based authentication. Before I

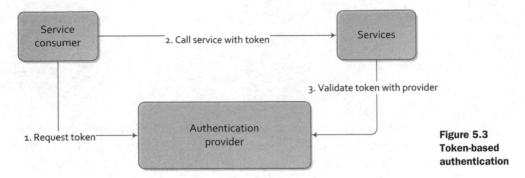

Figure 5.3
Token-based
authentication

show you how you can implement this policy for your own services, we'll look a bit deeper at what token-based authentication is. Figure 5.3 shows the process of token-based authentication.

This figure shows the required steps for token-based authentication:

1 The consumer requests a token from the authentication provider. This is normally done by providing a username and password to the authentication provider. The authentication provider checks whether the user's provided credentials are correct. If so, a token is returned to the service consumer. This token is valid only for a specific period but can be used to call multiple services.

2 The client includes this token in the request to a service. Depending on the type of service this token can be provided as a cookie, an HTTP header, a SOAP header, or a request parameter.

3 The service makes a call to the authentication provider to check the validity of the token. If the token is valid, the consumer is allowed to access the resource; if not, an access-denied message can be returned to the consumer.

How do you implement this for the services provided by OpenGov? You need to install an authentication provider, configure your clients to first request a token, and configure your services so that they check for authentication with the authentication provider. For this you need to take the following steps:

■ *Install an authentication provider*—You need an authentication provider to handle your authentication requests. In this example we'll use the open source OpenAM server. Note that there are also other authentication providers we could use; I've chosen the OpenAM server because it provides a clean REST interface you can use to integrate your own applications with, and it provides support for OAuth, which you'll see in the next section.

■ *Configure the authentication provider*—After installing the authentication provider, you need to configure it. You don't need to do much; just define the users who can access your services.

■ *Create a simple authentication service for your consumers*—You don't want to expose your OpenAM server directly to your consumers, because it provides much more functionality than just SSO. Besides, it's good practice to expose as little about your authentication solution as possible. So you'll create a simple service façade that handles all authentication-related requests. Another option could be to use an ESB to handle incoming requests and route these to OpenAM.

- *Create an authentication filter for your services*—Finally, you need to protect your services. For this you'll create a simple service filter that checks the incoming tokens for validity.

5.3.1 Installing the authentication provider

OpenAM is an open source project that used to be hosted by Sun. When Sun was taken over by Oracle, this open source project was forked and became OpenAM. OpenAM is currently actively maintained by the guys at ForgeRock. You'll be using the latest stable version from http://forgerock.com/downloads.html.

You can find additional information on how to install the OpenAM authentication software in the appendix.

5.3.2 Configuring the authentication provider

Once the authentication provider is installed, you need to create some users you can test with. To do this you need to set up a couple of things within OpenAM. First, open http://localhost:8080/opensso in your browser and log in as amadmin and the password you selected during the install.

When you've logged in, you'll be presented with the administration console. From here you can configure the complete OpenAM environment. There are many different ways to do SSO, and one of the most common ones is by using SAML2. SAML2 is an international standard for federated identity. Configuring and using SAML2 is a bit complex and out of the scope for this book. Luckily, though, OpenAM provides a REST-based interface you can use that hides the complexity of SAML2. You'll need to create a user that you can use in your tests. To do this, click the Access Control tab, and from the list of realms select /. You'll be shown a page with the properties of this realm. Now click the Subjects tab, and you'll be shown a page where you can add users. Click the New button and create a couple of users; see figure 5.4 for an example. For the examples I've created test1, test2, test3, and test4 users. The password I've used for all these users is secretsecret.

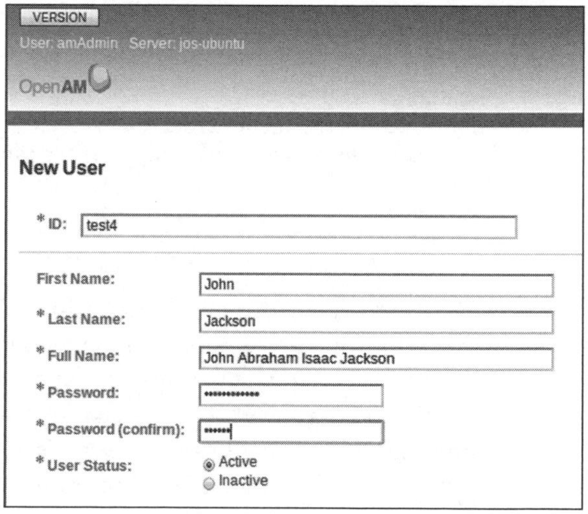

Figure 5.4 Create a new user to test the authentication process.

To quickly test whether everything is configured correctly, you can use OpenAM's REST interface to check the credentials of one of the users you've just added. If you open the following URL, http://localhost:8080/opensso/identity/authenticate?username =test4&password=secretsecret, you should see something like the following response in your browser:

```
token.id=AQIC5wM2LY4SfcyV8sf6EMSonuwOqrI-h343iRkGKcWqya4.*AAJTSQACMDE.*
```

This is the token that's now associated with this user. As you'll see in the following sections, when a consumer wants to call your service, or you want to check whether a consumer has authenticated, you use this token.

The next step is to create your authentication façade, so that your clients don't need to access the OpenAM server directly.

5.3.3 *Creating the authentication façade*

Your authentication façade doesn't just need to handle the request for a token from a client. There are two other operations that this façade should provide:

- *Check token validity*—Your service should be able to validate a token. This operation will be used by the filters that handle the authentication.
- *Get the user's attributes*—For logging and auditing purposes, it's important to know the details of who accesses your service. Without this operation the only information you'd have would be the user's token.

The service you'll create is a simple REST-based service that delegates to the REST interface provided by OpenAM. Let's look at how each of these operations is implemented.

AUTHENTICATION OF A USER

The first operation we'll look at handles the authentication of a user. To use this operation a consumer should make a call like this:

Request:
```
http://localhost:9002/opengov/identity/
    authenticate?username=test4&password=secretsecret
```

Response:
```
{"result":{"token":"AQIC5wM2LY4Sfczjyohqojab3K-
    9foRAY76mid12JArc8f0.*AAJTSQACMDE.*","status":"authenticated"}}
```

The response of this call contains the token the user should use in its follow-up calls. Note that in this example this service is provided over plain HTTP; this means that your password gets sent in plain text. In a production environment you might want to run this service on HTTPS to make sure nobody can intercept any credentials. For specific details on how this REST service is configured using JAX-RS, look at the source code for this chapter. The interesting part from this service is how the call to the OpenAM URL is made. This is shown in the following listing.

Listing 5.9   Authenticating a user using OpenAM

```
private String authenticateThroughOpenAM(String username, String password)
                                throws IOException {
    HttpClient client = new HttpClient();                          ① Create a GET
    GetMethod method = new GetMethod();                               method
    try {
      method.setURI(new URI(openAMAuthenticateLocation,false,"UTF-8"));
      method.setQueryString(new NameValuePair[] {
      new NameValuePair(USERNAME, username),                       ② Set the
      new NameValuePair(PASSWORD, password)}});                       parameters
      client.executeMethod(method);                                   Invoke the
      String responseBody = method.getResponseBodyAsString();      ③ operation
      if (responseBody.startsWith("token.id=")) {
        return StringUtils.trim(StringUtils                        ④ Parse the
            .substringAfter(responseBody, "="));                      response
      } else {
        return null;
      }
    } catch (URIException e) {
      LOG.error("Error in setting URI",e);
      throw new IllegalArgumentException(e);
    }
}
```

You've seen before that you use JAX-RS to define your REST services. JAX-RS, however, doesn't define a client API you can use to invoke other REST services. So for this example you use Apache Commons HttpClient. Listing 5.9 shows that you first define the type of method you want to use ①, which is GET in this case. Next, you specify the request parameters ②, and finally you execute the method ③ and parse the response ④.

After a user is authenticated, they can use the token received from this operation to call your services. The services will validate the token by using the isUser-Authenticated operation provided by your façade.

VALIDATION OF A TOKEN

Token validation is done in the same manner as you used to authenticate a user. OpenAM offers a REST call that you can use to validate a token. If you send the following request to OpenAM

Request:
```
http://localhost:8080/opensso/identity/isTokenValid?tokenid=
    AQIC5wM2LY4Sfczjyohqojab3K-9foRAY76mid12JArc8f0.*AAJTSQACMDE.*
```

you'll receive a Boolean response, boolean=true if the token is valid and boolean=false if the token couldn't be validated. The corresponding code to make this REST call is shown in the next listing.

Listing 5.10   Validating a token using OpenAM

```
method.setURI(new URI(openAMValidateTokenLocation,false,"UTF-8"));
method.setQueryString(new NameValuePair[] {
```

```
    new NameValuePair("tokenid", token)));              | Make the call
int responseCode = client.executeMethod(method);    <--| to OpenAM
if ("boolean=true\n".equals(method.getResponseBodyAsString())) {  <-- Validate
  result = true;                                                      the results
}
```

The final operation to include in your façade is getUserDetails. With this operation you allow a service to retrieve a set of user details from OpenAM based on a token. The OpenAM REST call you use for this is the following:

Request:
```
http://localhost:8080/opensso/identity/
    attributes?subjectid=AQIC5wM2LY4Sfcx90UoYFnzbyO8dxhdMTArVpwnlhcab53M.*AA
    JTSQACMDE.*
```

Response:
```
userdetails.token.id=AQIC5wM2LY4Sfcx90UoYFnzbyO8dxhdMTArVpwnlhcab53M.*AAJTSQA
    CMDE.*
userdetails.attribute.name=uid
userdetails.attribute.value=test4
userdetails.attribute.name=userpassword
...
userdetails.attribute.name=cn
userdetails.attribute.value=John Abraham Isaac Jackson
userdetails.attribute.name=givenname
userdetails.attribute.value=John
```

From your façade make this REST call using the following code.

Listing 5.11   Operation to get a user's attributes

```
Map<String, String> result = new HashMap<String, String>();
method.setURI(new URI(openAMUserDetailsLocation,false,"UTF-8"));      ① Set up
method.setQueryString(new NameValuePair[] {                             method
new NameValuePair("subjectid", token)});
int responseCode = client.executeMethod(method);        <--
String responseBody = method.getResponseBodyAsString();    ② Make REST call

if (responseCode == 200) {                              <--
  BufferedReader reader = new BufferedReader(new           ③ Check response code
              StringReader(responseBody));
  String propertiesLine = reader.readLine();                  ④ Process
  while (propertiesLine != null) {                     <--       results
    String key = StringUtils.substringBefore(propertiesLine, "=");
    String value = StringUtils.substringAfter(propertiesLine, "=");

    if (key.equals("userdetails.attribute.name")) {
      String valueLine = reader.readLine();
      String returnedValue = StringUtils.substringAfter(valueLine, "=");
      result.put(value, returnedValue);
    }
  propertiesLine = reader.readLine();
  }
}
```

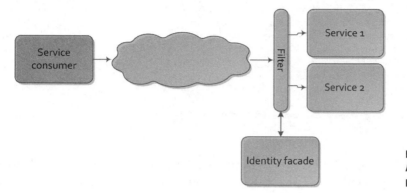

**Figure 5.5
Authentication filter
protecting services**

In listing 5.11 you use the HttpClient to invoke the REST ❷ call to the OpenAM server ❶ and store the result into a Map ❹ if you have a response code of 200 ❸. This Map is returned to the calling service to provide it with information on the user who called the service.

With this façade you've created a simple service that hides the details of your authentication provider. In the next section you'll learn how you can use this façade from a filter to check whether a consumer is authenticated or not.

5.3.4 *Creating the authentication filter*

The authentication filter you'll create, shown in figure 5.5, sits between the service consumer and your services.

Whenever a request for a service reaches the filter, the filter will check with your identity façade to see if the user is authenticated. If the user is authenticated, they are allowed access to your service; if not, an access-denied message is returned to the user. The core part of this filter is identical for both REST- and WS-* based services. In your filter you make a call to the authentication façade you created and check whether the supplied token is valid. To check whether a token is valid, you need to make a call to the façade that looks like this:

Request:
```
http://localhost:9002/opengov/identity/
    isUserAuthenticated?token=AQIC5wM2LY4SfczuGdTjARdzooXKuKZE360FwzVFd_ZrDU
    Q.*AAJTSQACMDE.*
```

Response:
```
{"result":{"token":"AQIC5wM2LY4SfczuGdTjARdzooXKuKZE360FwzVFd_ZrDUQ.*AAJTSQAC
    MDE.*","status":"valid"}}
```

The following listing shows how you can make this call to the authentication façade.

Listing 5.12 Calling the identity façade to validate a token

```
GetMethod method = new GetMethod();
method.setURI(new URI(validTokenURL,false,"UTF-8"));
method.setQueryString(new NameValuePair[] {
```

```
                    new NameValuePair(TOKEN, token)});
client.executeMethod(method);
String responseBody = method.getResponseBodyAsString();
JSONObject response = (JSONObject) JSONSerializer.toJSON(responseBody);
String result = response.getJSONObject("result").getString("status");
  if (result.equals("valid")) {
    return true;
  } else {
    LOG.info("Received invalid authentication response: " + responseBody);
    return false;
}
```

This code in listing 5.12 is similar to the previous listings where you made REST calls. You use HttpClient to execute a GET method, where you supply the token, provided by the user, as argument. If the response returns status `valid`, you return `true`, meaning the user is authenticated and may access this service. If not, you return `false` and the user is denied access to the service. One thing we haven't discussed yet is how a service consumer can get a token to your service. As mentioned, there are a number of different ways to do this, and in this example you require your clients to add the token, which they can request by calling `authenticateThroughOpenAM` on the façade, as an HTTP header with the name `opengov_token`.

The next section shows you how to do this for a REST service.

REST AUTHENTICATION FILTER

In chapter 2 we discussed a filter that sends events to the Bamos server. For the authentication filter you'll use the same approach. To add a filter for your REST service you need to add the information from the following listing to the applicationcontext.xml file.

Listing 5.13   Configuring authentication filter for REST service

```
<jaxrs:server address="http://localhost:9002">
<jaxrs:serviceBeans>
    <ref bean="serviceToProtect"/>                          ❶ The service
</jaxrs:serviceBeans>                                            to protect
<jaxrs:providers>
    <ref bean="authenticationFilter" />                     ❷ The filter
</jaxrs:providers>                                               to apply
</jaxrs:server>
```

Listing 5.13 defines a single REST service ❶ with a reference to a custom `authenticationFilter` ❷. This filter is called each time a request to your service is made. The configuration from listing 5.13 works great in a test or development environment. When you have many services to protect, a good idea would be to use an ESB or an authentication proxy. That way you can centralize the authentication check for all your services.

The next listing shows the implementation of this filter.

Listing 5.14 REST authentication filter implementation

```
public class AuthenticationFilter implements RequestHandler {          ◄── ❶ Implement
                                                                            RequestHandler
  private static final String TOKEN = "token";
  private static final String OPENGOV_TOKEN = "opengov_token";
  private String validTokenURL;

  public Response handleRequest(Message msg, ClassResourceInfo classinfo) {
    if (AuthenticatedService.class
            .isAssignableFrom(classinfo.getServiceClass())) {
      Map headers = (Map)                                              ◄── ❷ Get HTTP
      msg.get(org.apache.cxf.message.Message.PROTOCOL_HEADERS);            headers

      if (headers.containsKey(OPENGOV_TOKEN)) {                        ◄── ❸ Get our
        ArrayList<String> opengovHeader = (ArrayList<String>)             custom header
                            headers.get(OPENGOV_TOKEN);
        if (opengovHeader != null && opengovHeader.size() > 0) {       ◄── ❹ Check
          String token = opengovHeader.get(0);                            authentication
          if (authenticate(token)) {
            return null;                                               ◄── ❺ If valid,
          } else {                                                        continue
            LOG.info("Authentication failed for token: " + token );
            return  Response.status(401).build();                     ◄── ❻ If invalid,
          }                                                               return 40I
        }
      } else {
        return Response.status(401).build();
      }
    }
    return null;
  }
}
```

Because this class implements the CXF-specified `RequestHandler` interface ❶, it will be called whenever a request is sent to one of the services specified in listing 5.13. Whenever a request is received, you retrieve the HTTP headers from this request ❷ and check for the availability of your custom header ❸. The value from this header is used to authenticate ❹ against your façade, and based on the result you let the request through by returning `null` ❺ or return a 401 (Unauthorized) response ❻. If you want to test this filter, check out the sources for this chapter, where a soapUI test project is available.

WS-* AUTHENTICATION FILTER

The filter for WS-* based services isn't that different. This time, though, you won't be using HTTP headers (which would be a valid option for our use case), but you'll add the token information to a custom SOAP header. In this example you'll add a header that looks like this:

```
<soapenv:Envelope
      xmlns:soapenv="http://schemas.xmlsoap.org/soap/envelope/"
   xmlns:gov="http://www.opengov.org/identity">
  <soapenv:Header>
    <gov:token>AQIC5wM2LY4Sfcz500RurzwH0i735_9bPbQZHmr8-
    XOcONU.*AAJTSQACMDE.*</gov:token>
```

```
</soapenv:Header>
...
</soapenv:Envelope>
```

When a WS-* client wants to make a call to your service, they have to add this header to their SOAP message. Now that you know what the client should do, let's look at how to configure the server side. Just as you did for REST, you need to configure your service to use your filter. This is done in the applicationcontext.xml file as shown in the following listing.

Listing 5.15 Configuring the WS-* authentication filter

```
<jaxws:endpoint id="protectMe"
      implementor="soa.governance.chapter6.
                   identity.services.ws.ServiceToProtectImpl"
      address="http://localhost:9001/protectMe">
  <jaxws:inInterceptors>
    <ref bean="authenticationFilter"/>
  </jaxws:inInterceptors>
</jaxws:endpoint>
```

In listing 5.15, you define an inInterceptor on the endpoint you want to protect. All requests to this endpoint will now pass through this filter. The next listing shows the implementation of this filter.

Listing 5.16 Filter for WS-* based services

```
public class AuthenticationFilter
           extends SoapHeaderInterceptor {                        ❶ Extend CXF base class
  public void handleMessage(Message msg) throws Fault {
    SoapMessage message = (SoapMessage) msg;
    List<Header> headers = message.getHeaders();                  ❷ Get SOAP headers
    boolean found = false;
    for (Header header : headers) {
      QName name =header.getName();
      if (name.getNamespaceURI()                                  ❸ Check if token is present
            .equals("http://www.opengov.org/identity")
            && name.getLocalPart().equals("token")) {
        found = true;
        Node node = (Node) header.getObject();
        String token = node.getTextContent();
        if (!this.authenticate(token)) {                          ❹ Authenticate token
          throw new Fault("Token can't be validated",
              java.util.logging.Logger.getAnonymousLogger());
        }
      }
    }
    if (!found) {                                                 ❺ Throw SOAP fault
      throw new Fault("No token found",
        java.util.logging.Logger.getAnonymousLogger());
    }
  }
}
```

When a SOAP request is received, this filter ❶ intercepts the request and the handle-Message operation is invoked. In this method you extract the SOAP headers ❷ and check the availability of your own custom header ❸. If it's available, you check whether it's a valid token ❹. If the token is found, you do nothing and accept the request; if the token isn't valid or no token is found, you throw a SOAP fault ❺. If you want to test this, you can use the soapUI project that's provided with the rest of the source code.

In this section we focused on whether a user is authenticated to access a specific service. You set up this environment to comply with the "Use centralized identity system" policy. By using OpenAM you can easily comply with this policy and introduce a standard way of doing authentication within your environment.

There is, however, another scenario that we haven't covered yet, and one that you see more and more on the web. This is the scenario where you don't want to authenticate whether a specific user has access to your service but whether another service or application can access your service on behalf of that user. Twitter, for instance, provides an interface that other services and applications can use to access information from your Twitter account, if you grant those other applications access. The standard mechanism used for this is called OAuth. In the following section we'll look at how you can implement OAuth for your own services.

5.4 *Using OAuth to allow other services to access your service*

With OAuth you can grant applications and services access to your private information stored in a different service. If you, for instance, want to allow third parties to access your Facebook profile, you must use OAuth for this. In chapter 3 we defined a number of services that store information for a specific resident. One of the services allows a user to track the routes they drove by storing GPS data. This is information that would also be useful for other services to access. With OAuth you have a mechanism to do this, in a controlled and standard way. An example could be a third-party web application that allows you to plot your GPS data on a map. This third-party web application could use OAuth to request this information from your own service on behalf of a resident.

Before we look at how you can implement OAuth for your own service, I'll show you an overview of how OAuth works.

The easiest way to understand OAuth is by looking at the steps shown in figure 5.6.

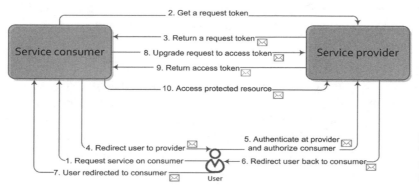

**Figure 5.6
The various steps
used in OAuth
authentication**

In this figure you can see the scenario a user goes through when they want to authorize a specific service (called the service consumer) to access protected information on a second service (called the service provider). For this example let's assume that your user has an account on the service provider that stores all their favorite movies. The service consumer is a *TV Guide* website that wants to access these movies, so it can show the user personalized information whenever one of their favorite movies is playing. For this the service consumer will need to access private information on the service provider. Implementing this with OAuth requires the following steps:

1   The user is browsing the *TV Guide* website and notices that they can use the information from the service provider, where their favorite movies are stored, in this website. They click the button Use Favorite Movies.

2   The first step in the OAuth negotiation is that the service consumer must acquire a request token from the service provider. This request token is used to identify the user and service for which you're executing this OAuth scenario.

3   The service provider checks whether the consumer website is allowed to access information on the service provider and returns a request token.

4   The service consumer redirects the user to the login page of the service provider.

5   The user authenticates themselves at the service provider and is asked whether to authorize the consumer access to its resources at the provider.

6   If the user allows this, the user is sent back to the consumer website by a redirect. At the service provider site, this request token is now marked as being valid and authenticated.

7   The consumer can now upgrade their request token to an access token.

8   The redirect from step 6 contains the request token, so the consumer knows which user it's dealing with. The consumer now makes a request to upgrade a request token to an access token.

9   The provider checks the received request token to determine whether the user has allowed the consumer access to its protected resources. Because the consumer was authenticated and authorized in step 5, an access token is returned to the service consumer.

10 With this access token, which the consumer should store somewhere to use later, the consumer can access protected resources on the provider. In this example, the consumer can use this access token to make a call to the provider and get a list of favorite movies.

If you look through the steps, you'll see that OAuth is a fairly straightforward authentication mechanism; the user explicitly grants a specific consumer access to a provider, which results in a unique access token that the consumer can then use to access the provider, without user interaction. Implementing OAuth for your own services, though, is a bit harder. You need to follow the exact steps from this scenario: the messages sent between consumer and provider need to be signed, they must be provided in a specific format, and you need to keep track of the consumers who have access to a specific provider. Luckily, though, there are a couple of open source libraries and tools that can help you in using and implementing OAuth. For this section you'll use OpenAM, which you used in the previous section, to handle all the OAuth specifics at the service provider side. And you'll use the Java libraries from http://oauth.googlecode.com/ to help you implement the service consumer.

REGISTERING A CONSUMER WITH THE SERVICE PROVIDER

I'll walk you through the steps and show you how to configure them. Before you start, though, you first need to tell the service provider that there's a consumer who wants to access its resources. If you look back at the favorite movies and *TV Guide* example, this would mean the Favorite Movies service must know beforehand that it can expect requests from the *TV Guide* service to access information for some users.

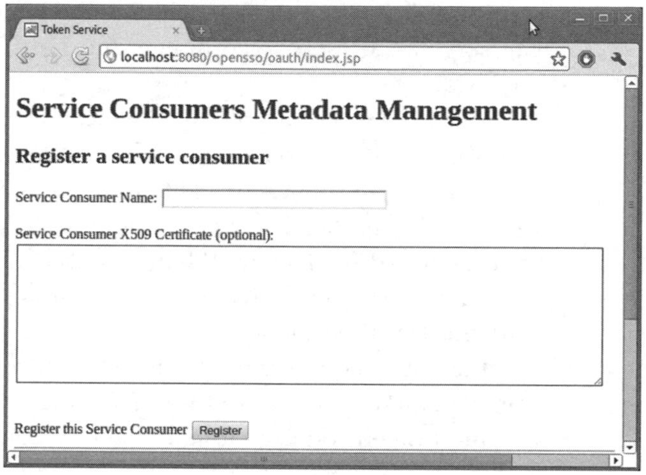

Figure 5.7   OpenAM consumer registration screen

If you don't restrict this to specific service consumers, any service could access information from the service provider. For this you need to get a consumer key and secret, which the consumer can use to identify itself and sign its messages. OpenAM provides functionality for this that you can use. If you open the following URL in your browser, http://localhost:8080/opensso/oauth/index.jsp, you'll be shown a basic form (see figure 5.7) that you can use to register OAuth consumers in OpenAM.

In this form you can register a consumer by entering a name in the Service Consumer Name field (in this example you use opengov) and clicking the Register button. You can optionally also use X.509 certificates for authentication, but for this example you won't do that. After you click the button you're shown the details of your registration (shown in figure 5.8).

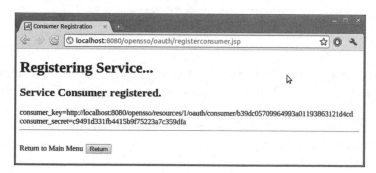

**Figure 5.8
Consumer key and secret**

Write these values down somewhere; you'll need them later on to identify your service consumer.

GET A REQUEST TOKEN FROM THE SERVICE PROVIDER

Now that you have a consumer key and secret, you can start with the scenario. If you look back at the steps, the first thing you need to do is create a simple website, as shown in figure 5.9, that can serve as the service consumer and start the scenario.

Figure 5.9 shows a demo web application that can be accessed on http://localhost:9002/ oauth/exampleApplication. The source code for this simple application can be found in the sources for this chapter. When you click the Search button (step 1 from the scenario), you start the OAuth scenario. For the next step you

Figure 5.9   OpenGov OAuth demo application you can use to test an OAuth scenario

need to get a request token from your service provider. Just as it does for authentication, OpenAM provides REST interfaces that you can use to get a request token. To get a request token you need to send the information shown in table 5.6 to OpenAM.

Table 5.6   OAuth get request token

Parameter	Description
oauth_consumer_key	This key uniquely identifies the consumer website. This is the key you were shown when you registered a consumer.
oauth_signature_method	All the messages sent between consumer and provider need to be signed. This is done to detect modified messages and guarantee message integrity. OAuth supports HMAC-SHA1, RSA-SHA1, and PLAINTEXT.
oauth_signature	This is the signature the consumer generated. This is checked at the provider side.
oauth_timestamp	This is the time when the request was sent. This can be used to detect old messages and avoid replay attacks.
oauth_nonce	This random string needs to be unique in each request.
oauth_version	This is the OAuth version you're using. OpenAM supports version 1.0.

How do you make this request? You could do this all yourself: set up the correct HTTP method, normalize the request headers, create the signature, and make the call to the service provider. But this is error prone and cumbersome, because it can quickly go wrong, which will often result in unclear error messages from the service provider. Luckily, the Java libraries from http://oauth.googlecode.com/ can handle the gritty details for you. In the following listing you use these libraries to get a request token from OpenAM. As you can see in this listing, you don't have to specify the headers from table 5.6 yourself. You only have to specify the consumer key and consumer secret (from figure 5.7) and you can make the call.

> **Listing 5.17 Use Java OAuth library to get request token**

```
HttpClient3 client = new HttpClient3();
OAuthClient oauthClient = new OAuthClient(client);

OAuthServiceProvider provider = new OAuthServiceProvider(          ❶ Define the
        requestTokenURL, userAuthorizationURL, accessTokenURL);        service
                                                                       provider

OAuthConsumer consumer = new OAuthConsumer(                        ❷ Define the
      super.getURL().toString(),                                      service
                  consumerKey, consumerSecret, provider);             consumer

consumer.setProperty(OAuthClient.PARAMETER_STYLE,                 ❸ Set OAuth style
                ParameterStyle.AUTHORIZATION_HEADER);

accessor = new OAuthAccessor(consumer);

Map<String,String> parameters = new HashMap<String, String>();    ❹ Add for
parameters.put("oauth_callback", super.getURL().toString());         OpenAM

oauthClient.getRequestToken(                                       ❺ Get the
          accessor,OAuthMessage.POST,parameters.entrySet());          request
//accessor.requstToken now contains the requestToken                  token
```

Listing 5.17 shows how to retrieve a request token. First, you need to specify what the various OAuth specific endpoints are and where the login page is that's shown when the user is asked for its password ❶. For OpenAM you specify the following URLs:

requestTokenUrl=http://localhost:8080/opensso/resources/1/oauth/
get_request_token
userAuthorizationUrl=http://localhost:8080/opensso/oauth/userconsole.jsp
accessTokenUrl=http://localhost:8080/opensso/resources/1/oauth/
get_access_token

The next step is to initialize your consumer ❷. Here you use the consumerKey and consumerSecret you created in OpenAM earlier. These two properties uniquely identify this service. The first parameter in ❷ is the URL where you want to be redirected; in this case it's the URL where your web application is running. Next, you specify how the OAuth request message should be sent ❸. Because OpenAM only supports the OAuth information being sent in an HTTP header, you specify that here. Before you can request the token, you need to explicitly add the oauth_callback property ❹. Even though this isn't a required property for this call, OpenAM checks for this property, and the OAuth client you use doesn't explicitly add this property. Finally, you can make the call ❺, and you'll get a request token.

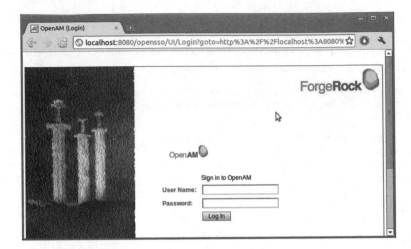

Figure 5.10 **After redirect the user is asked to identify themselves with the service provider.**

REDIRECTING, LOGGING IN, AND AUTHORIZING THE CONSUMER

Now that you have a request token, you should redirect the user to the login page for the service provider. In this case this is the login page provided by OpenAM. The following code snippet shows how to create the redirect URL:

```
String encodedToken = URLEncoder.encode(requestToken,"UTF-8");
String encodedCallbackURL =
            URLEncoder.encode(super.getURL().toString(),"UTF-8");
String urlToCall = userAuthorizationURL + "?"  +
                   "oauth_token=" + encodedRequestToken + "&" +
                   "oauth_callback=" + encodedCallbackURL;
  getMainWindow().open(new ExternalResource(urlToCall));
```

With this code snippet you redirect the user to the login page of OpenAM. To identify for which user you're executing this scenario you include the requesttoken. You also add a callback URL. This is the URL where you want to be redirected after authentication. When the user is redirected, they will be shown the standard OpenAM login screen (figure 5.10).

Here you can log in with your OpenAM credentials or with one of the test credentials you created earlier. After you've logged in, you're asked whether you want to allow the consumer access to the service provider; see figure 5.11.

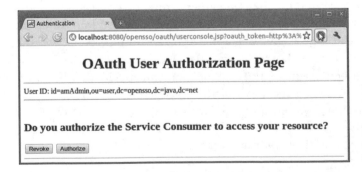

Figure 5.11 **Authorize the consumer to access the service on your behalf.**

After you authorize the service, you'll be redirected to the application with the following URL:

http://localhost:9002/oauth/exampleApplication/?oauth_token=http://localhost :8080/opensso/resources/1/oauth/rtoken/1d4b876ee3c149ee958e483a6be56b7b &oauth_verifier=4d44ad8ab8264096b89cfbc621ec251b

At this point your request token has been authenticated with the service provider and you've granted the consumer access. All that needs to be done now is upgrade the request token to an access token that can be used to access the service provider on behalf of the user you logged in with.

GETTING AN ACCESS TOKEN AND ACCESSING A PROTECTED RESOURCE ON THE PROVIDER

To get a request token from the service provider, you use pretty much the same code as you did to retrieve a request token, as shown in the next listing.

Listing 5.18   Using the Java OAuth library to get the access token

```
Map<String,String> parameters = new HashMap<String, String>();
parameters.put("oauth_verifier", verifier);
parameters.put("oauth_callback", super.getURL().toString());
oauthClient.getAccessToken(
        accessor,OAuthMessage.POST,parameters.entrySet());
return accessor.accessToken;
```

To get the access token you reuse the `accessor` from listing 5.17 and add two specific OpenAM parameters: `oauth_verifier` and `oauth_callback`. These properties aren't necessary in this call if you follow the OAuth specification but are required by the OpenAM OAuth implementation. The `getAccessToken` call will return an access-Token this service consumer can now use to access the service provider.

If you look back at figure 5.6 at the beginning of this section, you'll see that you've pretty much done everything. We've walked through steps 1 through 9 and you've retrieved an access token. But how can you use this token?

USING THE ACCESS TOKEN TO ACCESS A PROTECTED RESOURCE

If you want to make a call to the service provider, you must include all the required OAuth headers. This is needed because your service provider must be able to validate the OAuth headers to see if the access token is valid. To make this call you use the same `accessor` and `oauthclient` you used to retrieve the request and access token. To access a resource at the following URL, http://localhost:9002/opengov/accounts/1, use the following call:

```
OAuthMessage result = oauthClient.invoke(accessor,
        "http://localhost:9002/opengov/accounts/1",null);
```

This will make sure the correct access token and other OAuth parameters are set before the call is made. On the service provider side you now need to validate this request before you access the resource. In this example I've created a simple filter, which is configured for the service you want to protect, just as you did in section 5.3.4.

The code from this filter that handles the OAuth verification is shown in the following listing.

Listing 5.19   Using a filter to validate the OAuth access token

```
if (headers.containsKey("Authorization")) {
  OAuthMessage oAuthMessage =
              new OAuthServlet().getMessage(request, null);

  String accessToken = oAuthMessage.getToken();
  String consumerKey = oAuthMessage.getConsumerKey();

  String secret = getSecret(consumerKey,
                  oAuthMessage.getSignatureMethod());

  String sharedSecret = getSharedSecret(accessToken);
  String subject = getSubject(accessToken);


  // check OAuth authentication
  SimpleOAuthValidator validator = new SimpleOAuthValidator();
  OAuthConsumer consumer = new OAuthConsumer("", consumerKey,
                          secret, null);
  OAuthAccessor accessor = new OAuthAccessor(consumer);
  accessor.tokenSecret = sharedSecret;
  validator.validateMessage(oAuthMessage, accessor);


  // if we get here the token is validated and we've
  // got an OAuth authenticated user
  System.out.println("Subject: "
      + URLDecoder.decode(subject, "UTF-8")
      + " authorized through OAuth");
  return null;
}
```

① Create an OAuth message from request
② Get OAuth parameters
③ Get consumer secret from OpenAM
④ Get shared secret from OpenAM
⑤ Get subject from OpenAM
⑥ Use supplied OAuth validator
⑦ Authentication successful

In this filter you again use the OAuth client libraries to help parse OAuth headers. You first create an OAuthMessage ① so that you can easily access the OAuth headers. Based on these headers ② you can make calls to OpenAM (③, ④, and ⑤) to get all the information you need to validate the access token (these are basic REST calls, not shown here). Your OAuth library also provides a validator you can use ⑥ to validate the incoming OAuth message. If this validator doesn't throw an exception, the access token is authenticated ⑦. At this point you know the subject belonging to the token, and you can continue processing the request, just as if the request was made directly by this user instead of by the service consumer.

In these last couple of pages we've walked through a complete OAuth scenario. OAuth involves many steps, and there are a lot of places errors can occur. With the code from this section and the example code, you should be able to set up your own OAuth service consumer and provider. Remember that if you play around with the example code, make sure you use the correct consumer key and secret and replace the ones that are configured in the code.

So far we've only looked at a user's authentication. If a user was authenticated, that was enough to access all the functionality provided by the service; you didn't check whether the consumer had the correct permissions. In the next section I'll show you how you can make use of a federated authorization provider. For this we'll once again use functionality provided by OpenAM.

5.5 *Reusing existing authorization services*

When you know which user you're dealing with, the next step is to get this user's permissions. Often authorization isn't done in a centralized system but is created specifically for a service or application. The reason is that, unlike authentication, authorization isn't the same for all applications. With authentication the goal is to get an authenticated user; this is something that can easily be externalized because how you get this authenticated user isn't important for the application. With authorization, on the other hand, it's a bit more complex. You need to be able to create a fine-grained authorization model that's usually hard to externalize. OpenAM, however, provides a federated authorization mechanism where you can create these fine-grained authorization rules and easily access these rules from your service or application. This functionality is provided by the Entitlement service. In this section you'll implement an example where you protect a REST service using authorization rules stored in OpenAM.

The service you'll protect in this example is the `ParkingPermitService`. This service allows residents to get an overview of the parking permits that have been issued by the city and allows city officials view all the parking permits. The last group of users is from the Permit Bureau. These users are also allowed to revoke permits. These rights and users are shown in figure 5.12.

In chapter 3 I defined policy SEC_POL_4 that described that access to our services must be restricted to authorized persons. That policy didn't specify any details on

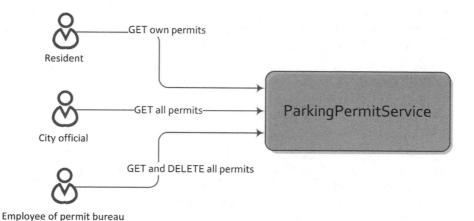

Figure 5.12 Actors and the rights they have on the `ParkingPermitService`

what needs to be protected. For this authorization example we'll go one step deeper than the original policy with the following three detail policies:

- *Policy 1*—Any authenticated user may issue GET operations on the resource identifying a parking permit. The system will check whether the issuer is the owner of the permit, and if so the permit will be returned.
- *Policy 2*—City officials may issue GET operations on all parking permits.
- *Policy 3*—Employees of the Permit Bureau may use DELETE operations to revoke a parking permit.

The first thing you need to do is configure OpenAM to support this configuration. After that you'll look at a filter to validate whether the calling user has the correct credentials.

5.5.1 *Configuring the OpenAM entitlement service*

The first thing to do is create the users and groups who can access your service. In section 5.3.2 I showed you how to create users. For this example create the users listed in table 5.7.

Before we go on to the groups, you need to set an extra property on your residents. In your policy you've defined that the residents can access only their own resources. In your service you assume you identify a resident's parking permit by their social

Table 5.7 Users to test federated authorization with

Name	Password
Resident1	secretsecret
Resident2	secretsecret
Resident3	secretsecret
Official1	secretsecret
Official2	secretsecret
Permit1	secretsecret
Permit2	secretsecret

security number (SSN). If you add the value of the SSN to your residents, you use it later on in your filter to test whether the user is allowed to view a specific parking permit or not. To do this, select the resident from the list of subjects and add 10000001 into the User Alias List for Resident1, 10000002 for Resident2, and 10000003 for Resident3. This same value will be used in the GET queries, for example: http://local host:9002/opengov/parkingpermits/10000001.

Besides users, you'll also create the following three groups: residents, officials, and permitbureau. Creating a group is done in the same place that you add the users. This time, though, click the Groups tab, and in that tab click the New button. This will open a basic screen, where all you can add is an ID. Do this for each of the groups. When you've done this you should have the groups shown in figure 5.13.

You need to add the users you've created to these groups. Click the residents group you just created, and on the screen that opens you'll see a General tab and a User tab. Click the User tab and you'll see a screen where you can select the users to

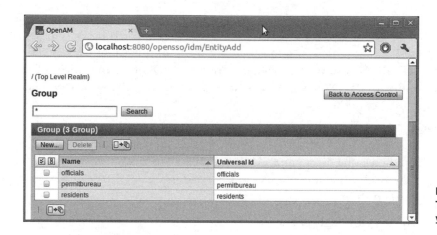

**Figure 5.13
The three groups
you've added**

add to this group. Select the Resident users and click the Add button. Add the Official users to the officials group and the Permit users to the permitbureau group.

CONFIGURING THE APPLICATION

With your test users and groups in place, we'll look at how to configure the permissions and the rights for the `ParkingPermitService`. The first thing you need to do is configure an application in OpenAM. An application in OpenAM defines the resources that are protected, the operations allowed on these resources, and the policies that apply to this application. To create an application in OpenAM, from the start screen select the Test Beta Console. From the screen that opens select the Entitlements > Applications > Create Applications menu option. This will present you with a wizard where you can create an application in a couple of steps. In the first step you specify the name and the description:

> *Name*—`ParkingPermitService`
>
> *Description*—Application describing the rights for the `ParkingPermitService`
>
> *ApplicationType*—WebAgent (base for services and applications)

Click Next and you're shown the second step, where you can specify the resources you want to protect. Enter the following two URLs:

> http://localhost:9002/opengov/parkingpermits/*
>
> http://localhost:9002/opengov/parkingpermits

The first URL is used to identify a single parking permit, and the second URL is used to get an overview of all the parking permits. Click Next, and you'll be shown a list of subject types. Enable the check box for Identity Repository Group, because you'll be authorizing users based on the group they're in. In the next step you define the actions you can execute on a specific resource. The default actions that are specified here are GET and POST. For this example you won't need POST, so delete that one, and click the Add button to add an action with the name DELETE. If you click Next here, you can also define the conditions that can be applied (time of day, day of week, IP addresses, and so on). You won't be using those in this example, so click Finish to end this wizard. You've now created an application that defines a set of resources, actions, and subjects. Now you can define the security policies in OpenAM that are applied to this service.

CREATING THE POLICIES

Select the Entitlements > Policies > Create Policies menu option. In this wizard you'll create the policies that determine whether a specific user may access a resource. You'll start with the policy that allows users in the residents group to read parking permits. In this wizard configure the following values:

> *Name*—Residents policy
>
> *Application*—`ParkingPermitService`
>
> *Resources*—http://localhost:9002/opengov/parkingpermits/*
>
> *Subjects*—Drag the residents group to the subject area.
>
> *Actions*—Allow only GET operations.

When you're configuring the actions for this policy, click the User Attributes tab. Here, drag the user attribute iplanet-am-user-alias-list to the list of attributes you want to return from an authorization call. This is the property you used to store the SSN of the resident. If you specify this property here, you can use the information stored in this property later on in your filter. These steps will create a policy where you allow all users from the residents group to access the specified resource, but only with the GET action. In the same manner create the other two policies:

> *Name*—Officials policy
>
> *Application*—`ParkingPermitService`
>
> *Resources*—Select both resources.
>
> *Subjects*—Drag the officials group to the subject area.
>
> *Actions*—Allow only GET operations.

> *Name*—Permit bureau policy
>
> *Application*—`ParkingPermitService`
>
> *Resources*—Select both resources.
>
> *Subjects*—Drag the permitbureau group to the subject area.
>
> *Actions*—Allow both GET and DELETE actions.

You've now created a set of test users, configured an application for the `Parking-PermitService`, and defined the three policies we discussed earlier. The next step is to create a filter that you can use to check whether a user has the correct rights for your service.

5.5.2 *Creating an authorization filter*

Creating a filter for your REST services shouldn't be too difficult. You've already created two other REST filters in the previous section, and this one isn't that different. Before we dive into the code, let's look at the REST service OpenAM provides to check whether a user is authorized for a specific operation. You can check a specific authorization request using the following HTTP call:

```
GET /opensso/ws/1/entitlement/decision
              ?subject=45Qn48Yibgakz5PPfKknAJ7mqxA%3D
              &action=GET
              &application=ParkingPermitService
              &resource=...%2Fparkingpermits%2F1000001

Cookie:  iPlanetDirectoryPro=AQIC5wM2LY4Sfcxu0LqCUHE
         AyUWV32cHNaQmx19P4yk5gyo.*AAJTSQACMDE.*;
```

In this call you specify a number of parameters OpenAM uses to determine whether the supplied subject is authorized for this action; see table 5.8.

Table 5.8   Required parameters to check for a user's authorization

Parameter	Description
subject	SHA-1 hash of user token. Base64 encoded. Used as extra check on user's token.
action	The action performed on the resource. Matches the actions you defined in the application and policy configuration in OpenAM.
application	Name of the application you're dealing with.
resource	Name of the resource to check a user's authorization on. Matches the URLs you defined in OpenAM's configuration.
iPlanetDirectoryPro	Cookie that contains the user's token.

The following listing shows the filter and utility methods that are needed to use OpenAM's authorization functionality.

Listing 5.20   Authorization filter using OpenAM's entitlement service

```
public Response handleRequest(Message msg, ClassResourceInfo classinfo) {
if (AuthorizedService.class
      .isAssignableFrom(classinfo.getServiceClass())) {

  HttpServletRequest request =
      (HttpServletRequest) msg.get("HTTP.REQUEST");
  Map headers = (Map)
      msg.get(org.apache.cxf.message.Message.PROTOCOL_HEADERS);
  ArrayList<String> opengovHeader = (ArrayList<String>)
      headers.get(OPENGOV_TOKEN);

  if (opengovHeader != null && opengovHeader.size() > 0) {
```

❶ Get HTTP request and headers

```
    try {
      String token = opengovHeader.get(0);
      String verb = (String) msg.
                get("org.apache.cxf.request.method");
      String resource = request.getRequestURL().toString();

      String[] results = authorize(token, verb, resource);

      if (results[0].equals("allow")) {
        if (results.length > 1) {
         // check if ssn matches
        } else {
          return null;
        }
      } else {
          LOG.info("Authorization failed for token: " + token );
          return Response.status(401).build();
      }
    } catch (Exception e) {
      LOG.warn("Error while auhtorizing" e,e );
      return Response.status(401).build();
    }
    return null;
  } else {
    return Response.status(401).build();
  }
}
```

② Get input for authorization call

③ Make call

④ Process results

⑤ Return `null` to let the request proceed

Listing 5.20 shows a basic filter you've seen before in this chapter. When a request is received you get the headers and request **①**, because you need those to retrieve the input for your authorization call. With this input, you get all the request parameters **②** and make the REST call **③**. This call returns `allow` or `deny`, which indicates whether you're authorized or not. Besides this, if you requested additional parameters to be returned (which you did for the users in the residents group), those are also returned as additional String values in the array. This response is then checked **④**, and either a 401 message is returned or the incoming request is accepted. If authorization succeeds, you return `null` **⑤**, which will cause your request to be processed normally.

Listing 5.20 didn't show how to make the REST call to OpenAM. This call is made from the `Authorize` method **③**. The details of this method are shown in the following listing.

Listing 5.21   Method used to execute the authorize call to OpenAM

```
private String[] authorize(String token, String subject,
       String action, String resource)
           throws HttpException, IOException {
String subject = shaDigest(token);
HttpClient client = new HttpClient();

 GetMethod method = new
     GetMethod("http://localhost:8080/opensso/ws/1/entitlement/decision");
 method.setQueryString(new NameValuePair[] {
   new NameValuePair("subject",subject)
 , new NameValuePair("action", action)
```

① Create an SHA hash from the token

② Configure HTTP method

```
    , new NameValuePair("application", "ParkingPermitService")
    , new NameValuePair("resource", resource)

});

method.setRequestHeader("Cookie", "iPlanetDirectoryPro=" + token + ";");
client.executeMethod(method);
String[] resultLines =
        StringUtils.split(method.getResponseBodyAsString());

return resultLines;
}


private String shaDigest(String msg) throws NoSuchAlgorithmException,
                  UnsupportedEncodingException {
MessageDigest digest = MessageDigest.getInstance("SHA-1");
digest.update(msg.trim().getBytes("UTF-8"));
byte[] hash = digest.digest();

return new String(Base64.encodeBase64(hash));
}
```

Make the authorization call ❸

Listing 5.21 creates two methods that are used to make the REST call to OpenAM. The Authorize method first creates an SHA-1 hash ❶ from the token and creates a new GetMethod ❷, sets the required cookie, and executes this method ❸. The shaDigest method is a simple helper method that creates the Base64-encoded SHA-1 hash for your token.

If you want to test this policy, it's easier to use the supplied JUnit tests in the source code from chapter 5, because you first have to authenticate yourself with OpenAM (or with your façade) and use that token in the next call for the authorization to succeed. In the JUnit tests you can find various tests that let you access the service as a member of the residents, the officials, and the permitbureau groups.

5.6   *Summary*

- Security is an important part of service design. The policies in this chapter can help you in getting a good security basis for your services.
- A good basic level of security can be introduced by using HTTPS instead of HTTP when providing services to your consumers.
- When working with WS-* services a good place to start is WS-Security. This specification can provide all message-based security features you require.
- For REST-based services there aren't any security-related standards. HTTPS together with an HMAC-based integrity scheme offers a good solution.
- When you have multiple services or applications, it's a good idea to centralize authentication and authorization. OpenAM provides a reliable and easy-to-integrate solution for this.
- When you want to authorize services to access your private data on other services, using the OAuth standard is a reliable method. This can also be done using OpenAM.

Testing, performance, and the cloud

This chapter covers

- Testing your service
- Enforcing code quality and test coverage
- Developing for the cloud

In the final chapter for this section on design-time policies we'll look at testing, performance, and how to run your service in the cloud. Even though these aren't strictly policies, it's important that during the design phase of your service you take these subjects into account.

In this chapter we'll specifically look at the following areas:

- *How to test your service*—There are many different ways you can test a service. In this section I'll show you the different levels on which you can test your service and provide you with an example service and test cases, which you can use as a starting point for your own services.

- *How to enforce code quality and test coverage*—Once you have a service and a set of test cases, you need to find a way to measure the quality of your tests and the service you've created. I'll provide you with an environment using open source tools that can help you in measuring the quality of your service.

- *Developing for the cloud*—When your services need to scale, or maybe for economic purposes, you might want to run your services in the cloud. This section will provide you with some guidelines on how to create a service that can run in the cloud. I'll explain this based on a service that uses Amazon's cloud services.

We'll start by looking at how you can effectively test your service.

6.1 How to test your service

In this book we talk about how to apply SOA governance, so why is there a section on testing your services? The reason is that just following policies, creating well-defined interfaces, and following security-related requirements is not enough. A standard policy should be that each service that's created is well-tested, regardless of whether it's defined by a SOA governance board. The service you're creating will probably be used by many different consumers. Some of them will use your service from inside your own company and others from outside your organization. You create contracts with these consumers regarding how they may use your service and what level of uptime, performance, and so on that they can expect. Without properly testing your service, you run a big risk that you can't fulfill your contract with these consumers. This can result in bad press and a loss of customers and might cause your service to be abandoned altogether. If you have tests covering the complete contract of your service, including the positive and negative scenarios, you can ensure that your service behaves as expected and that it keeps on behaving as expected whenever you make changes to it.

In chapter 2 I explained that, in most cases, a service is divided into a few different layers: a service remoting layer that provides a REST- or WS-* based interface for your service, the logic layer that provides the business functionality, and a data layer that handles the persistency of the model used in the services. Each of these layers can and should be tested separately. If you have multiple services that depend on each other or need to be called in a specific sequence, you can add another layer, which we'll call the integration layer and which should also be tested. Table 6.1 summarizes what you should test in each of these layers.

Table 6.1 Layers of service

Layer	What to test
Integration layer	Test to see if all the different components work together as expected. This may include calls using multiple services.
Service remoting layer	Test to see if you can make a call to the service remoting layer and whether this layer correctly handles the conversion of data from the remoting format to the internal format. For this you need to create a mock of your service layer, but more on that later.
Logic layer	Here you test whether the business logic of the service layer and the model is implemented correctly. To test this layer you again need to use mock objects, this time for the data layer.
Data layer	In the data layer you test whether the information gets persisted correctly.

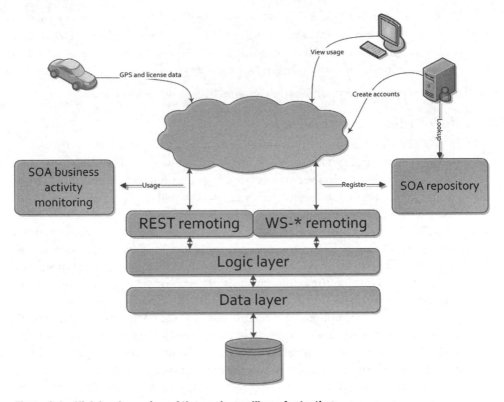

Figure 6.1   **High-level overview of the service we'll use for testing**

In the section we'll look at each of these layers in more detail and show you how you can test these layers as well as the complete service you've created. As an example we'll use the traffic service from chapter 2, because it provides a basic implementation of all the different layers shown in table 6.1. All the code examples shown in this chapter can be found in the test folders from the projects from chapter 2. As a reminder, this service is shown in figure 6.1.

Figure 6.1 shows that this service has two distinct remoting interfaces, REST-based and WS-* based. Both these remoting layers delegate their calls to the logic layer. This logic layer uses various repositories to store and retrieve the data from the datastore. In the next couple of sections I'll show you how you can test all these different layers. You'll start by testing the logic and data layers.

6.1.1   *Logic layer and data layer testing*

You're probably already comfortable with testing the internal logic and data layers if you write unit tests. There are many good books, for instance *JUnit in Action*, that show you how to create unit tests for these two layers, so I won't go into too much detail here. I'll show you how to test one specific service method using mock objects and how to create a unit test to test a NoSQL/Cassandra–based repository.

TESTING THE INTERNAL SERVICE USING MOCK OBJECTS

In chapter 2 you created a simple service that could be used to create accounts. An account is a simple POJO that's stored in Cassandra. You'll see how you can easily test this service using mock objects so that you don't have to start up a database. A mock object can be used to simulate behavior of real objects in a controlled manner. In this example you'll use such a mock object to simulate the `AccountRepository`, which you'll use to access the datastore. The method you're going to test, shown in the following listing, is a simple one. This method checks the validity of the supplied account object and stores this in the database.

Listing 6.1 Method to test with mock objects

```
public Account createAccount(Account account) {
    notNull(account,"Account to create may not be null");
    account.validate();
    accountRepository.createAccount(account);
    return accountRepository.getAccount(account.getSsn());
}
```

Not much explanation is needed for the operation; all you do is check whether the supplied account is valid, create an account, and then retrieve this account, which is returned. Because you only want to test this specific service and not the underlying database, you're going to create a mock for the repository used in the `createAccount` method. The next listing shows how to do this using EasyMock.

Listing 6.2 Unit test to test the `createAccount` method

```
private AccountRepository mockRepository;
private AccountServiceImpl accountService;

@Before
public void setup() {
    mockRepository = createMock(AccountRepository.class);     ← ❶ Create the mock
    accountService = new AccountServiceImpl();
    accountService.accountRepository = mockRepository;
}

@Test
public void TestCreateAccountWithValidAccount() {
    Account account = createTestAccount();
    mockRepository.createAccount(account);                    ❷ Record expected behavior
    expect(mockRepository.getAccount(account.getSsn()))
            .andReturn(account);
                                                              ❸ Reset the mock
    replay(mockRepository);
    Account result =                                          ❹ Run the service method
        accountService.createAccount(account);
    assertEquals(account, result);                            ❺ Normal JUnit assertion
    verify(mockRepository());                                 ❻ Verify the behavior
}
```

In this listing you first create a mock version of your repository ❶. You can use this mock in your tests instead of the real implementation. This mock is used to test whether your service calls the repository with the arguments you expected and the calls are made in the correct sequence. You do this by first recording ❷ the calls that will be made to the repository. In this example you expect this service method to first call the createAccount operation on your mock, and after that you expect it to call the getAccount operation. If the method that you expect to be called returns a result, you can use expect() to specify the return value. If the expected method call doesn't return a value, you don't have to use the expect() method.

Once you've finished recording, you reset the mock object ❸ so it can be used for testing and call the method you want to test ❹. You next check whether the response you received from the call is equal to what you used as an argument ❺. The final step to complete this scenario is to test whether your mock repository was called in the manner you expected ❷; you do this by using the verify method ❻. If this test succeeds, you've written the first test you can use to test this service method. To completely test the createAccount operation, you should also write tests with a null input or with an Account object that contains null values.

Now let's look at how you can test the data layer.

TESTING THE DATA LAYER

In the data layer you want to test whether your repository stores and updates your values correctly. Usually when you write tests for the data layer, you use an embedded database (for example, HSQL) to test this layer. Unfortunately, there isn't something like that for NoSQL databases. Luckily though, it's possible to run Cassandra itself as an embedded server. The code in the following listing shows how to set up a test case, which starts Cassandra in embedded mode and, at the end of the test, cleans up all the files Cassandra has created.

Listing 6.3   Setup and teardown of Cassandra test case

```
@BeforeClass
public static void setup() throws Exception {
    embedded = new EmbeddedServerHelper();          Create embedded
    embedded.setup();                               server
}

@AfterClass
public static void teardown() throws IOException {        Stop embedded
    EmbeddedServerHelper.teardown();                      server
    CassandraServiceDataCleaner cleaner
                = new CassandraServiceDataCleaner();   Clean up the
    cleaner.cleanupDataDirectories();                  server data
}
```

With the code from listing 6.3 at the top of your test case, you can easily test Cassandra in isolation. Note that the @beforeClass and @afterClass annotations are called respectively once before the tests start and after all the tests have finished. This means that you should carefully consider what data you use in your tests, because the data stored is shared among all the tests in the class.

We won't dive too deeply into the actual testing code, because that isn't so interesting (see the provided source code if you're interested). We'll just look at how to test a single operation: the `createAccount(Account account)` method from the `Account-Repository`. The following listing shows you how to test this method.

Listing 6.4 Using the embedded server for testing

```
@Test
public void testCreateAccount() throws HectorException {
    AccountRepository repo = createRepository();
    Account testAccount = createTestAccount();
    repo.createAccount(testAccount);
    Account account = repo.getAccount("31415");
    assertEquals(testAccount,account);
}

private AccountRepository createRepository() {
    Cluster c = getOrCreateCluster("TestCluster", "localhost:9160");
    c.addKeyspace(new ThriftKsDef("Keyspace1"));
    createColumnFamily(c);

    AccountRepository repo = new AccountRepository();
    repo.setKeyspace(createKeyspace("Keyspace1", c));
    repo.setCluster(c);

    return repo;
}
```

① Store a test account

② Get the account and compare

③ Set up the test environment

In listing 6.4 you first do the Cassandra-specific stuff **③**. You need to do this because the embedded server doesn't have any ColumnFamilies (the table synonym for Cassandra) or Keyspaces (schemas) defined. If you use the same configuration for the repository in every test, you could also move this piece of code to the `@beforeClass` operation you saw in listing 6.3. Testing the repo itself is just like normal JUnit testing. You store a test account **①**, retrieve it **②**, and assert its equality.

So far, you've seen how to set up an environment in which you can test the data and service layers; if you want more information on how to write good test cases, you might find Peter Tachiev's *JUnit in Action*, Second Edition, interesting.

The next layer from your service to test is the service remoting layer.

6.1.2 Remoting layer testing

When you look back at the initial architecture you saw in chapter 2, you'll note that the remoting layers don't do much. The remoting layer in a service architecture usually has just the following two responsibilities:

- Handle the communication between the client and the server using a specific protocol.
- Convert the data from the format used by the transport to the internally used format.

When you want to test this part of your service, you should limit your tests to these two areas. At this point you're not interested in whether the business logic of the internal service runs correctly or whether the information is stored in the database. You just want to test whether your communication layer behaves as it should. We'll start with testing the communication, and then we'll look at the data conversion.

TESTING COMMUNICATION FOR A REST-BASED SERVICE

For this example we're still using the example from chapter 2 (see figure 6.1). In this section I'll show you how you can test the REST remoting layer, and in the next section I'll do the same for the WS-* remoting layer.

Calling a REST service is easy. You make an HTTP call with a specific verb (PUT, GET) and get a response back from the server. To test this you can use one of the available HTTP libraries and manually parse the responses to see whether they're in the expected format. For our examples you'll use the Apache Commons HttpClient. This client allows you to make REST calls with a minimum of configuration.

The operation you'll be testing is the registerGPSData operation from chapter 2. This operation expects a PUT HTTP call and, based on information from the URL and the supplied JSON data, creates a GPSData object. This object is stored in the database by using the CarService. Let's look at this operation, shown in the following listing, to see what you need to mock and what needs to be tested.

Listing 6.5   The registerGPSData method that you'll test

```
public Response registerGPSData(String jsonData,
            @PathParam("license") String license,
            @PathParam("route") int route,
            @PathParam("timestamp") long timestamp,
            @Context UriInfo info) {

    GPSData data = jsonToGPSData(jsonData, timestamp);
    carService.addGPSData(license, route, data);
    URI us = info.getBaseUriBuilder().segment("trafficavoidance", "gps",
            license, Integer.toString(route),
            Long.toString(timestamp)).build(new Object[]{});

    return Response.created(us).type("application/json").build();
}
```

You'll write a test for this operation in which you'll test the following items:

- If an error occurs, you expect a response 500.
- If the data is added, you expect a response 201 (created).
- The type of response should be application/xml.
- The body of the response should be a URL pointing to the resource.

Before you write the tests, you need to create an environment in which you can start this service in isolation and mock the CarService. For this example I've created a separate Spring applicationcontext.xml file. In chapter 2 you let Spring handle the dependencies completely by using annotations and also let Spring handle the injection of the correct dependencies; in this test you'll set up the REST service and its dependency manually. That means you can inject a mock object instead of the real service. The following listing shows the relevant portion from this new applicationcontext .xml file.

> **Listing 6.6 Manually wired dependencies to test the REST service**

```
<bean name="restTrafficService"                                    ❶ Define the
      class="...services.rest.RestTrafficService"/>                   implementation

<bean id="carService"
   class="org.easymock.EasyMock" factory-method="createMock"
   name="carService">                                              ❷ Create a
     <constructor-arg index="0" value="...services.CarService"/>      mock object
</bean>

<jaxrs:server address="http://localhost:9002">
  <jaxrs:serviceBeans>                                             ❸ Point to the
    <ref bean="restTrafficService"/>                                 implementation
  </jaxrs:serviceBeans>
</jaxrs:server>
```

This applicationcontext.xml starts a REST service ❸ on port 9002. This time, however, the service ❶ doesn't call into a real `CarService` implementation but uses the mock implementation ❷. The next step is to create a test case, shown in the following listing, that calls this service to run the four tests specified earlier.

> **Listing 6.7 Test case to test REST remoting layer**

```
@BeforeClass                                                      ❶ Create Spring context
public static void setup() throws Exception {                        and get mock service
appContext =
    new ClassPathXmlApplicationContext("applicationcontext-test.xml");
    mockService = (CarService) appContext.getBean("carService");
}

@Test
public void testInvalidMessage() throws Exception {
    HttpClient client = new HttpClient();
    PutMethod method = new PutMethod(location);
     method.setRequestEntity(new StringRequestEntity(
            "invalid json",                                        ❷ Make the
            "application/trafficavoidance.gpsdata+json",              POST method
            "UTF-8"));

     assertEquals(500, client.executeMethod(method));              ❸ Make the call and
}                                                                     check response code

@Test
public void testResponseContentType() throws Exception {
    reset(mockService);                                            ❹ Set the
    mockService.addGPSData(eq("112233"),eq(2),isA(GPSData.class));    expected
    replay(mockService);                                             mock call
```

```
HttpClient client = new HttpClient();
PutMethod method = new PutMethod("location");
method.setRequestEntity(new StringRequestEntity(
      testData,
      "application/trafficavoidance.gpsdata+json",
      "UTF-8"));

client.executeMethod(method);
assertEquals("application/json",                             ❺ Check if content
      method.getResponseHeader("content-type").getValue());      type is correct
}
```

In listing 6.7 you create a standard JUnit test case. In the setup method ❶ (annotated
with @BeforeClass) you create a Spring ApplicationContext and retrieve your mock
service. In the test cases (annotated with @TestCase) you use HttpClient ❷ to make
the calls to the REST service you started during setup. To validate whether the
response is what you expected, you use a standard JUnit assertion ❸. Note that you
catch an error 500 here. The reason is that the REST framework you use treats all
uncaught exceptions, which an invalid JSON string will cause, as server errors. This
causes the service to return a result code of 500. You could add more fine-grained
exception handling to the service to return other error code, for example 40x codes.
You configure your mock service ❹ to expect a specific method invocation. If this
method isn't invoked in this manner, an exception will be thrown, which will result in
the test failing. For the test that checks for the content type of the response, you use
normal JUnit assertions ❺. Listing 6.7 doesn't show the tests for the response code
and location. These two tests are pretty much the same as the ones in this example.
They are included in the source files, if you're interested. Next, you'll do the same for
your WS-* based remoting layer.

TESTING COMMUNICATION WITH A WS-* BASED SERVICE

You'll see in this section that testing a WS-* based service in isolation isn't that hard. In
chapter 2 you used a WSDL to generate the server-side code; you'll use this generated
code to test your WS-* service. The next listing shows the operation you'll be testing.

Listing 6.8   The operation in the `AccountService` that you'll test

```
@Override
public String createAccount(Account account) {
    soa.governance.chapter2.traffic.model.Account result =
      service.createAccount(ConvertUtil.convertFromWS(account));
    return result.getSsn();
}
```

This listing shows a piece of trivial code. In this method the incoming data is converted to your internally used model, and the internal AccountService is called with
this account.

So how do you test this operation? You need to do the following:

- Create a test application context for Spring.
- Define a WS-* client, which you can use to invoke the WS-* service.

- Configure a mock implementation of the internal AccountService.
- Make a new JUnit test case that starts the application and uses the client to invoke the service.

The first thing on your list is creating a custom applicationcontext.xml file to test with. Just as you did for the REST service, you create a new minimal file that defines the beans required for this test. This applicationcontext.xml file is shown in the following listing.

Listing 6.9   Spring configuration for testing the WS-* based service

```
<jaxws:client id="accountServiceClient"
  serviceClass="...service_1_0.AccountServicePortType"      ❶ Client for the
  address="http://localhost:9001/accountService" />            web service

<bean id="accountServiceImpl" class="org.easymock.EasyMock"   ❷ Mock
    factory-method="createMock" name="accountServiceImpl">       implementation
  <constructor-arg index="0"
            value="...traffic.services.AccountService"/>
</bean>
                                                              ❸ WS-* remoting
<bean name="accountService"                                     implementation
      class="...traffic.services.ws.impl.AccountServiceImpl"/>

<jaxws:endpoint id="trafficService"                           ❹ Expose as
  implementor="#accountService"                                 WS-* service
  address="http://localhost:9001/accountService"
  wsdlLocation="/contract/accountService.wsdl">
  <jaxws:schemaLocations>
    <jaxws:schemaLocation>
       ./contract/traffic-avoidance-types.xsd
    </jaxws:schemaLocation>
  </jaxws:schemaLocations>
</jaxws:endpoint>
```

You've already seen most of the elements in the listing in previous code fragments. The only new one here is ❶. With this configuration you create a WS-* client for the interface specified by the serviceClass attribute. This is the client that you'll use in your tests. The rest of the listing looks a lot like the one in the previous section on REST; you define a mock implementation of the internal service ❷ and define a WS-* based service ❹ that uses ❸ as its implementation. Looking back at the four points of our list, we've already covered the first three with the configuration shown next in listing 6.10.

The only thing left to do is create a JUnit test class, which starts the service and runs the tests, as shown here.

Listing 6.10   Unit test to test the WS-* based service

```
@BeforeClass
public static void setup() throws Exception {          ❶ Set up the test
  appContext =
    new ClassPathXmlApplicationContext("applicationcontext-test-ws.xml");
```

```
    client = (AccountServicePortType) appContext.getBean("helloClient");
    accountServiceMock = (AccountService)
                appContext.getBean("accountServiceImpl");
}

@Test
public void testValidCall() throws Exception {
    reset(accountServiceMock);
    expect(accountServiceMock.createAccount(isA(...del.Account.class)))
                    .andReturn(getModelAccount());
    replay(accountServiceMock);
    String response = client.createAccount(getTestAccount());
    assertEquals(getTestAccount().getSsn(), response);
    verify(accountServiceMock);
}
```

Create the mock service ❷

❸ **Use the WS client**

Validate ❹ **the response**

In this listing you create an `ApplicationContext` and from that `ApplicationContext` retrieve the mock service and the WS-* client ❶. These beans are used in the rest of your tests. In the `testValidCall` test, you want to test the happy flow. If you make a call with valid arguments, does the service behave as it should? Because you use a mock service, the first thing you need to define is what this mock service can expect for calls ❷. For this test you know that the `createAccount` operation will be called with an `Account` as an argument and that this operation should also return an `Account`. You configure this on your mock service using the `expect` method. When you've defined the expected behavior for the mock service, you can use the client ❸ to make the WS-* based call and check whether the result from this call is what you expect ❹.

So far in this section you've tested whether the remoting layer works and responds correctly to your requests. You've done this by mocking the internal service, so that you can focus your test on this layer and not on the complete application. In the introduction to this section I mentioned that besides testing the transport, it's also important to test the conversion between the domain model used by the remoting layer and the one used by the internal services. If there are errors in the conversion layer, you'll get unexpected behavior in the service and data layers that can be hard to track down. In the last part of this section we'll look at how to test the conversion.

TESTING THE CONVERSION

Testing the conversion can be done completely in isolation from all the other tests—at least if the conversion code is externalized in its own utility class. In the code from chapter 2, you can see that for the WS-* based service the conversion between the internal service model and the generated model is done in a separate utility class called `ConvertUtil`. This class can be tested with JUnit without the need for additional configuration. For the REST service, however, the conversion code is done in the service itself. Even though the code looks trivial, this setup makes it much harder to test the code in isolation, especially when the conversion becomes more complex. If you want to test your conversion code in isolation, you must externalize it to a separate utility class. If you don't want to do that, for instance if the conversion code is trivial, you can often also test it using the methods used for testing the remoting layer shown in this section.

The last item I'm going to show in this testing section is how you can test whether the integration between all of the different services and components works as expected.

6.1.3 Integration testing

In the next couple of paragraphs I show you how to write and run tests that use multiple services. This is useful when you have services that depend on each other, and you want to make sure that these services work correctly together. You can choose to write such an integration test in the same manner as you did for the various layers in this section. If you choose this approach, you need to make sure all the services, databases, and other resources are up and running before the test fires, and if something goes wrong you'll probably need to manually clean up various databases.

In this section you'll take a different approach. You'll record a scenario that can be easily played back. This allows you, for instance, to run your integration tests against your "acceptance" environment to quickly determine whether everything is deployed correctly, before your testers start with their functional tests. For our integration tests you'll use SoapUI to record a scenario, and I'll show you how you can run this SoapUI scenario directly from Maven.

INTEGRATION TESTING FROM SOAPUI

For this integration test you want to test whether the following scenario can be executed successfully:

1. Create a new account, using the `AccountService` (WS-* based).
2. Store three `GPSData` events through the REST-based `CarService`.
3. Update the account. This is also done through the `AccountService`.

Even though in this example you use SoapUI to test this scenario, if you want you could also program this test in Java using HttpClient and a WS-Client.

Start SoapUI and open the SoapUI project: chapter2/traffic-service-general/src/test/resources/integration-soapui-project.xml. You'll see a project outline similar to figure 6.2.

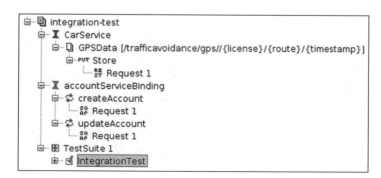

**Figure 6.2
Layout of the integration
test SoapUI project**

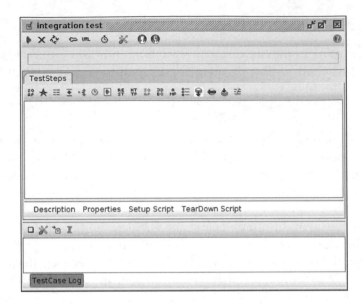

Figure 6.3
Empty integration test; steps can be added using the buttons from the TestSteps tab.

Figure 6.2 shows the configuration of the SoapUI project for this test. You've created a client for the REST-based `CarService` and for the WS-* based `AccountService`. This is nothing new so far. What's different in this project is that you've created a test suite (`TestSuite1`) and a test case (`IntegrationTest`). Right-click the `IntegrationTest` label and select Show TestCase Editor. This will show you an overview of all the steps that are part of this test case. In the provided SOAP project all the steps are already filled in. Select these and press Delete to remove them. You'll see the window shown in figure 6.3.

In the TestCase editor click the SOAP button (the button located in the middle of the menu bar below the TestSteps tab), and select the `createAccount` operation (figure 6.4). This allows you to select an operation of a service that's configured in this SoapUI project.

Figure 6.4   Select the operation to add to your test case.

After you've added this operation, fill in the data you want to test with. This is shown in figure 6.5.

The next step is to add the REST calls. I won't show you the details of how to do this, because this is done in exactly the same manner as you did for the SOAP request. Add three Add GPSData requests and a final SOAP call that uses the `updateAccount` operation. At this point you have something like what's shown in figure 6.6.

If you click the green play arrow at the top, the test will launch, and the results will be shown. In this example you call only two services; you can expand this to more

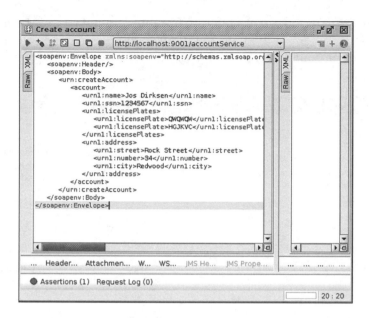

Figure 6.5
Create the test request for the `createAccount` operation.

services and use the result from one step as input for the next. In this way you can easily set up complex integration tests for your specific environment.

USING THE SOAPUI TEST CASE FROM MAVEN

If you have many integration tests and want to run those, doing that manually from
SoapUI isn't very effective. You'd have to manually start the test cases and analyze the
results. Luckily though, SoapUI allows you to run test cases from Maven. This means
you can create a Maven project that stores all the integration tests and run these tests

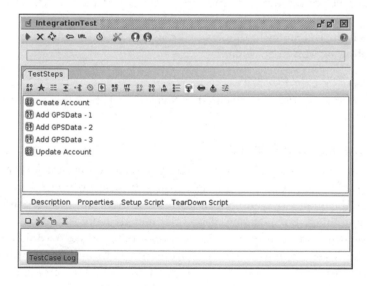

Figure 6.6
Our complete test case for the integration test

at your convenience. To run the SoapUI test case from this example using Maven, you have to add an extra element to the pom.xml file. For this example I've added this configuration to the pom.xml file for the chapter2/traffic-service-general project. The following listing shows these additions.

Listing 6.11   Configure a Maven project to run SoapUI test cases

```
<pluginRepositories>
    <pluginRepository>
      <id>ewiarePluginRepository</id>
      <url>http://www.eviware.com/repository/maven2/</url>       Configure where
    </pluginRepository>                                          plug-in can be
  </pluginRepositories>                                          found
...
<plugin>

<groupId>eviware</groupId>
<artifactId>maven-soapui-plugin</artifactId>                      Define plug-in
<version>3.6.1</version>                                          to use
<configuration>
  <projectFile>
     src/test/resources/integration-soapui-project.xml           Point to project
  </projectFile>                                                  to execute
  <outputFolder>target</outputFolder>
  <junitReport>true</junitReport>
 </configuration>
</plugin>
```

You need to add two different elements. The first one is the `<pluginRepositories>` element. This element is needed to specify where Maven should get the SoapUI plug-in from. The other element you add is the SoapUI plug-in configuration. The interesting part of this configuration is the `<projectFile>` element. This element points to a SoapUI configuration file. If you run a Maven build with the correct goals on this pom.xml, all the test suites in that SoapUI configuration file will be executed. You can use the following Maven command:

```
mvn eviware:maven-soapui-plugin:test
```

This will run the integration test you specified in SoapUI and show the output to the console.

6.2   *Using quality management tools*

In the previous section we looked at how you can write tests to test the various layers of your application. Just having tests isn't enough. You still have no metric—no numbers—to determine the quality of your code and your tests. Without numbers it's difficult to measure something. For instance, if you defined that the service you create should be "pretty secure" and the response within a "reasonable" time, it would be hard to determine whether you comply with these requirements. The same applies when you want to measure software quality. You can't say your software should be of a high quality; you should say it complies with 80% of these rules and 100% of those rules.

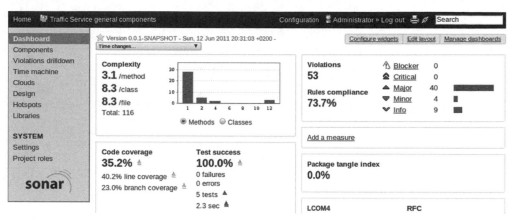

Figure 6.7   Example of metrics harvested by Sonar

If you look at this from a governance point of view, it would be great to have such a metric you can use in your policy definition. There are various tools that can help you with this. For this example I'll show how you can accomplish this by using another open source tool: Sonar (see figure 6.7).

With Sonar you can define a whole set of metrics you can use to determine the general health and quality of your project. The metric definition page for Sonar, http://docs.codehaus.org/display/SONAR/Metric+definitions, gives an overview of the metrics that are available to you. Besides this basic set, Sonar allows additional metrics to be added through a plug-in mechanism, so if the one you need isn't listed, you could write your own using Sonar's standard plug-in mechanism.

When using Sonar it's a good idea to select a number of key metrics and based on these metrics define minimal levels for your services to comply with. A good starting point when measuring the quality of services is the set of metrics shown in table 6.2.

Table 6.2   Metrics used to measure the quality of services

Reporter	Description
Code coverage	This reporter shows the results of the unit tests that are run and the total code coverage of your service. **Goal:** Minimum amount of code coverage: 80% Test success: 100%
Security rules	This custom plug-in checks for the violations of a set of security rules. **Goal:** Maximum number of security issues: 0
Rules compliancy	The rules compliancy reporter provides an overview of violations reported by Checkstyle, PMD, and FindBugs. From this plug-in you can easily drill down to the offending class and see what needs to be fixed. **Goal:** Rules compliancy: 90%

With these metrics as a starting point you can quickly get up to speed and start improving and measuring the quality of your code. Before we look at the details of how to run Sonar on your projects, let's take a step back and look at how this relates to SOA governance and policies. We can translate this set of metrics into a policy.

Policy: QA_POL_1	Services must have a minimal level of quality
Statement	We want our services to have a minimal measurable level of quality. The services must be well tested and must confirm to the coding standards we've defined. We define the following levels of compliance: Code coverage: minimum of 80% Test success: 100% Security issues: 0 Rules compliance: 90%
Rationale	Within our organization we have many different applications and services. They're created and maintained by different people and different teams. To make it easy for people to read and maintain other people's code, we want to make sure code is created in a uniform manner. In addition, we want to have a certain level of quality in our services. This will help in maintaining a high-quality code base and will result in less time spent on rework and fixing bugs.
Implications	Code must be extensively tested to conform to specific quality demands. A quality build must be set up to automatically check code quality.

Let's look at the steps you need to take to configure Sonar so that you can measure whether your projects comply with this policy. As an example you'll create a Sonar report for the traffic-service-general project from chapter 2. Before we start, make sure you've installed Sonar. Installation instructions for Sonar can be found in the appendix.

6.2.1 *Running a maven build for Sonar*

You can run Sonar from Maven without having to change the pom.xml file. You just tell Maven you want to generate a Sonar report:

```
mvn -Dsonar.host.url=http://localhost:10100 sonar:sonar
```

If you followed the installation instructions from the appendix, you'll probably understand the additional parameter you specify here. With `sonar.host.url` you can specify the URL Sonar is running on. Because you changed the default port during the installation, to avoid port conflicts you need to specify this port here explicitly. When you execute this command from the project directory, all the information Sonar needs will be gathered. If you now point your browser to http://localhost:10100 and log in with admin/admin, you'll be shown the following screen (figure 6.8).

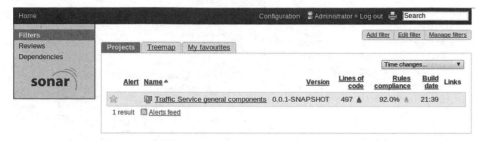

Figure 6.8   Sonar project overview screen

In this screen Sonar shows all the projects it has information for. In this case you see only the project you just ran Sonar for. From here on you can drill down by clicking the project. This will open a dashboard with a number of reports (figure 6.9).

Figure 6.9   Dashboard showing the reports for the selected project

Your dashboard will probably look a bit different. If you click the Configure Widgets link at the top, you can select which widgets you want to see. From here you can select one of the reports to see more detailed information. Figure 6.10, for instance, shows the violations for this project.

**Figure 6.10
Report showing the
violations for each
package**

Coverage
42.0%

🔍 📁 soa.governance.chapter2.traffic.services.impl	33.3%
🔍 📁 soa.governance.chapter2.traffic.data	35.4%
🔍 📁 soa.governance.chapter2.traffic.model	42.3%
🔍 📁 soa.governance.chapter2.traffic.data.util	72.2%

📄 AccountServiceImpl	41.7%
📄 Address	46.1%
📄 AbstractRepository	53.3%
📄 Account	53.9%
📄 RepositoryUtil	72.2%
📄 AccountRepository	95.2%

Figure 6.11   Report showing code coverage for each package in the project

As you can see from the report, your test coverage isn't what you need it to be. To determine where you need to add additional tests, you can use the Coverage report (figure 6.11).

So far we've looked at how to test the different services and how you can make quality measurable by using Sonar. With a Sonar report you can confirm whether your service complies with the policy that defines a specific level of code quality.

The services you've developed in this and the previous chapters run in the traditional way. In the next part of this chapter we'll look at how you can create services that can be run in a cloud environment.

6.3   *Developing for the cloud*

If you look back at chapter 3 you'll see that one of the policies OpenGov defined was that it should be possible for its applications to run in the cloud. Before we look at this policy and show you an example of how you can create a service that can run in the cloud, we'll look a bit closer at what *running in the cloud* means.

When we talk about cloud computing we usually mean that instead of accessing computing resources (for example, CPU and storage) locally, you access them remotely. For instance, you can create a set of services and deploy those to a cloud provider, and this provider will make sure enough CPU, IO, and storage are available for your services. The big advantage of this model is that you, as a company, don't have to make big investments in hardware and data centers. You can use the resources from your cloud provider and don't have to worry about adding extra hardware when the number of consumers grows. An added advantage is that with most cloud providers you pay only for what you use. So running in the cloud allows you to start quickly, with minimal expenses and lots of flexibility.

6.3.1   *Different types of cloud services*

There's a lot of talk about running services in the cloud, but this doesn't mean you can just select one of the cloud providers, upload your service, and expect it to work. You have to make sure you select a cloud provider that offers the functionality you need. If we look at the available cloud providers, we can divide these into three distinct categories:

- *Software as a service (SaaS)*—When you use an SaaS environment, you get access to a full application or service hosted somewhere online. You don't deploy your own applications or services on this cloud but make use of what is offered by the SaaS provider. Google Docs, Salesforce, and Office 365 are all examples of SaaS.
- *Platform as a service (PaaS)*—If you want to deploy your own applications, you might use a PaaS. With a PaaS you're offered a complete computing platform or software stack that you can use to create your own applications and services. Google Apps, Amazon's AWS, Microsoft's Windows Azure, and many more provide this service.
- *Infrastructure as a service (IaaS)*—IaaS provides computing infrastructure such as CPU resources, data storage, and network IO. Often PaaS makes uses of the services provided by IaaS. There are many IaaS providers: Cloud.com, Rackspace, Amazon, and HP to name but a few.

Because you're looking for a platform to run services on, we'll focus on PaaS. We aren't interested in using computing resources or already available software services such as Salesforce. Because you'll be deploying services, you need to take governance into account. Chapter 3 defined a number of policies that are important for the OpenGov organization. If you look a bit closer at these policies, you'll notice that the platform on which a service runs doesn't invalidate any of these policies. All the policies we defined also apply when running a service in the cloud; for instance, you still need to define who can access your service. This is even more important because the service might be running on a public cloud. And service versioning, documentation, and backward compatibility are at least as important in a cloud environment as they are when you deploy a service internally.

If you want to run a service in the cloud, you have to closely look at the features and functionality provided by a specific provider. In the next section I provide an overview of what to look for in your cloud provider.

6.3.2 Requirements for the cloud provider

There are many cloud providers available. On the one hand you have specialized cloud providers that offer computing resources for CPU-intensive tasks to analyze complex mathematical problems. On the other hand you have general cloud providers that offer complete software stacks to build your applications with. This makes choosing the correct cloud provider for your specific requirements rather difficult. The following requirements can help you in determining which cloud provider to use:

- *Functionality*—Not all cloud providers offer the same functionality. Some might only offer computing resources, whereas others offer a complete software stack. When looking at a possible cloud provider, you must determine the functionality you need. Do you need an online database, email functionality, or maybe a messaging system? Try to find a provider that covers all these requirements. If you can't find one, try to find a few that can integrate well with each other.

- *Software stack*—Not all services are created using the same technology. In this book I show you examples using Java, but you could just as well be developing in .NET, Ruby, Python, Scala, or something else. When choosing a cloud provider, look for one that supports your development stack, and if it offers additional features (such as key/value–based storage), look for one that provides an API in your language.

- *Portability of data*—When you run your services in the cloud, make use of the storage options provided by the cloud, and make sure this provider allows you to easily export your data. If this isn't the case, you can quickly become locked into a specific cloud provider.

- *Scalability*—An important advantage of using a cloud provider is that you don't have to worry about adding extra resources when your application grows. When you're looking for a cloud provider, look for one that provides transparent scalability. Should your resource requirements grow, the cloud provider should automatically be able to scale up. If your resource requirements decrease, the cloud provider should scale down.

- *Data security*—When you use a cloud provider, you store your sensitive information in the cloud. This data might even be stored in a different country. When you're selecting a cloud provider, make sure that the data security options provided by this provider match your and your customers' requirements.

- *Backup policy*—If you use the cloud platform for storage, it's important to determine what the backup policies of the cloud provider are. Do they back up the data regularly, are databases replicated, or do you have the control to restore backups yourself?

- *Manageability*—The cloud platform should be easy to manage by you. There should be a management interface with which you can easily see the resource usage of your services and add extra functionality. You should also be able to easily view the logging and audit records for your application.

- *Cost*—Cost is always an important factor. Look at what you have to pay for the services offered. Is there a minimum price you have to pay each month? Does your average price go down when you use a lot of resources?

Now that you have a set of requirements you can use to choose a cloud provider, let's look at how to run one of our examples in the cloud. For our example we'll use Amazon AWS. Amazon provides an easy-to-use cloud environment with all the features you require for your architecture. The Amazon AWS environment is also free to use for the first year. If you want to use the Amazon cloud, you'll have to register an account. An account can be created from http://aws.amazon.com/.

6.3.3 *Creating a service that can run in the Amazon cloud*

In chapter 3 you saw an overview of the set of applications OpenGov offers. Most of these services focus on allowing residents of a city to communicate with various local city departments. One of the applications offered by OpenGov provides all different kinds of information regarding the city, for example, the opening times for the shops, when garbage is collected, and when festivals are scheduled. Open-Gov wants to extend this platform so that residents themselves can share information with the rest of the city's residents. In their first iteration they decide that they'll offer a service where residents can share images and comment on those images. For instance, if you took an interesting photo of the ancient church located in the center of your town, you can

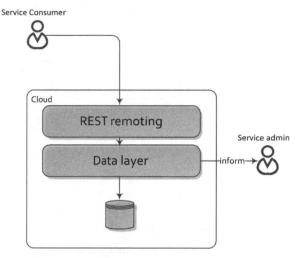

Figure 6.12   Components of the `ImageCommentService`

share this image, along with a comment, with other people through this service. It's a bit like Flickr but much simpler. Besides storing the image, OpenGov wants to provide a simple query function, where a set of images and comments can be retrieved based on location. Because they expect much use of this service, and it's one of the policies defined by the OpenGov organization, this service will be created to run in the cloud. Figure 6.12 shows a high-level overview of this service, which we'll call the `Image-CommentService`.

Figure 6.12 shows a REST layer that the users of your service can use to add their images. Through a data layer this information is stored in a datastore. In this section you'll see how to map these various components to the components provided by Amazon. We'll start with the data layer and show how you can implement that layer with Amazon Web Services.

THE DATA LAYER

With this service the user can store an image with some metadata. This means that the data layer needs to be able to store binary data, the image, and a set of metadata information. The following listing shows a simple POJO that captures the information that you want to store.

Listing 6.12   The model for the `ImageCommentService`

```
public class ImageComment {
    private InputStream stream;
    private String comments;
    private String location;
    private String timestamp;
    private Map<String, String> userdata;
}
```

Figure 6.13   All the services offered by Amazon Web Services

Listing 6.12 shows binary data (the `InputStream`), a number of `Strings`, and a `Map` containing an arbitrary amount of custom user information. What options does Amazon offer that you can use to store this image and its metadata? In figure 6.13, you can see the complete set of AWS products offered by Amazon. One of these products should be able to meet your requirements.

The interesting services to us here are the ones in the Database and Storage lists. From these lists you could use the following products to store data in the cloud:

- *Amazon Simple Storage Service (S3)*—With S3 Amazon offers a simple REST interface that you can use to store objects in the cloud. These objects can be anywhere from 1 byte to 5 terabytes. Each object can be retrieved using a unique, developer-assigned key.
- *Amazon SimpleDB*—With Amazon SimpleDB you can easily store and query information in a key/value–based manner. This is stored somewhat like the `column-Families` in Cassandra, which I showed in chapter 2. All the values stored are indexed for easy searching.
- *Amazon Relation Database Service (RDS)*—Amazon RDS provides a relational database that you can use in the cloud. You can choose to use a MySQL or Oracle-based database.

If you look back at the model from listing 6.12, you'll see that you have two different types of data to store. You have the binary data representing the image, and you also have a set of key/value pairs. For this example you'll store the image in S3, because it's a blob of unstructured data, and you'll store the key/value pair in Amazon SimpleDB, where you'll also store the reference to the object stored in S3. You store this object using the `storeImageComment` operation of the `AmazonImageCommentRepository`. The first part of the `storeImageComment` method is shown in listing 6.13, and the second part is shown in listing 6.14. The following listing shows the basics of storing objects using S3.

Listing 6.13   Using Amazon S3 to store an object (`AmazonImageCommentRepository`)

```
@PostConstruct                                                    Create a S3 client  ❶
public void init() {
  s3 = new AmazonS3Client(new BasicAWSCredentials(sharedKey,secret));
  bucket = s3.createBucket(SOAGOV_BUCKET);                        ⟵      Create
  ...                                                                 ❷ a bucket
}

public void storeImageComment(ImageComment comment) {            ❸  Generate a
  String key = KEY_PREFIX + UUID.randomUUID();                  ⟵      unique key
  s3.putObject(bucket.getName(), key ,comment.getStream(), null);  ⟵   Store
  ...                                                               ❹ the data
}
```

To store object you use the Amazon-provided Java client. This client handles all the low-level REST calls. All you have to do is specify the shared key and the secret to use with the call ❶. If you've registered with AWS, you can get this information from your account page. Once you've set up a client, the next step is to make sure you have a bucket. A *bucket* is a container in which you store your objects. The code at ❷ will create a new bucket if one with the specified name doesn't already exist. All you need to store the object is the input stream, a unique key ❸, and the name of the bucket to store the data in. If you call `s3.putObject` with these arguments ❹, the object will be stored in the Amazon S3 cloud.

Now that you've stored the image, you also need to store the metadata of the object. The following listing shows how you can use Amazon SimpleDB to store this information.

Listing 6.14   Use Amazon SimpleDB to store the metadata

```
@PostConstruct
public void init() {
  ...
 sdb = new AmazonSimpleDBClient(                                  ❶  Create client
   new BasicAWSCredentials(sharedKey,secret));                        for SimpleDB
 sdb.createDomain(new CreateDomainRequest(SOAGOV_DOMAIN));       ⟵      Create
}                                                                   ❷ domain

public void storeImageComment(ImageComment comment) {
  ...
  List<ReplaceableAttribute> attributes = new                     ❸  Attributes
    ArrayList<ReplaceableAttribute>();                                to store
  attributes.add(new ReplaceableAttribute(
    TIMESTAMP, Long.toString(System.currentTimeMillis()), true));
  attributes.add(new ReplaceableAttribute(
    COMMENTS, comment.getComments(), true));
  attributes.add(new ReplaceableAttribute(
    LOCATION, comment.getLocation(), true));
```

```
   Map<String,String> otherData = comment.getUserdata();
   for (String userelement : otherData.keySet()) {        4  Add user data
     attributes.add(new ReplaceableAttribute(
       userelement, otherData.get(userelement), true));
   }
   sdb.putAttributes(new PutAttributesRequest(             5  Store in
     SOAGOV_DOMAIN, key, attributes));                        the database
}
```

In listing 6.14 you see how you can use the `AmazonSimpleDBClient` to store the non-binary information from your `ImageComment` class. You first get a client, just as you did for S3 ❶. This time, you also need to create the location where your information needs to be stored. For SimpleDB this is called a domain, which you create in ❷. You can then use this client to store the rest of the data. You do this by creating a list of attributes ❸, which are simple name/value pairs. You also add the user-specified data ❹ to this attribute list, and finally you use the `putAttributes` method to store the information. One thing to notice is that you use the same key in this operation ❺ as you did for the call to S3 in listing 6.13. In this way you can easily correlate the information from S3 with the information you stored in SimpleDB, because both keys are the same.

I also mentioned that we would like to support searching for `ImageComments` based on location. I won't show you the complete code for this (look at the code examples for chapter 6 if you're interested), but I'll show you how to query SimpleDB and retrieve information from S3. Querying SimpleDB can be done in a way similar to SQL. For our scenario you use the following statements for your search function:

```
String selectExpression = "select * from `"+ SOAGOV_DOMAIN
  +"` where location like '%" + location + "%'";
SelectRequest selectRequest = new SelectRequest(selectExpression);
List<Item> queryResut = sdb.select(selectRequest).getItems();
```

With these statements you create a SQL-like query and use `AmazonSimpleDBClient` to execute the query. This will return a set of `Item` objects, where each item contains a name that contains the value of your key and all the attributes you stored. Because the image you stored in S3 was stored with the same name as the metadata in SimpleDB, you can also use this name to retrieve the image data from S3:

```
InputStream data = s3.getObject
            (bucket.getName(), key).getObjectContent();
```

With this information you can create list of `ImageComment` objects, which you return as search results.

Note that in this simple cloud example you haven't defined an internal service layer. The remoting layer directly uses the data layer to store and query data.

THE REMOTING LAYER

For the REST remoting layer you can use the same setup as you did for the other REST-based services. You create a Spring bean and use JAX-RS annotations to define which method should be invoked when a specific resource location is requested with a specific HTTP verb. The following listing shows the remoting layer for this service.

Listing 6.15 The REST remoting layer

```
@Service
@Path("/opengov/govdata/")
public class GovDataCloudService {

  @Resource(name="ImageCommentRepository")
  private ImageCommentRepository repository;

  @PUT
  public Response addImageComment(String jsonData) {
    ImageComment imagecomment =
            jsonToToImageComment(jsonData);                    ❶ Convert and store
    repository.storeImageComment(imagecomment);                   the JSON request
    return Response.ok().build();
  }

  @GET
  @Produces("application/cloudservice.imagecomments+json")
  public Response searchImageComments(@QueryParam("loc")  String query)
                    throws IOException {
    JSONObject responseData = new JSONObject();

    List<ImageComment> comments =                              ❷ Find all Image-
            repository.findImageCommentsForLocation(query);       Comment objects
    List<JSONObject> foundElements = new ArrayList<JSONObject>();
    for (ImageComment imageComment : comments) {
      foundElements.add(imageCommentToJson(imageComment));
    }

    return Response.ok().entity(responseData
      .element("imagecomments", foundElements).toString(3,1)).build();
  }
}
```

In this listing you don't do anything that's specific to Amazon or for running in the cloud. It's just a basic JAX-RS–based service that uses the repository ❶ to store incoming data and to find ❷ ImageComments based on a location.

So far, you've seen how the data layer and the REST layer are implemented. The final step you need to do is create the Spring application context that glues everything together. The next listing shows the Spring configuration file that's used in this example.

Listing 6.16 Spring configuration for the Amazon cloud-based service

```
<import resource="classpath:META-INF/cxf/cxf.xml" />
<import resource="classpath:META-INF/cxf/cxf-extension-jaxrs-binding.xml" /
  >
<import resource="classpath:META-INF/cxf/cxf-servlet.xml" />

<jaxrs:server id="customerService" address="/cloud">
<jaxrs:serviceBeans>
  <ref bean="cloudServiceBean" />
```

```
    </jaxrs:serviceBeans>
</jaxrs:server>

<bean id="cloudServiceBean" class="...services.rest.GovDataCloudService" />

<bean id="ImageCommentRepository"
   class="...data.impl.AmazonImageCommentRepository" >
     <property name="sharedKey" value="sharedkeyfromyouraccount"/>
     <property name="secret" value="secretfromyouraccount"/>
   </bean>
```

Listing 6.16 shows a basic JAX-RS configuration. The main difference is that in this instance you don't specify the full address for your service but just the context /cloud. The reason is that you'll be running this service in the container provided by Amazon, so the hostname and port are defined by this container.

PACKAGE, DEPLOY, AND TEST THE SERVICE

All you need to do now is to package all your classes, deploy this service to Amazon, and test to see if the service is working. For this you'll use the Amazon Elastic Beanstalk. With this product you can easily deploy and manage application on Amazon's cloud, without having to worry about the underlying platforms and products. The standard platform used by the Elastic Beanstalk is a Tomcat-based software stack. To deploy your application you need to package it as a .war file and upload it to the Elastic Beanstalk.

If you look at the pom.xml for this example (in chapter6/cloud) you'll see that I've specified the following: <packaging>war</packaging>. If you use Maven to package (execute mvn package) this project, Maven will create a .war file for you. If you want to test this .war file locally, you can deploy it to a locally installed Tomcat instance. The behavior should be the same as when you deploy the .war file to the Amazon cloud.

To deploy this .war file go to the AWS page and log in to the AWS Management Console. Open the Elastic Beanstalk tab and you'll be greeted with the welcome screen shown in figure 6.14.

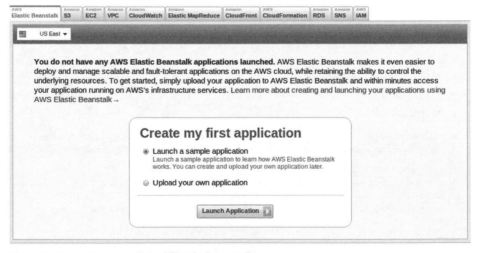

Figure 6.14   Welcome screen of Elastic Beanstalk

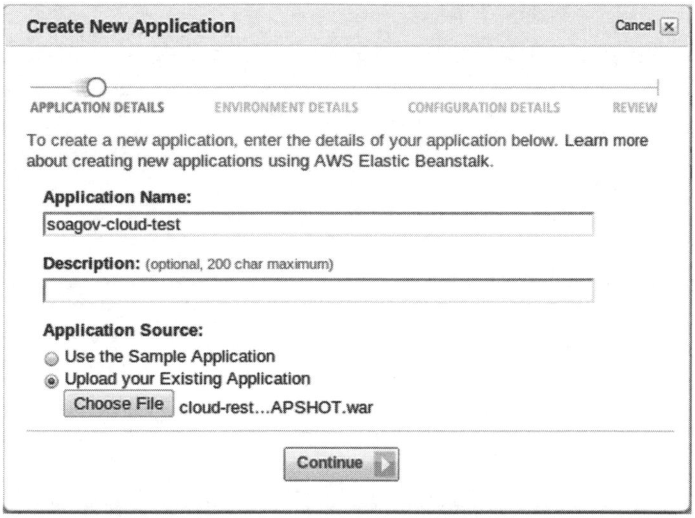

Figure 6.15 Create a new application for Elastic Beanstalk deployment.

From this screen select the Upload Your Own Application option and click the Launch Application button. This will bring you to the screen shown in figure 6.15.

In this form as Application Name fill in `soagov-cloud-test` and browse to your cloud/target folder in your workspace where the .war file was created. After you've done this, click Continue again. In the next step you're going to configure the environment in which your service will run. This is shown in figure 6.16.

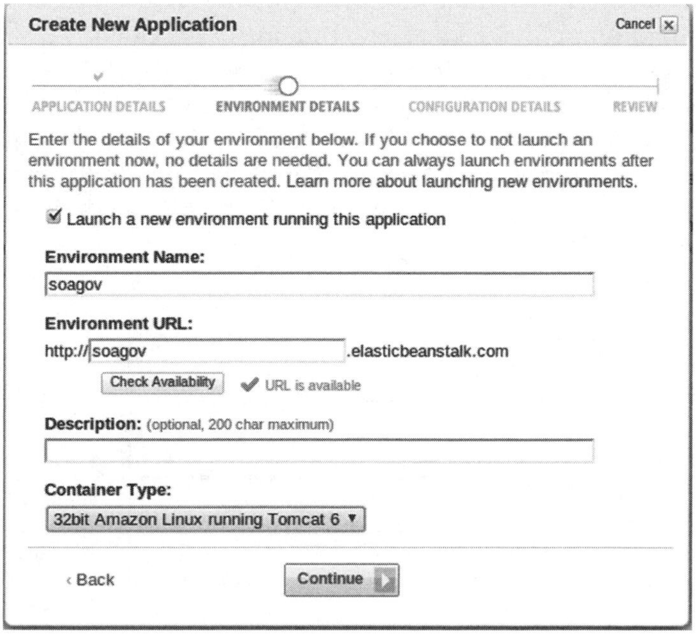

Figure 6.16 Configure the environment in which to run the service.

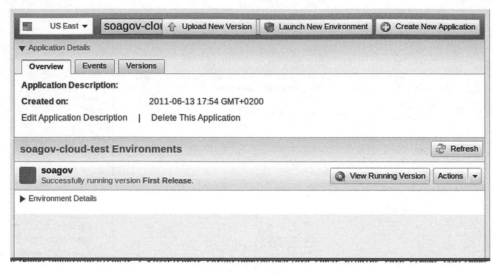

Figure 6.17   Overview of your Beanstalk-deployed applications

Check the 'Launch a new environment running this application' check box, and fill in the hostname you'd like your service to run on. For Container Type select the 32bit Tomcat 6 one, and click Continue. On the next screen make sure the instance type is set to t1.micro and click Continue. Check whether you've filled in everything correctly in the review screen and click Finish. Now you'll have to wait a bit while your application is uploaded and deployed. After a couple of minutes you'll get a message stating successful deployment, and after closing that screen you'll see the screen shown in figure 6.17, which shows the applications you have running in the cloud.

The easiest way to test whether deployment was successful is to click the View Running Version button. This will bring you to the home page of your web application, which lists the available RESTful services. This should look something like figure 6.18.

Now that you have your service running in the Amazon cloud, you'll want to test it. In the test/resources folder for this chapter you'll find a sample JSON request you can use to test your cloud-enabled service.

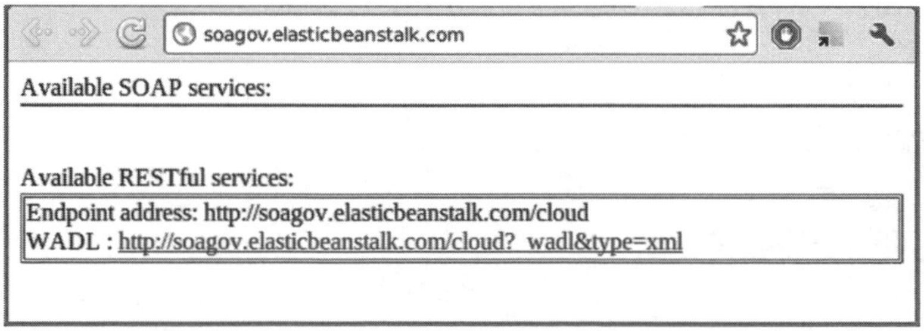

---

soagov.elasticbeanstalk.com

Available SOAP services:

Available RESTful services:

Endpoint address: http://soagov.elasticbeanstalk.com/cloud
WADL : http://soagov.elasticbeanstalk.com/cloud?_wadl&type=xml

**Figure 6.18
Welcome screen of your application in the cloud**

6.4 *Summary*

In this chapter I showed you how testing applies to services and how you can make your tests and the quality of your code measurable. We also looked at running services in the cloud, and I showed you an example using Amazon Web Services. The most important points from this chapter are as follows:

- It's important for the quality of your services to test them thoroughly. It's good to make this one of your design-time policies.
- Each layer of an application should be tested in isolation.
- Integration tests shouldn't be run as part of an automated test suite.
- To make tests and quality measurable you can use Sonar.
- Choose a set of metrics and compliance levels to serve as a minimum baseline your services should comply with.
- Base your choice for a cloud provider on your specific requirements.
- Try to find a single cloud provider that offers the features you need; if you can't find one, try to find a couple that integrate well with each other.
- Deploying and developing for the cloud aren't that difficult. Most practices you're used to when developing services for a normal environment can be applied to services that run in the cloud.

Part 3

Runtime policies

In the second part of the book we looked at the policies that can be applied during design time. Once a service is created and is ready to be deployed, we enter the runtime governance phase. In this phase we want to be able to monitor our services and make sure they comply with the policies we defined. In this last part of the book we'll look at runtime governance and how tools can help you in creating such a monitoring environment.

You'll start by creating a runtime governance environment using the open source Bamos server. This is an easy-to-use event processing server that you can easily integrate with your existing services and applications. In chapter 7 I'll show you how to use the Bamos server to monitor various metrics of your application.

Besides monitoring your services it's important to have a well-defined lifecycle for your services and policies. A well-defined service lifecycle helps in communicating when your service is ready to be tested, can be used by your consumers, and finally becomes obsolete and is removed. Besides a service lifecycle I'll also show you how you can define a lifecycle for the policies you define.

In the last chapter of this part, we'll focus on how you can integrate the various tools and techniques we discussed in this book with existing tools. I'll show you examples of how to integrate ESBs, BPM tools, and various non-Java languages.

Using tools for
runtime governance

This chapter covers

- Setting up the Bamos runtime governance environment
- Monitoring performance metrics for your services
- Visualizing information using various gadgets

In this chapter I'll show you how you can set up a runtime governance environment based on the open source Bamos server, which you can use to monitor your services. I'll start by introducing the various parts that make up this runtime monitoring solution and then show you, through various examples, how you can use this server to monitor various aspects and performance indicators of your services.

7.1 Runtime governance

In this section we'll start with the various components that make up a runtime governance solution. When you want to monitor your services for compliancy with your policies, you'll need some tools to help you with this. As mentioned in chapter 2, there are, unfortunately, no generic open source tools available to accomplish this. Luckily, though, there are a lot of standard open source components available that

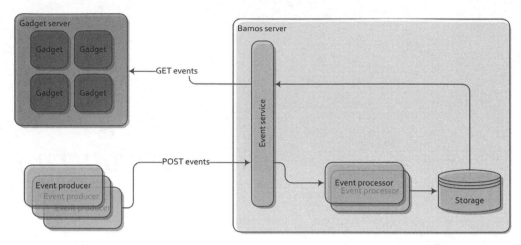

Figure 7.1 Components of runtime monitoring

you can combine to create your own runtime monitoring solution. For this book I started a new open source project, Bamos (http://www.smartjava.org/bamos), with which you can monitor your services and create reports about the various policies you defined in a generic manner.

In this section we're going to look at the various parts of this solution, and I'll show how all these components can be combined to form a complete runtime service monitoring environment.

Figure 7.1 shows all the components you need for runtime monitoring. In the following sections we'll look at each of these components individually, and I'll explain how you can use and configure them.

We'll be looking at the components shown in table 7.1.

Table 7.1 Explanation of the components that make up the Bamos server

Component	Description
Gadget	A visualization component that shows a specific metric of your server or services. You could, for instance, create a bar chart that shows which users use your service, a line chart that lists the unprotected services, or a funnel chart that shows possible sales opportunities. The gadgets follow the OpenSocial Specification, so they can be run in any gadget server that supports that specification.
Gadget server	To show the gadgets you need a container to run them in. For this we use WSO2's gadget server, but you could use any OpenSocial-compatible gadget server. The gadget server handles the rendering of the components, keeps track of the gadgets' configurations, and allows users to create their own pages based on the available gadgets.

Table 7.1 Explanation of the components that make up the Bamos server *(continued)*

Component	Description
Event producer	Without information from your services, you won't have anything to show or measure. Event producers send information to the Bamos server in the form of events. Events follow a predefined format and can contain anything from average task execution times to failed login attempts.
Event service	The events produced by the event producers are sent to the event service. This service will store them so that they can be retrieved at a later time.
Event processor	When you want to show information, it can be useful to correlate information from more than one event. It's not interesting to know the average processing time of a single service call. You could retrieve all the events and calculate the average time using JavaScript, but that isn't practical. With event processors you can process and correlate events the moment they're received. You can do this by implementing a simple Java interface or using Esper, which provides complex event processing (CEP) functionality.

Let's look a bit closer at each of these components.

7.1.1 Gadget

A gadget is used to visualize information to the end user. You could, for instance, create gadgets that show how many requests a specific customer has made, which employees have the most assigned tasks in a specific business process, or the geographical distribution of your clients. In figure 7.2, you see a simple gadget that shows which services for a specific server are used the most. The gadgets we discuss in this chapter all get their data from the Bamos server using REST calls and can be configured directly on the gadget server.

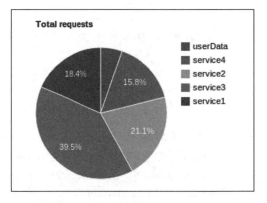

Figure 7.2 Example gadget showing which services are used the most

Gadgets aren't limited to showing information provided by the Bamos server. You can also include other gadgets that follow the OpenSocial (http://docs.opensocial.org/) specifications.

7.1.2 Gadget server

The gadgets will need an OpenSocial-compatible gadget server to run in. For this you use the WSO2 Gadget Server; see figure 7.3.

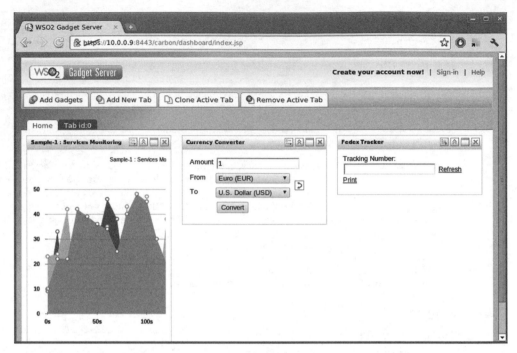

Figure 7.3   Gadget server in which you'll show the gadgets

In this server you'll add the gadgets you create in this chapter. This server will allow you to create your own dashboards using Bamos gadgets and other gadgets that are available.

7.1.3   Event producer

So far we've looked at the front end of the Bamos server, the visualizations the end user sees and can use to track various metrics and policies regarding their services. But, without any services producing events, there won't be much to see. We call the components that create events *event producers*. An event producer can be anything from an Apache web server module, a CXF interceptor, or an enterprise service bus (ESB)— you name it.

In the next section we'll look a bit closer at what the event that the Bamos server expects looks like. If you want to write your own event producer, you can create a JSON-based event and do an HTTP post (see the next section). We also provide a simple client that provides a simple Java class with which you can send events. Its method signature is shown in the following listing.

Listing 7.1   Bamos client method you can use to send `events`

```
public void sendEvent(String server, String serviceName, String eventClass,
      long timestamp, Map<String,Object> userData);
```

As you can see from this listing, this is a simple client to use to send events.

7.1.4　*Event service*

The event service is used to store and query for events. It provides a simple REST-based API that you can use to do this. To store events you make a POST request, as shown here:

```
POST /services/event HTTP/1.1
Content-Type: application/json
Content-Length: 139

{"event":
  {"timestamp":"1310294128455",
   "service":"service1",
   "eventclass":"class"
   "server":"server1"
   "userdata1":1344,
  }
}
```

This will store this event in the Bamos server so that it can be retrieved later. The properties of this event are explained in table 7.2.

Table 7.2　Event properties

Property	Description
timestamp	This property contains the timestamp when the event was created.
Service	An event is usually for a specific service. Use this property to define the service that created this event.
Eventclass	The Eventclass property can be used to classify an event. For instance, you could use this to group all security violations together.
Server	This property describes the server from which the event was sent. For instance, this could be the name of an application or a specific server you're monitoring.
User data	Besides the previous fixed properties, the user can provide a set of additional properties, which are stored with the event.

Once you store an event, it's also practical to be able to retrieve the stored event again. For this, this service provides the following search functionality at /services/event/list. With a GET operation on this URL you can search for events. This URL supports the query parameters shown in table 7.3.

Table 7.3　Query parameters available for searching

Property	Description
from	Use this together with the to property to define a time range for which you want to query the events. The time you specify here is in the standard Unix timestamp.
to	Use this together with the from property. See the from property description.

Table 7.3   Query parameters available for searching *(continued)*

Property	Description
class	On your events you can define a class property. With this property you can search for the events that belong to a specific class.
server	On your events you can define a server property. With this property you can search the event from a specific server.
service	On your events you can define a service property. With this property you can search the events for a specific service.
limit	With this property you can limit the results you receive from this service. The default behavior is to return all the events that match the query.
reverse	This property allows you to reverse the events that are received. The default is to return the events sorted on timestamp. The newest events would be returned first. If you set this property to true, the oldest events will be returned first.
lastms	This property allows you to specify that you want to retrieve all the events for the last *n* milliseconds. This property can't be combined with the from and to properties.

All the events that are received are stored in a NoSQL (Cassandra) database. That means you'll have minimal overhead when writing and querying events, and you'll be able to easily deal with large numbers of events. This does, however, impose some limitations on the query options. When you want to query for events, you can only specify one of the service, server, or class properties. You can't use these properties together. The following queries show you how you can use this service:

```
http://localhost:9003/services/event/list?service=serviceName&lastms=100
http://localhost:9003/services/event/list?server=server2&count=1&reverse=true
http://localhost:9003/services/event/list?class=performanceEvents&limit=1000
```

The final component is probably the most important one. The event processor allows you to process and enrich the events you receive.

7.1.5   *Event processor*

The event processors are the most interesting parts of the Bamos server. With an event processor you can analyze the events as they come in, and based on these events an event processor can create new events or alter existing ones. For instance, you could use an event processor for the following use cases:

- Count the number of times a specific method is invoked.
- Calculate the time it takes to execute a complete business process.
- Filter out duplicate events.
- Enrich events with backend information.

Bamos provides a few event processors out of the box, as shown in table 7.4.

Table 7.4   Example event processors provided by the Bamos server

Property	Description
EventCountProcessor	A simple processor that counts events and groups them based on service name.
EsperProcessor	A processor that can be configured with Esper statements. Esper is a complex event processing (CEP) tool, which provides all kinds of advanced functionality for event processing and correlation. With this processor you can execute statements on the incoming events and process your events using all the functionality provided by Esper. More information on Esper can be found at http://esper.codehaus.org/.
LocationProcessor	This processor can take an IP address and convert it to a location. You can use this information to draw geographical maps and determine where the users of your services come from.
NagiosProcessor	This processor allows you to send events to an external Nagios installation. You can use this external Nagios installation to monitor your services or send out escalation mails and messages if a specific threshold is reached.

Now that you've seen the various components that make up our runtime monitoring solution, let's see it in action by monitoring performance and service usage.

7.2   *Monitor performance and service usage*

In this section I'll show you how you can use the Bamos tools, which I first introduced in chapter 2, to monitor how your services are used and how they perform. We'll discuss the set of reports listed in table 7.5 in this section.

Table 7.5   Performance and service usage reports

Name	Description
Average response time	This report will show the average response time of a service call. This will show a report in a gauge.
Location-based usage	It's interesting to see where the users of your service come from. This report uses their IP address to determine their location and shows a map of the geographical distribution of your customers.
Service-based usage	This report uses a pie chart to give you an overview of which service is used the most on a specific server.
Usage based on time window	In this line chart you'll see the number of queries per time period. You can use this to get insight into the usage of your service over a specific period of time.

In each of the following sections we'll look at these aspects of monitoring:

- *Event producer*—What information the event needs to contain and how you can produce such an event.
- *Event processor*—You might need to alter an event, or a set of events, before you can store it in the database.
- *Report visualization*—How to show this event to the user and what properties an end user can use to alter the visualization.

We'll start by looking at the first of the reports, which is a simple gauge that shows the average response time of a specific service.

7.2.1 *Average response time*

Let's first look at what we're aiming for in this report. In figure 7.4 you can see a gauge that shows the average response time in milliseconds for one of the services.

Before you see how to connect everything together, we'll first look at what the event looks like that you'll send to the Bamos service. This event (shown in the following listing) is used to determine the average time for events based on the processingTime attribute.

Figure 7.4 Gauge showing the average response time of a service

---

Listing 7.2 Event used to determine the average time

```
{"event":
    {"timestamp":"1310294128455",
     "service":"serviceName",
     "processingTime":1344,          Time for service to
     "server":"expServer"            process request
    }
}
```

In previous chapters you've already seen how you can create interceptors and request handlers for WS and REST services, so I won't show you the details of how to integrate this with a specific service. Remember that we provide a simple Java-based client, which you can use to easily send events to the Bamos server. If you don't want to use Java, have a look at chapter 9, where you'll see how to send events using other languages.

In chapter 2 I showed you an example of how you can use a REST call to retrieve the events from Bamos and used client-side JavaScript to calculate the average processing time. Even though this is a flexible approach, it's also one that can quickly lead to errors and doesn't allow you to do complex aggregation of events. In the examples in this chapter you'll process the events at the server at the moment you receive them. For this you'll use an EventProcessor to calculate the average response time. Because an EventProcessor is just a Java class, you have many options to calculate the average processing time. For instance, you could write a custom class that keeps track of all the events you receive and calculates the average. In this example, though, I'll show you how you can use Esper, an open source complex event processor framework, to handle the processing of events.

Esper: complex event processing

Esper is an open source project that you can use to process complex events. With Esper you can analyze a set of events over a specific period of time to find specific correlations. For this Esper offers its own domain-specific language (DSL), which you can use to describe how events should be processed. An example of how you can use Esper is by looking at how this could be applied for the stock market. If you want to automate transactions, it isn't enough to know what a single stock is doing. You'll want to know how it did during the last half hour and compare that with how other stocks in your portfolio faired. Maybe you'd also like to take into account the time of day— whether the stock market is near to closing or has just opened. All these factors should be taken into account when processing the single stock events. This kind of complex event processing is where Esper comes in handy.

In this chapter we look at analyzing events from various services. Most of these are pretty straightforward, but when you're working with complex processes using multiple event producers and you want to correlate these disparate events, Esper can help you with this. You can find more information on Esper from their website at http://esper.codehaus.org.

To use Esper you'll use `EsperEventProcessor`, a processor that's provided by the Bamos server. You'll configure the `EventProcessor` using Spring with an expression. This expression is executed on each event that's received. Let's look at the configuration (which can be found in the chapter 7 source directory), which calculates the average processing time based on the event shown earlier, as shown in the following listing.

Listing 7.3 Configuring Esper to process events

```
<bean id="espereventprocessorAverage"
        class="...processors.event.esper.EsperEventProcessor">     ❶ Filter on
    <property name="filter" value="serverName == 'expServer'"/>          events
    <property name="esperStatement"
            value="select avg(cast(userValues('processingTime'),double))
                  as average from Event"/>                          Esper expression
    <property name="resultStatement" value="average"/>           executed on events ❷
    <property name="storagePrefix" value="average_"/>
    <property name="userClass" value="averageServiceTime"/>      ❺ Class used in
</bean>                                                              the event from
                                                                    this processor
```

❸ Result to use from Esper

❹ User property in which the Esper result is stored

When an event is received by this processor, the following steps are taken:

1 *Check event filter*—You can use the filter property ❶ to determine whether you want to process this event by this processor. In this case all events that have the property server set to expServer will be processed by this processor.

2 *Process event using Esper*—The event you received is now sent to the Esper processor. Esper processes this event using the configured statement ❷.

3 *Esper creates a new event*—Esper itself can create new events based on the original events it received. In this configuration every time an event is processed by Esper, Esper creates a new event where it sends the current average processing time ❸. To easily identify this event you add a custom class to the event ❺ that can be used to search for these events.

4 *Store events*—The original event and the event created by Esper are stored ❹ and can be retrieved using the REST interface we discussed in section 7.1.

Before we look at the events this processor produces, we'll look a bit deeper at the Esper expression we used:

```
select avg(cast(userValues('processingTime'),double))
                as average from Event
```

This expression uses the avg function to calculate the average processing time from the events it processes. It does this by retrieving the value stored in the userValues map of the events it receives. The current average is returned whenever a new event is processed. We won't dive too deeply into the configuration of Esper in this book. For more information on how you can create Esper statements, look at the Esper site at http://esper.codehaus.org/.

You've already seen what the original event looks like (see listing 7.2); events produced by this processor (for an example see the following listing) are stored in the same standard way. In this way you can easily retrieve the information using the event service we discussed in section 7.1.4.

Listing 7.4   Event created by Esper for the round function

```
{"event": {
    "timestamp": "1311504899604",
    "eventclass": "averageServiceTime",
    "average_EsperEventProcessor": "1344.0",
    "service": "EsperEventProcessor.service",
    "server": "EsperServer"
}}
```

As you can see in this listing, the storagePrefix and userClass defined in listing 7.3 are used here to identify the event. The final step is to hook up this event to a gauge, so that you can monitor this event and report the average processing time. Let's first look at what you can configure on a gauge; see table 7.6.

Table 7.6   Configuration options for the gauge

Property	Description
Interval	The interval used to update the gauge. This example uses 5000, which updates the gauge every 5 seconds.
jsonURL	The URL that you use to get your events from. The result is a JSON array of events. Because a gauge can only show a single value, the result should be a single event. In this example you use the following query: `http://localhost:9003/services/event/list?class=averageServiceTime&reverse=true&amp;count=1` This will return the last result that your Esper processor calculated.
Label	The label to show on the gauge.
Lower LimitGauge	The lower limit of the gauge.
Upper LimitGauge	The upper limit of the gauge.
Property Name	The property of the event to show in the gauge. In this example you use `average_EsperEventProcessor`.

You can now add the gauge gadget, which is available from http://localhost:9003/web/gadget/bamos-gauge.xml, in the same manner as you did in chapter 2, to the gadget server and configure it with the values from table 7.6. If you produce some events (using the Bamos client or soapUI), you'll now see the gauge respond, as shown in figure 7.5.

Figure 7.5   Configured gauge responding to received events

7.2.2   *Report usage based on service*

In this section I'll show you how you can use the Bamos processor together with the bar chart and pie chart gadgets to create usage-based overviews of your services. With such an overview you can quickly see how much a certain service is being used. In this example you'll create the overviews shown in figure 7.6 and figure 7.7.

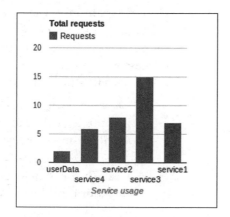

Figure 7.6   Bar chart showing service usage

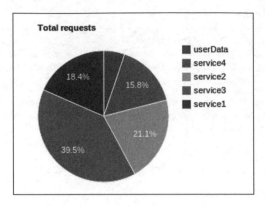

Figure 7.7   Pie chart showing the percentage of calls made to a specific service

To create these graphs you need to take the same three steps shown earlier:

- Make your services send events whenever a request is received.
- Use an EventProcessor to process these events in a form you can use in your gadgets.
- Configure the gadgets so that the correct information is retrieved and shown.

We start by looking at how the processor is defined in Spring. This time you use a simple Java-based processor, provided by the Bamos server, which counts all the events that are received. This configuration is shown in the next listing.

Listing 7.5   CountEventProcessor configuration in Spring

Filter events from server ❶

```
<bean id="counteventprocessor"
    class="org.bamos.core.processors.event.common.CountEventProcessor">
        <property name="filter" value="serverName == 'server2'"/>
        <property name="userClass" value="countServer2'"/>    ◁─┐
    </bean>
```

Created events have this userclass ❷

Here you can once again see that you only process events from server2 ❶, and with the userClass property ❷ you indicate that the events created by this specific processor get a custom class with the value countServer2. I won't show you the code for this processor (you can find it in the Bamos source code provided with this book), but this processor takes the following steps:

1. *Check incoming event*—This processor checks whether it should process the incoming event. For this it uses the configured filter. So in this case all the events from server2 will be processed.
2. *Retrieve current state from database*—This processor keeps its counts in the database. In this step it retrieves its current count from the database and increases the count for the received service.

3   *Update the state*—After updating the counter for the specific service, it stores the counts in the database again.

4   *Send count event*—Finally, it sends an event that contains an overview of the counts of the services that belong to this service.

The event that's sent by this processor, and which you'll use to visualize using a bar chart and a pie chart, is shown here:

```
{"event": {
    "timestamp": "1311507175285",
    "eventclass": "CountEventProcessor.class",
    "PROC_NAME": "CountEventProcessor",
    "countfor_userData": "2",
    "service": "CountEventProcessor.service",
    "countfor_service4": "6",
    "server": "server2",
    "countfor_service2": "8",
    "countfor_service3": "15",
    "countfor_service1": "7"
}}
```

As you can see, for each service you receive a `countfor` property. Each of these properties will be used in the bar and pie charts.

The final step is configuring the pie and bar charts. These can be found at the following locations:

http://localhost:9003/web/gadget/bamos-barchart.xml
http://localhost:9003/web/gadget/bamos-piechart.xml

Both these charts can be configured in the same manner, using the properties shown in table 7.7.

Table 7.7   Configuration options for the bar and pie charts

Property	Description
Interval	The interval used to update the gauge. In this example you use 5000, which updates the gauge every 5 seconds.
jsonURL	The URL that you use to get your events from. The result is a JSON array of events. Because a gauge can only show a single value, the result should be a single event. In this example you use the following query: `http://localhost:9003/services/event/list?server=server2&service=CountEventProcessor.service&count=1&reverse=true`. This will return the last result from your count processor.
prefix	The `prefix` value determines which values you're going to show in your visualizations. Because the values start with `countfor_`, you set this property to that value.
title	The title shown at the top of the chart.
dataLabel	The label shown when you hover over a chart.

If you now add one of these charts to your dashboard (see chapter 2 or the appendix for instructions on how to do this), you can use this to monitor the number of requests your services receive. In figure 7.8, you can see the distribution of calls made to services on server2.

It's also possible to enrich an event with information from an external source. In the following section I'll show you how you can enrich an event with location-based information.

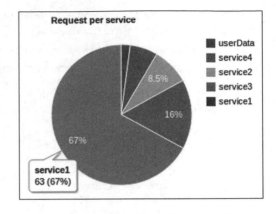

Figure 7.8   Pie chart showing the distribution of the service calls made on server2

7.2.3   *Report usage based on location*

For this report we're going to look at how you can add a report that shows from where in the world people are using your service. If you've defined specific uptimes during business hours and you have worldwide consumers of your service, it's good to know which country most of your users come from. If you have to bring your service down for maintenance you can make sure it's done outside the business hours or on a country's specific holiday.

We're going to create the report shown in figure 7.9.

In this figure you can see which country your users come from, and when you hover over a country, you see the number of calls that were made from that specific country. To accomplish this you take the following steps:

1   *Include IP address in event*—You need a way to determine where a consumer comes from. You can do this based on the IP address of the consumer. You need to include the IP address in the event the client sends.

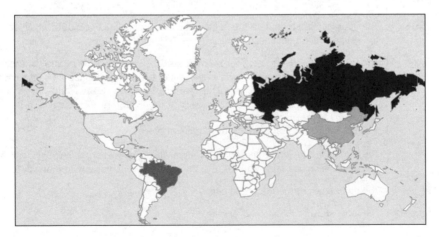

Figure 7.9   Service usage based on location

2　*Convert IP address to country code*—When you receive an event that has an IP address, you need to convert this to a country code. For this you use the database from IPInfoDB.com. With this database you can convert an IP address to a location.

3　*Count requests*—The next step is to keep track of how many events are received for a specific country code. You do this by storing this information in Cassandra.

4　*Send accumulated event*—Every time you receive a new event with location information, you send out a new event that contains the accumulated data. Note that you could also choose to only send out events every 10 minutes if you want to decrease the load.

5　*Show map*—This last event is retrieved every couple of seconds from a gadget and rendered as a map.

First, let's look at how the event looks that you're going to send. This is just an event like any other, but this time you also include some custom user data that contains the IP address of the consumer:

```
{"event":{"timestamp":"1310294128455",
        "service":"service3",
        "ipaddress":"92.241.173.211",
         "server":"server3"}
}
```

To process these types of events you create a new custom Java-based `EventProcessor`. This processor converts the IP address to a country code and keeps track of how many events are received for a specific country. The code for this `EventProcessor` is shown in the following listing.

Listing 7.6　InfoDB processor

```
@Override
public Event processEvent(Event event) {
  String ipaddress = (String) event.getUserValues().get("ipaddress");
  String countryCode =
          infodbservice.getCountryCodeFromIp(ipaddress);        ❶ Convert IP address
                                                                    country code

  String rowKey = event.getServerName() + event.getServiceName();
  Map<String, String> locationData =
          stateRepo.getProcesData(rowKey, IPINFOKEY);            ❷ Get the
                                                                    current state

  String columnKey = LOCATION_EVENT_PROCESSOR_PREFIX + countryCode;
  if (locationData != null && locationData.size() > 0) {

    if (locationData.get(columnKey) != null) {
      String newCount = increaseCount(locationData.get(columnKey));
      locationData.put(columnKey,newCount);
      stateRepo.storeData(rowKey, IPINFOKEY, locationData);
    } else {
      locationData.put(columnKey, "1");
      stateRepo.storeData(rowKey, IPINFOKEY, locationData);
    }
```

```
    } else {
      locationData.put(columnKey, "1");
      stateRepo.storeData(rowKey, IPINFOKEY, locationData);
    }

    Map<String,Object> userData = new HashMap<String, Object>();
    userData.putAll(locationData);

    String uc = LOCATION_EVENT_PROCESSOR_CLASS;
    if (getUserClass() != null) {
      uc = getUserClass();
    }

    Event result = new Event(event.getServerName(),                    ❸ Send a new
                    LOCATION_EVENT_PROCESSOR_CLASS, uc,                    event
                    System.currentTimeMillis(), userData);
    return result;
  }
```

The first thing you see in this listing is that you use the infodbservice service ❶ to convert an IP address to a country code. The implementation of this service is out of scope for the current subject we're discussing. If you're interested in how to do this, you can look at the bamos-extensions-services-ipinfodb project, which you can find in the supplied source code. In this project you can also find a test case you can use to load in the IP location database.

After you retrieve the country code, you update the current state ❷ to keep track of how many events from a specific country you've received. You use the same mechanism here as you did in section 7.2.2, Report usage based on service. Finally, you send the event that contains the number of calls for each country ❸ that you show on the map. This final event looks like this:

```
{"event": {
    "timestamp": "1312106551702",
    "eventclass": "iplocation'",
    "PROC_NAME": "IPINFODBPROCESSOR",
    "location_RU": "35",
    "location_BR": "20",
    "location_US": "1",
    "service": "LocationEventProcessor.class",
    "location_NL": "11",
    "server": "server3",
    "location_CN": "12",
    "location_UK": "22"
}}
```

To use this custom processor you have to configure it once again in Spring, as shown in the following listing. This configuration can also be found in the bamos-extensions-services-ipinfodb project.

> **Listing 7.7   CountEventProcessor configuration in Spring**

```
<bean id="counteventprocessor"
    class="...ipinfodb.IPInfoDBProcessor">
  <property name="expression" value="serverName == 'server3'"/>
```

```
    <property name="userClass" value="iplocation'"/>
</bean>
```

The last step you need to take is to configure the gadget to show a map based on this event. This gadget can be added from the following location:

http://localhost:9003/web/gadgets/bamos-geochart.xml

On this gadget you can use the configuration options shown in table 7.8.

Table 7.8　Configuration options for geo chart

Property	Description
Interval	The interval used to update the gauge. In this example you use 5000, which updates the map every 5 seconds.
jsonURL	The URL that you use to get your events from. The result is a JSON array of events. You want to retrieve a single event that contains all the information for the chart. You use the following query: `http://localhost:9003/services/event/list?eventclass=iplocation&amp;reverse=true&amp;count=1` This will return the last result from your InfoDB processor.
prefix	The `prefix` value determines the values you use as input for the map. Because the values start with `location_`, you set this property to that value.

If you add this gadget with the previously mentioned configuration, you'll get a chart that looks something like the one shown in figure 7.10.

So far you've seen static information. In the next two sections I'll show you how to visualize information over a specific period of time. You can use this kind of information to, for instance, determine when your service is used the most or when the performance is the worst.

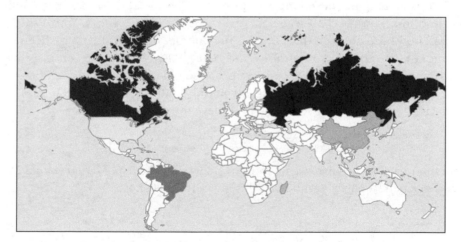

Figure 7.10　Final gadget showing where your service is called from

I'll start by showing you how you can easily plot the number of queries a specific service receives over a specific period of time.

7.2.4 *Number of requests per time period*

Before we look into the specific configuration, I'll show you what we're aiming for. In figure 7.11, you can see an area chart that shows the number of requests received in a period of 10 seconds.

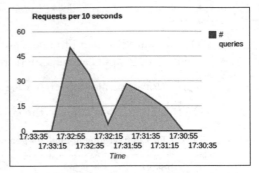

Figure 7.11 Area chart showing the number of requests received in a period of 10 seconds

To achieve this you'll use the Esper-based EventProcessor you also used in section 7.2.1. For this scenario, configure this processor as shown in the following listing.

Listing 7.8 EsperEventProcessor configuration to measure time windows

```
<bean id="espereventprocessor10Seconds"
    class="org.bamos.core.processors.event.esper.EsperEventProcessor">
  <property name="expression" value="serverName == 'expService'"/>
  <property name="esperStatement" value='select count(*) from
              Event.win:time_batch(10 sec,"FORCE_UPDATE")'/>
  <property name="resultStatement" value="count(*)"/>
  <property name="storagePrefix" value="countAll10Sec_"/>
  <property name="userClass" value="countAll10Sec"/>
</bean>
```

This configuration looks much like the previous one in section 7.2.1. The main difference is the Esper statement used. Let's look a bit closer at this statement:

```
select count(*) from Event.win:time_batch(10 sec,"FORCE_UPDATE")
```

With this statement you count all the events (count (*) from Event) that are received in a window of 10 seconds (.win:time_batch(10 sec)). Your Esper processor will now send an event that contains the number of events that have been received in the last 10 seconds. You also use the FORCE_UPDATE option to ensure that Esper sends updates even when no events are processed in this time window.

You can now query these events as you did in all the previous examples. For this scenario use the following REST call to retrieve the events:

```
http://localhost:9003/services/event/
    list?class=countAll10Sec&reverse=true&count=10
```

This query will return the last 10 events produced by the Esper-based EventProcessor just described. A partial result from this query is shown here:

```
{"events": [
   {"event":      {
      "timestamp": "1311530255693",
      "eventclass": "countAll10Sec",
```

```
        "countAll10Sec_EsperEventProcessor": "60",
        "service": "EsperEventProcessor.service",
        "server": "EsperServer"
   }},
   {"event":       {
       "timestamp": "1311530235693",
       "eventclass": "countAll10Sec",
       "countAll10Sec_EsperEventProcessor": "13",
       "service": "EsperEventProcessor.service",
       "server": "EsperServer"
   }},
   {"event":       {
       "timestamp": "1311530215693",
       "eventclass": "countAll10Sec",
       "countAll10Sec_EsperEventProcessor": "12",
       "service": "EsperEventProcessor.service",
       "server": "EsperServer"
   }},
 ...
]}
```

The final step is to configure the chart to use this REST call and show an area chart based on these events. This chart can be added to your dashboard from the following URL: http://localhost:9003/web/gadgets/bamos-areachart.xml. In table 7.9 (where I've skipped the `interval` and `jsonURL` properties because they're the same for all charts) you can see how this chart can be configured.

Table 7.9 Configuration options for `areachart`

Property	Description
title	The name of the area chart, shown at the top of the chart.
valueTitle	The type of data you want to show; in this example we've used # of queries.
property	The property that contains the value you need to show. If you look at the JSON data shown earlier, you can see that the name of the property is countAll10Sec_EsperEventProcessor.

When you add this chart to your dashboard and configure it like I've just shown you, you'll get a chart that shows you how often your service is called over a specific period of time (see figure 7.12).

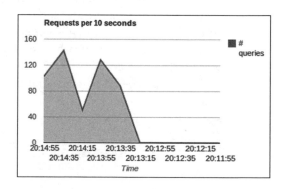

Figure 7.12 Area graph based on recently received events

7.3   *Security and documentation*

So far you've seen how to monitor various usage-related policies. These aren't the only types of policies you can monitor at runtime. In this section we'll focus on some different policies that you can easily monitor using the tools shown in this chapter.

7.3.1   *Failed authentication and authorization*

In chapter 5 we looked at how you can comply with various security-related policies at design time. In this section we'll look at how you can monitor how your customers use your secured services. More specifically, I'll show you how you can create a simple line chart that shows the failed authentication and authorization requests that are made during a specific time. We'll create the two line charts shown in figure 7.13 and figure 7.14.

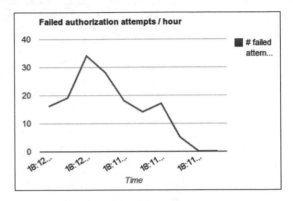

Figure 7.13   Line chart showing the failed authorization requests per hour

If you want to show failed authentication and authorization attempts, the first thing you need to do is send an event when such an event occurs. If you look back at chapter 5, you can see that you've used interceptors that check specific headers for authentication information. Based on that information a call was made to the federated identity server to check whether a user was authenticated or authorized for a specific service. You could easily expand these inter-

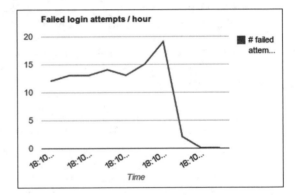

Figure 7.14   Line chart showing the failed authentication requests per hour

ceptors to send an event when such an event occurs. For an example of this see the provided source code.

To show this graph you need to collect information on the failed attempts. The first step is always to define the events you want to work with. For this report you'll work with the following events:

```
{"event":{"timestamp":"1310294128455",
        "service":"service12",
        "authenticationFailure":"true",
        "eventclass":"ev",
        "server":"authService"}
}
```

And

```
{"event":{"timestamp":"1310294128470",
          "service":"service12",
          "authorizationFailure":"true",
          "eventclass":"ev",
          "server":"authService"}
}
```

These two events both specify a single custom property. The first event specifies the `authenticationFailure` event and the second event defines the `authorization-Failure` event.

With these events specified we can look at how you'll process these events in the Bamos server. This time you'll use Esper. As you saw in section 7.2.1, Average response time, with Esper you can easily process events for a specific time window. The Bamos server provides you with an Esper-based `EventProcessor`, which you'll configure in this section to count the failed authentication and authorization attempts. To accomplish this you'll configure the `EsperEventProcessor` as shown in the following listing.

Listing 7.9 Configure the Esper-based `eventprocessors`

```
<bean id="espereventprocessorFailedAuthorization"
    class="org.bamos.core.processors.event.esper.EsperEventProcessor">
  <property name="expression" value="serverName == 'server10'"/>
  <property name="esperStatement" value='select count(*) as count
          from Event(userValues("authorizationFailure") =
          "true").win:time_batch(1 hour,"FORCE_UPDATE")'/>     ❶ Esper statement
  <property name="resultStatement" value="count"/>
  <property name="storagePrefix" value="count_"/>
  <property name="userClass" value="authorizationcount"/>      ❷ Identifying event class
</bean>

<bean id="espereventprocessorFailedAuthentication"
    class="org.bamos.core.processors.event.esper.EsperEventProcessor">
  <property name="expression" value="serverName == 'server10'"/>
  <property name="esperStatement" value='select count(*) as count
          from Event(userValues("authenticationFailure") =
          "true").win:time_batch(1 hour,"FORCE_UPDATE")'/>     ❸ Esper statement
  <property name="resultStatement" value="count"/>
  <property name="storagePrefix" value="count_"/>
  <property name="userClass" value="authenticationcount"/>     ❹ Identifying event class
</bean>
```

In the configuration in listing 7.9 you define two processors. The first one listens for specific events that have an `authorizationFailure` property ❶ and have the class `authorizationcount` ❷, and the second one listens for events that have the `authenticationFailure` property ❸ and the class `authenticationcount` ❹. Let's look a bit closer at the Esper statement used for these two processors:

```
select count(*) as count from
          Event(userValues("authenticationFailure")
          = "true").win:time_batch(1 hour,"FORCE_UPDATE")
```

This statement counts all the events (count(*)) that have a user value property with the name authenticationFailure with the value true. It does this for one hour, and even if no events are received it still sends an update after the hour (win:time_batch(1 hour,"FORCE_UPDATE")). The update this provider sends is also in the form of an event. This event looks like this:

```
"event":        {
        "timestamp": "1312130271359",
        "eventclass": "authenticationcount",
        "count_EsperEventProcessor": "0",
        "service": "EsperEventProcessor.service",
        "server": "EsperServer"
    }
```

You can see that this is the event for the authentication failures because the event-class is set to authenticationcount. The final step is to configure the line chart to query for these events and show them in the graph. The configuration for this chart, shown in table 7.10, is pretty much the same as you saw in section 7.2.4.

Table 7.10   Configuration options for line chart

Property	Description
title	The name of the line chart, shown at the top of the chart.
valueTitle	The type of data you want to show.
property	The property that contains the value that you need to show. If you look at the JSON data shown earlier, you can see that the name of the property is count_EsperEventProcessor.
jsonURL	The URL that you use to get your events from. The result is a JSON array of events. http://localhost:9003/services/event/ list?class=authenticationcount&reverse=true&count=10

When you add this chart to the gadget container (http://localhost:9003/web/gadgets/bamos-linechart.xml) and configure the gadget with the values shown previously, you'll see the graph shown in figure 7.15.

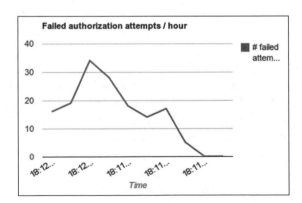

Figure 7.15   Line chart showing the failed authorization requests per hour

7.3.2 *Documentation compliance*

In chapter 8 I'll show you how you can combine the WSO2 registry and the Bamos server, but in this section I'll go ahead and provide you with a short preview of what's possible. In chapter 4 I talked about documenting your services and registering them in the repository. In chapter 8 I'll show you how to create the pie chart from figure 7.16.

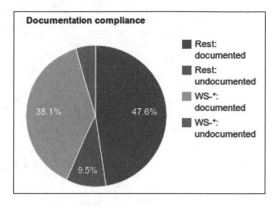

Figure 7.16 Information from the services stored in the service repository

In figure 7.16 you can see how well you comply with your documentation policy. You've documented most but not all of your WS-* and REST-based services. More information on how you can integrate the repository and the Bamos server is shown in section 8.5.

7.4 *Summary*

In this chapter you've learned the following:

- What the various parts of a runtime monitoring solution are
- How you can use the Bamos server to capture events
- How you can use the REST interface to retrieve event information
- How simple it is to process events using Esper
- How you can extend the functionality of the Bamos server with your own event processors
- How you can map events to a specific location

Lifecycle support
and discovering resources

This chapter covers

- What a service lifecycle is and how to register it in the registry
- What a policy lifecycle is and how to register it in the registry
- How to locate the resources that have been stored in the registry
- How to visualize the information in the WSO2 registry using the Bamos server

Using policies will make sure that your services are of a certain quality level and follow the regulations and standards set out by your company. This will ensure that your services are well understood by you as well as your customers and can be used effectively. So far, however, we've skipped two important aspect of SOA governance: service and policy lifecycle and resource discovery.

Besides these main subjects I'll also show you how to extend the WSO2 user interface to make registration of resources easier. We'll start with the definition of a service lifecycle.

8.1　*Defining the lifecycle of a service*

A lifecycle, as the name implies, defines the stages a service goes through during its existence. A service lifecycle is important for the following reasons:

- It helps to identify which services need to be created or updated, because it provides a complete overview of all the services currently running in production.
- It helps to make sure all the necessary steps are taken before a service is put in production or is made obsolete.
- It can be used to determine which policies need to be complied with in each stage.

8.1.1　*Standard service lifecycle*

You can make the lifecycle of a service as fine-grained or coarse-grained as you want. But usually four distinct phases are identified: model, assemble, deploy, and manage, as shown in figure 8.1. Let's look at each of these phases before you define a pragmatic lifecycle that you'll implement using the WSO2 SOA registry.

The first step in the lifecycle of a service is usually called the model phase.

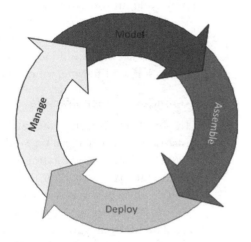

Figure 8.1　Standard service lifecycle

THE MODEL LIFECYCLE PHASE

In this phase you look at the business requirements that need to be fulfilled. Say that the OpenGov organization gets a number of requests from its customers, the municipalities, which specify that they would like functionality that allows them to publish information on events that take place in their city. For instance, there's a grand opening of the new museum, and they want to easily publish information about this event. In this case the business requirements are clear. The next step in this phase is to identify the business services that are needed to offer this new functionality. Is this functionality already available from one of the existing services? Do you need to create a completely new service? Can you extend one? All these questions will need to be answered in this phase of a service lifecycle. In our example you don't have any services that can fulfill this requirement, so you need to create a new service.

THE ASSEMBLE PHASE

The next phase is the assemble phase. During the assemble phase you take the business services identified in the model phase and, in our scenario, create the service. This means that in this phase you define the contract for the service, create the service, and test the service. These steps will result in either a new service or an updated one. In this stage you'll also publish the contract of this service to a service repository, so that service consumers can view the contract and start preparing to consume this service.

DEPLOY PHASE

After a service is created, you can start deploying it; this is the deploy phase. This means that the service is deployed to a service container, integrated with other services it might use, and made available to be used by the service consumers.

MANAGE PHASE

The final phase is the manage phase. In this phase you look at how the service operates at runtime. You determine whether the policies you've defined for this service are met, whether new functionality might be required, and whether all the services you've defined meet the business objectives set out during the model phase. If there are any new requirements or if changes need to be made to your existing service, you start a new cycle, in the model phase.

These four phases can be applied to pretty much every service. These are, however, coarse-grained and can't be used in this form to keep track of the state of a service. In the next section we'll look one step deeper into these four steps and define a pragmatic service lifecycle, which you'll then implement using the WSO2 registry.

8.1.2 *OpenGov service lifecycle*

In the WSO2 registry you can create custom lifecycles and attach a lifecycle to each resource, even if it isn't a service. When you attach a lifecycle to a resource in the WSO2 registry, the resource is automatically given the first state of this lifecycle. On each state you can then define a set of checklist items that need to be completed before the resource is moved to its next lifecycle state. Let's expand the four-phase model from the previous section and define a pragmatic lifecycle for your service.

The lifecycle you'll use for your service is shown in table 8.1.

Table 8.1 The lifecycle phases of the OpenGov service lifecycle

Lifecycle phase	Description
Identify business process	In this phase you'll define which business processes might need to be changed if you want to fulfill the new business requirements. This lifecycle phase occurs before you've defined any services, so it won't be included in the service lifecycle you'll define in the repository.
Identify required services	After you've identified the business processes that are involved, you can use those to identify the services that might need to be updated or newly created. Like the previous phase, this one will be kept out of the WSO2 registry, because you haven't created resources in the repository at this phase.
Define the contract	At this point you know the service you need to create. In this phase you'll define the contract (a WSDL in the case of WS-* and a set of documentation in the case of REST).
Register the contract	After you've defined the contract, you can register it in the WSO2 repository.
Realize the service	With the contract in the repository, you can start the realization of the service. In this phase you might make some small changes to the contract already stored in the repository.

Table 8.1 The lifecycle phases of the OpenGov service lifecycle (continued)

Lifecycle phase	Description
Test the service	Before you deploy the service so that your service consumers can use it, you first need to test the service.
Deploy the service	After testing, you can finally deploy the service to a container and inform the service consumers that they can start using it.
Service is available	After deployment, the service is made available. In this phase the service will be monitored to see whether it complies with its runtime policies.
Service is deprecated	When the service isn't used anymore or a new version is deployed, this service can be marked as being deprecated. If that's the case, service consumers can still use the service but should move to a different one, because this service will be retired shortly.
Service is retired	After a service has become obsolete and needs to be removed, you retire the service. If a service is retired, service consumers won't be able to access it anymore.

As you can see, table 8.1 defines a more fine-grained service lifecycle for your services. Let's look at how you can translate this to a service lifecycle inside the WSO2 registry. In the WSO2 registry for each stage, you can define a name and a set of conditions that need to be met before moving to the next stage. An example from the sample lifecycle that's provided by the registry is shown in figure 8.2.

Figure 8.2 Example of lifecycle usage in WSO2 registry

You can translate the lifecycle from table 8.1 to the one in table 8.2 that uses states and checklists in the WSO2 registry.

Table 8.2 The lifecycle as modeled in WSO2 registry

Status	Checklist before moving on to next status
Initial	Has a contract been defined? Has the documentation been written?
Registered	Has the service been created? Do the code quality and test coverage match the policy?
In test	Is the integration test with other components finished? Is the integration test with the service consumer finished? Has the service been deployed to the production environment? Has the service configuration been updated?

Table 8.2   The lifecycle as modeled in WSO2 registry *(continued)*

Status	Checklist before moving on to next status
Available	Have consumers been informed about deprecation? Has the service configuration been updated?
Deprecated	Have consumers been informed about service retirement?
Retired	End of service lifecycle.

The final step is to set up this lifecycle in the registry. Open the WSO2 governance registry and navigate to the Extensions > Configure > Lifecycles menu option. On the page that opens click the Add New Lifecycle button. This will open a sample lifecycle, which you'll configure with the information from table 8.2. This configuration is shown in the following listing.

Listing 8.1   Custom lifecycle definition in WSO2 governance registry

```
<aspect name="OpenGovLifecycle"                          ⟵⎤  Name of the lifecycle
class="org.wso2.carbon.governance.registry.extensions
      ➥.aspects.ChecklistLifeCycle">
  <configuration type="literal">
    <lifecycle>
      <state name="Initial">                             ⎤  Define each
        <checkitem>Has a contract been defined?</checkitem>   ⎟  state of
        <checkitem>Has the documentation been written?</checkitem>  ⎟  the lifecycle
      </state>
      <state name="Registered">
        <checkitem>Has the service been created?</checkitem>
        <checkitem>Do the code quality and test coverage match the
          policy?</checkitem>
      </state>
      <state name="In test">
        <checkitem>Is the integration test with other components
          finished?</checkitem>
        <checkitem>Is the integration test with service consumer
          finished?</checkitem>
        <checkitem>Has the service been deployed to the production
          environment?</checkitem>

        <checkitem>Has the service configuration been updated?</checkitem>
      </state>
      <state name="Available">
        <checkitem>Have consumers been informed about
          deprecation?</checkitem>
        <checkitem>Has the service configuration been updated?</checkitem>
      </state>
      <state name="Deprecated">
        <checkitem>Have consumers been informed about service
          retirement?</checkitem>
      </state>
      <state name="Retired">
```

```
      </state>
    </lifecycle>
  </configuration>
</aspect>
```

After you've entered this information, click Save and your lifecycle will be created. You can now attach this lifecycle to a service, and using the checklist items, you can promote a service to the next stage in its lifecycle.

To attach this lifecycle to a service, browse through the service you want to attach this lifecycle to; you can either use the direct Metadata > Services menu options or browse through the repository. Once you've opened the service, the segment from figure 8.3 shows where you can define a service's lifecycle.

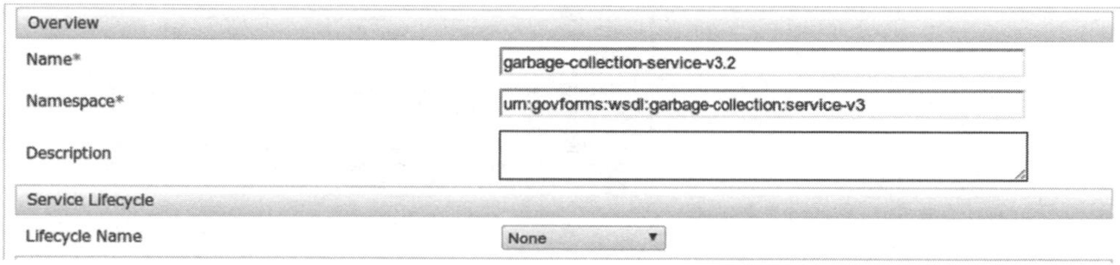

Overview	
Name*	garbage-collection-service-v3.2
Namespace*	urn:govforms:wsdl:garbage-collection:service-v3
Description	
Service Lifecycle	
Lifecycle Name	None ▼

Figure 8.3   Add a lifecycle to a service.

8.2   Creating a custom view for the policy

Before I show you how you can add a lifecycle to a policy, you first need to modify the WSO2 registry to support policies. The WSO2 registry only supports WS-Policy files. If you use one of those files, you get a nice custom UI with which you can manage your policy description.

What is WS-Policy?

WS-Policy is a W3C specification that allows consumers and providers of web services (the WS-* kind) to specify the requirements and capabilities of their services. By using the WS-Policy specification you can, for instance, specify that your service, specified by a WSDL, requires transport-level security. You do this by adding or referencing policy assertions to your contract. If the consumer uses a policy-aware client, this policy will tell the client to communicate using HTTPS. If your WSDL contains such policies, the WSO2 registry will automatically detect these and create policy resources for them.

There are additional specifications available that specify policies for subjects such as security, reliable messaging, atomic transaction, and business activity. These specifications, though, aren't used much. Interoperability between various platforms on these standards is difficult, and the added value is only minimal. In practice, when these kinds of requirements are needed, they're defined in the service's documentation. Policies should be meant for human consumption, not for machine-to-machine communication.

Add Resource	
Resource name *	SSD_POL_1
Policy name *	Service documentation
Statement	All services, REST and WS-* alike, must be self-documenting. There shouldn't be the need of extensive user manuals on how to use the services we provide.
Rationale	We want our customers to be able to use our services without the help of online documentation or calling the helpdesk. Creating self-documenting services will help us in keeping the available documentation succinct and up to date. If our services are self-explanatory, consumers will have less need to call the helpdesk and we can focus on creating new services and functionality.
Implication	• For all the WS-* based services the WSDL will serve as the base for the documentation. When registering a service in the repository, from this WSDL human readable documentation must be created and linked to this service. • The REST services should use relations and links to show the intent on how these services should be used. • For REST services a text document must be created and stored in the repository together with the REST service definition. This document explains, in a human readable manner, how the service is to be used.

Save

Figure 8.4   Custom input form to add a policy to the repository

The policies we're talking about in this book don't follow that format. We've defined general policies, meant for human consumption, not to be automatically processed, such as WS-Policy descriptions. If you want to register your policies in the registry, this poses a bit of a problem. You can register them as plain-text files, but it would be much nicer if you could create a custom view for your policy descriptions. That would make it much easier to read, edit, and keep the policies up to date. The WSO2 registry lets you create custom handlers for this, which allows you to present custom resources in a formatted manner. In this section I'll show you how you can accomplish this for policy files. The input and output screens you'll create are shown in figures 8.4 and 8.5.

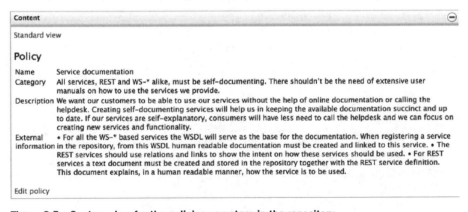

Figure 8.5   Custom view for the policies you store in the repository

You need to take the following steps to achieve this:

1 *Define policy format*—So far when we've discussed policies we've only talked about the content of the policy; we haven't talked about how this policy is described. You could make a Word document of it, but that would make it harder to manage in your repository. The first thing you should do is define a simple XML format in which you describe your policies.

2 *Link media type*—The WSO2 registry allows you to define custom handlers based on media type. This is done in a components.xml file where you define which .jsp files should be called when a certain action is executed.

3 *Create the logic*—WSO2 offers a couple of utility classes that you can use to store and update content in the repository. From your custom UI you use those functions to access your policy information.

4 *Create the pages*—The pages, which are standard JSP pages, define how the user of the repository sees your content. You need to create pages to add, view, and update your policy content.

5 *Deploy the custom pages*—The final step is to deploy your custom pages. These are deployed as a simple .jar file to a specific directory in the WSO2 registry.

In the following sections we'll walk through these steps to create the custom UI shown in figure 8.4. The source code for this complete example can be found in the supplied sources for this chapter.

DEFINING THE POLICY FORMAT

The first thing you need to do is determine how you're going to store the policy files in the repository. You don't want to define a policy file used in machine-to-machine communication; you want to create a format that can easily be read by users of your repository. For this example I've defined the XML-based policy format shown in the following listing.

Listing 8.2 Policy format to be stored in the repository

```xml
<policy name="Service documentation">
    <statement>All services, REST and WS-* alike, must be self-documenting.
        There shouldn't be the need of extensive user manuals on how to
        Use the services we provide.
    </statement>
    <rationale>We want our customers to be able to use our services without
        the help of online documentation or calling the helpdesk.
        Creating self-documenting services will help us in keeping the
        Available documentation succinct and up to date. If our
        services are self-explanatory, consumers will have less need
        to call the helpdesk and we can focus on creating new services
        and functionality.
    </rationale>
    <implication>For all the WS-* based services the WSDL will serve as
        the base for the documentation. When registering a service in
        the repository, from this WSDL human readable documentation
        must be created and linked to this service.
```

```
        The REST services should use relations and links to show the
        Intent on how these services should be used.
        For REST services a text document must be created and stored in
        The repository together with the REST service definition.
        This document explains, in a human readable manner, how the service
        is to be used.
    </implication>
</policy>
```

As you can see in listing 8.2, you define a simple policy format that contains three fields. You use the `name` attribute to set the name of the policy, the `statement` element to describe what this policy is about, and the `rationale` to show why this policy is important. Finally, you have the `implications` element, which is used to highlight the implications of using this policy.

LINKING THE MEDIA TYPE

Now that you've defined the format in which you'll store the policy, the next step is to tell the WSO2 server which pages should be used when it encounters one of your policy files. The WSO2 registry does this based on the media type of the content you add. If you want to add a file with the WSDL media type, it will show the WSDL editor, and if the registry can't find the content type, it will just show the default editors. This means that for your custom content, you need to register a media type with the registry and tell the registry which pages it should use when it encounters this media type. This is done in a file named components.xml, as shown in the following listing.

Listing 8.3   Components.xml used to link a media-type to JSP pages

```
<component xmlns="http://products.wso2.org/carbon">
  <customUI>
    <uiType>view</uiType>
    <mediaType>policy</mediaType>
    <uiPath>../registry/custom/pol/policy_main_ajaxprocessor.jsp</uiPath>
  </customUI>

  <customUI>
    <uiType>add</uiType>
    <mediaType>policy</mediaType>
    <uiPath>../registry/custom/pol/policy_add_ajaxprocessor.jsp</uiPath>
  </customUI>
</component>
```

In listing 8.3 two `customUI` elements are defined. In each of these elements you link a specific media type, in this case `policy`, to a JSP page. The `uiType` in this element specifies the type of view you're in. The first `customUI` element specifies the page you see when you view your custom resource, and the second element defines the page you see when you add a resource.

CREATING THE LOGIC

Before I show you what the `jsp` pages from listing 8.3 look like, we'll look at some Java code that's used by the JSPs to store and retrieve the policy content. For this I've created three simple Java classes: `AddPolicyUtil`, `GetPolicyUtil`, and `SavePolicyUtil`.

AddPolicyUtil is used to store a new resource in the repository, GetPolicyUtil is used to retrieve content from the repository, and SavePolicyUtil is used to update existing content in the repository. Let's look a bit closer at the AddPolicyUtil class, shown in the following listing.

Listing 8.4 Helper class used to store your custom content in the repository

```
public class AddPolicyUtil {

  private final static String MEDIATYPE = "policy";

  public static void addEndpointBean(                          ❶ Called from
    HttpServletRequest request,ServletConfig config,              JSP page
    HttpSession session) {

    String parentPath = request.getParameter("parentPath");    ❷ Parameters
    String resourceName = request.getParameter("resourceName");   passed in
    String name = request.getParameter("policyName");             request
    String category = request.getParameter("policyCategory");
    String description = request.getParameter("policyDescription");
    String external = request.getParameter("policyExternal");

    OMFactory fac = OMAbstractFactory.getOMFactory();
    OMElement polElement = fac.createOMElement("policy", null);
    polElement.addAttribute("name", name, null);

    OMElement catElement = fac.createOMElement("category",null);
    catElement.setText(category);
    OMElement descElement = ac.createOMElement("description",null);
    descElement.setText(description);
    OMElement extElement = fac.createOMElement("external",null);
    extElement.setText(external);

    polElement.addChild(catElement);
    polElement.addChild(descElement);
    polElement.addChild(extElement);

    String content = polElement.toString();                    ❸ Store
    CustomUIServiceClient customUIServiceClient =                 the content
        new CustomUIServiceClient(config, session);              as string
    customUIServiceClient.addTextContent(parentPath,
        resourceName, MEDIATYPE, null, content);
  }
}
```

Listing 8.4 shows you the method that you'll call from your JSPs to store a new policy in the repository. In this code you do three main things. First, you get all the content from your custom form ❶, and you convert this information to the XML ❷ you specified in listing 8.2. In the last step you convert the XML to a String and use a Custom-UIServiceClient, ❸ which is provided by the repository, to create a new text resource in the repository at the path you specified.

In the other helper classes you do the same as in listing 8.4. You use request parameters to pass information from the form you show the user to the helper class and use the `CustomUIServiceClient` to interact with the repository. Now that you've seen how to store content from a custom form, let's look at how you define this form.

CREATING THE PAGES

Custom UI screens in the WSO2 registry are defined using standard JSPs, and information is submitted to the helper classes as a simple form submit. This means that the pages you need are basic. In the following listing you can see the JSP you use to define the Add New Policy page.

Listing 8.5   JSP used to show the Add New Policy page

```jsp
<%@ page contentType="text/html;charset=UTF-8" language="java" %>
<%  String parentPath = request.getParameter("parentPath"); %>
<br/>
<script type="text/javascript">
submitPolicyForm = function() {
    sessionAwareFunction(function() {                         ①  Add the policy
        var rForm = document.forms["policyAddForm"];
        rForm.submit();
        }
    }, "Session Timed Out");
    return true;
}
</script>
                                                              ②  Show the form
<form id="policyAddForm"
    name="policyAddForm"
  action="../registry/custom/endpoint/policy_add_handler_ajaxprocessor.jsp"
  method="post">

<input type="hidden" name="parentPath" value="<%=parentPath%>"/>
<table style="width:100%" class="styledLeft">
  <thead>
    <tr><th colspan="2"><strong>Add Resource</strong></th></tr>
  </thead>
  <tbody>
        <tr>
        <td class="leftCol-med">Resource name <span
            class="required">*</span></td>
        <td><input type="text" name="resourceName" /></td>
    </tr>
    <tr>
        <td>Policy name <span class="required">*</span></td>
        <td><input type="text" name="policyName" /></td>
    </tr>
    <tr>
        <td>Statement</td>
        <td><textarea name="policyStatement" rows="6"
            cols="30"></textArea>
    </tr>
    <tr>
```

```
        <td>Rationale</td>
        <td><textarea name="policyRationale" rows="6"
            cols="30"></textArea>
    </tr>
    <tr>
        <td>Implication</td>
        <td><textarea name="policyImplication" rows="6"
            cols="30"></textArea>
    </tr>
<tr>
    <td colspan="2" class="buttonRow">
     <input class="button" type="button"
         onclick="submitPolicyForm();"
            value="Save"/></td>
 </tr>
 </tbody>
</table>
</form>
```

❸ **Show the submit button**

As you can see, this is a standard JSP page. This page renders a simple form ❷ that a user can use to create a policy. When a user submits this form ❸, it gets sent to a different JSP page ❶: policy_add_handler_ajaxprocessor.jsp. This page is shown in the next listing.

Listing 8.6 Code for the `policy_add_handler_ajaxprocessor.jsp` page

```
<%
String parentPath = request.getParameter("parentPath");
try {
  AddPolicyUtil.addPolicyBean(request, config, session);
} catch (UIException e) {
        %>
Could not add policy
<%
  return;
}

  String resourcePagePath =
 ➥ "../../../resources/resource.jsp?region=region3&item=
 ➥ resource_browser_menu&viewType=std&path=" + parentPath;

  response.sendRedirect(resourcePagePath);
%>
```

This page makes use of the addPolicyBean operation defined in listing 8.4. After the policy is added, you're redirected back to an overview page, where you can see that the resource is added.

   If you look through the code and the listings from this and the previous section, you can see that creating custom pages is quite a bit of work. Currently there's no simpler way than shown here. But, because you're using standard JSP and Java, you could easily expand on this example and make the code you write a lot more reusable.

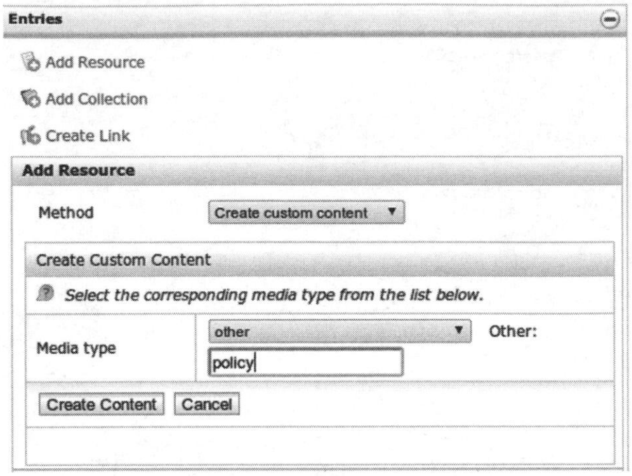

Figure 8.6   Add a resource as custom content with your specified media type.

DEPLOYING THE CUSTOM PAGES

There's one thing left to do, and that's deploying your custom component to the repository. If you browse to the source folder of this example, you can use Maven to create a deployable for this custom UI component. If you use the `mvn package` command, a .jar file will be created in the target directory of this project. Copy this .jar file to the <REPO_HOME>/ repository/components/dropins/ directory and restart the server.

To test if everything is working you'll create a new policy using the custom UI you just created. Log in to the repository and use the Resources > Browse menu option to navigate to the folder where you want to add a policy. Select the options shown in figure 8.6.

If you click Create Content on this page, you'll be shown the screen in figure 8.7, where you can enter your custom policy.

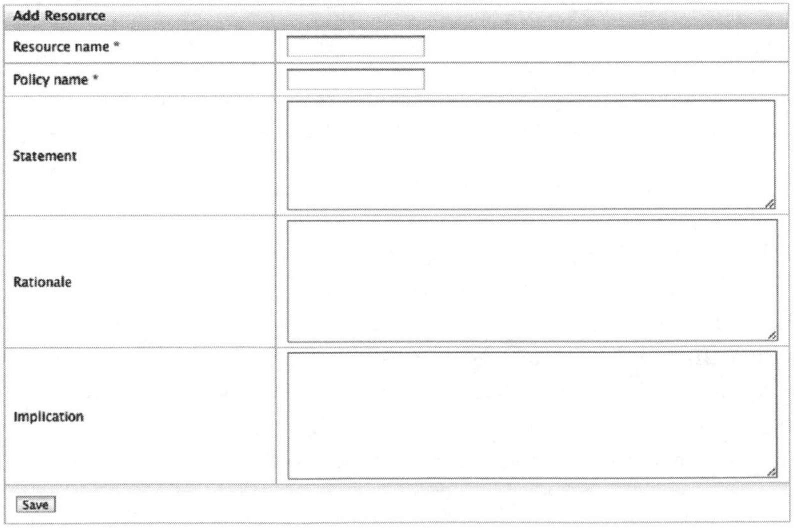

Figure 8.7 Add a custom policy.

If you click Save, this policy will be stored in the XML format you specified earlier.

8.3   *Defining the lifecycle of a policy*

Just as a service has a specific lifecycle, so does a policy. A policy doesn't just exist for all times but is defined based on internal or external factors. For instance, new legislation could cause a new policy to be defined, or a new industry standard that needs to be followed could lead to a new policy. The same goes for the policies that are already in place; a policy should be reviewed periodically to see whether it's still valid. It could be that legislation has been overturned, best practices have been updated, or the requirements from your customers have changed. All this could lead to policies being deprecated and made obsolete. In this section I'll define a basic policy lifecycle and once again show how you can apply this in the WSO2 repository.

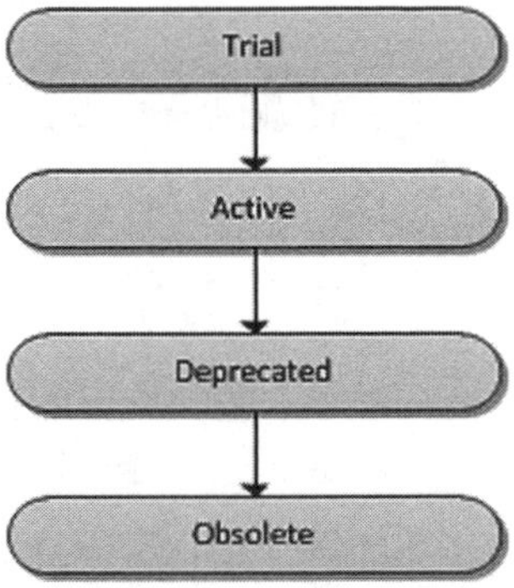

The lifecycle you'll use for your policies is shown in figure 8.8.

Figure 8.8   Basic policy lifecycle

The various states in a policy lifecycle are explained in table 8.3.

Table 8.3   The lifecycle as modeled in WSO2 registry

Lifecycle state	Description
Trial	A policy that's in the trial state has been identified as a potential new policy that can be used within the organization. This policy hasn't been tested completely or isn't completely understood yet. For instance, a policy could be that all the frontend applications that are built must be able to operate on Android and iPhone devices using HTML5. Before this policy can be adopted, there first should be a specific pilot project that checks whether this policy is viable and is fully understood. Once a policy is validated, it can be made active.
Active	When a policy is active, it means that services must follow this policy. Such policies have already been validated and their value has been proven.
Deprecated	A policy is based on legislation, open or industry standards, available technologies, or company guidelines. All these elements are subject to change. When a new government comes into power, certain legislation may change, or when new technologies become available, adopting these might increase productivity. These types of events will mean that some policies are no longer needed. This doesn't mean that you immediately scrap the affected policies. You mark these policies as deprecated, so the users of a specific policy are informed that with a new version of a service, they no longer need to comply with this policy.
Obsolete	After a specific amount of time when a policy has been deprecated, it will be moved to the obsolete state. In this stage no more services should use this policy. If there are still services that are using this policy, action should be taken to change these services.

As you saw in the previous section, when you define a lifecycle in the WSO2 repository, you do this by using states and checklists. A policy is in a specific state, and once all the checklist items are completed, it may move to the next state. You'll now define the policy lifecycle in the WSO2 registry that creates these states, as shown in listing 8.7. This is done in the same manner as you've done for the service lifecycle by defining an XML configuration file in the WSO2 registry.

Listing 8.7 Defining the lifecycle to apply to policies

```xml
<aspect name="PolicyLifecycle"
    class="org.wso2.carbon.governance.registry.extensions.aspects.ChecklistL
    ifeCycle">
  <configuration type="literal">
      <lifecycle>
          <state name="Trial">
              <checkitem>Pilot project executed?</checkitem>
              <checkitem>Policy accepted?</checkitem>
          </state>
          <state name="Active">
              <checkitem>Service owners informed?</checkitem>
              <checkitem>Policy documentation updated?</checkitem>
          </state>
          <state name="Deprecated">
              <checkitem>Services updated?</checkitem>
              <checkitem>Policy documentation updated?</checkitem>
          </state>
          <state name="Obsolete" />
      </lifecycle>
  </configuration>
</aspect>
```

When you enter this and attach it to a resource, this resource will get the lifecycle states, as shown in figure 8.9.

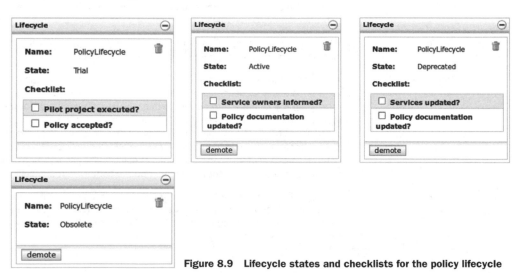

Figure 8.9 Lifecycle states and checklists for the policy lifecycle

To complete this example, let's attach this lifecycle to a policy. In the previous section you created a policy using your own custom pages. If you open this policy in the web application, at the right side of the screen you're shown the Lifecycle component. Open this component and click the Add Lifecycle button. In the drop-down menu that's now shown you can add the lifecycle you just created.

8.4 Discovery of a service and a policy in the service repository

In the previous sections you've seen how to register services and policies and attach lifecycles to them. I haven't yet shown you the various ways you can search for existing services and policies. It's important that before you start looking at creating a new service or policy, you first look in the repository to see if there's a service or policy available that specifies what you want to do or comes close to your requirements. In that case it might be better to modify the existing service or, if possible, change the requirements to fit the existing service.

In this section I'll show you the different ways you can find these services and policies in the repository. First, we'll look at the options provided by the user interface, and then I'll show you some more advanced uses of the WS-* based registry client.

8.4.1 Searching the repository from the web application

Within the WSO2 registry you can search resources from two different starting points. You can search in the content of the resources stored in the repository, or you can search the metadata of these resources.

CONTENT SEARCH

To open the content search, browse to the Search > Content menu option. You'll see the search, as shown in figure 8.10.

If you search using this form, you'll search through the content of the resources in your repository. All the content that's added to the repository is indexed through Solr/Lucene, and using this form you can easily search it. The WSO2 registry is standard, configured to index plain text, XML content, PDF files, Word documents, Excel documents, and PowerPoint documents. A more extensive search can be done by searching on metadata.

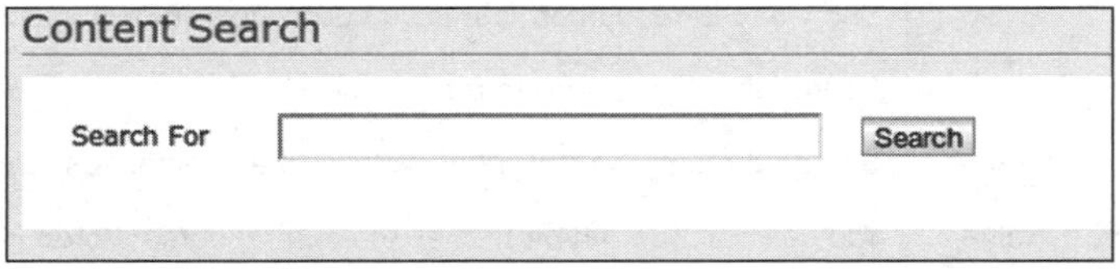

Figure 8.10   Search the content of your resources.

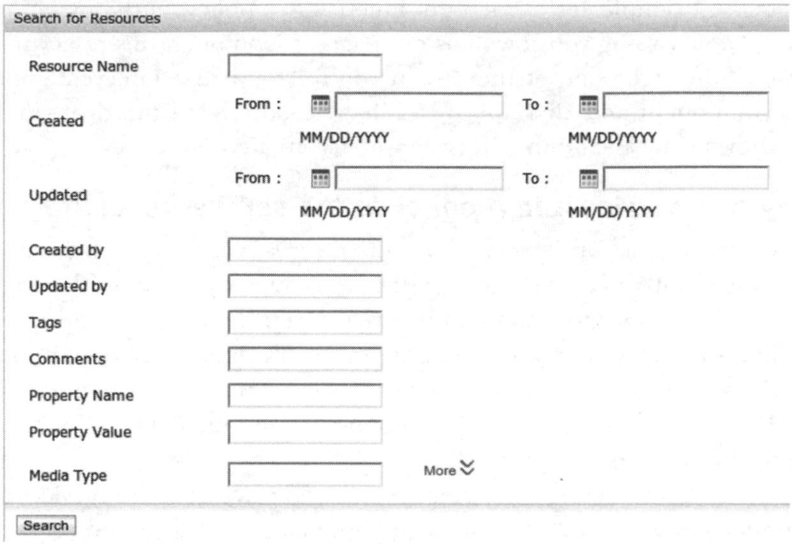

Figure 8.11
Metadata search

METADATA SEARCH

The metadata search (Resources > Search > Metadata) allows you to search on the metadata information stored with your resource. Figure 8.11 shows the various search options that are available.

Table 8.4 explains the various options you can use in searching for resources.

Table 8.4 Search options for metadata search

Search property	Description
Resource Name	If you know the resource name, you can directly search for it.
Created	List all the resources that have been created in a specific time period.
Updated	List all the resources that have been updated in a specific time period.
Created by	Show all the resources that have been created by a specific user.
Updated by	Show all the resources that have been updated by a specific user.
Tags	Search the tags added to a resource.
Comments	Search through the comments added to a specific resource.
Property Name / Property Value	You can add custom properties to each resource stored in the repository. With these two search fields you can search specifically on these properties.
Media Type	Show all the resources that have this specific media type, for instance, application/policy or plain text.

When you execute this query, a list of matching resource locations will be shown, and you can browse directly to the specific resource.

Besides searching from the web interface, the WSO2 repository also provides a Java client you can use to search for resources. You've already seen this client in chapter 2 but only used it to directly access a resource stored in the repository. In the following section I'll show you how you can search the repository from this client.

8.4.2 *Searching the repository from the repository client*

The repository client offers you one method to search the repository. Searching is done using the searchContent method. This operation allows you to search through the content of your repository just like the Search Content operation from the web application. An example of this operation is shown in the following listing.

Listing 8.8 Using the repository client to do a full-text search

```
WSRegistryServiceClient client;
client = initialize();
Collection col = client.searchContent("security");
String[] children = col.getChildren();
```

This query will return all the resources that contain the word "security." If you don't know the exact content you want to search for, you can also use the registry client to browse through the repository and list the content from a specific location. The following listing shows how you can retrieve all the services that are stored within the repository and determine their current lifecycle.

Listing 8.9 Walking through the repository tree to retrieve all the services

```
private final static String LC_PREFIX = "registry.LC.name";

public void listAllLifecycles() {
  List<Resource> paths = getServicePath(registry,            ❶ Get all the
              "/_system/governance/trunk/services");              resources
                                                                   in this path
  for (Resource service : paths) {
     Properties props = service.getProperties();
     for (Object prop : props.keySet()) {
     if (prop instanceof String
           && ((String)prop).equals(LC_PREFIX)) {          ❷ Get the
  lcName = (String) ((LinkedList)props.get(prop)).get(0);       lifecycle
  // lcName contains the lifecycle name                         property
  }
}

private static List<Resource> getServicePath(Registry registry,
  String servicesResource) throws RegistryException {

  List<Resource> result = new ArrayList<Resource>();
  Resource resource = registry.get(servicesResource);

  if (resource instanceof Collection) {
    Object content = resource.getContent();
```

```
for (Object path : (Object[])content) {
  result.addAll(getServicePath(registry,(String)path));
  }
} else if (resource instanceof Resource){
  result.add(resource);
}
  return result;
}
```

❸ **If the content is a
resource, add to list**

To determine in which lifecycle a specific service is, you first need to retrieve all the services **❶** from the repository. You do this by recursively walking through the path where the services are stored (/_system/governance/trunk/services), and if you encounter a resource element **❸** you add it to the result list. Next, you can iterate over these resources and, for instance, determine in which lifecycle a specific resource is **❷**.

In the next section we'll look a bit closer at what you can do with the information that's stored in the repository.

8.5   *Visualizing the information from the registry*

In this section I'll show you how you can integrate information from the WSO2 registry with the Bamos server. You're first going to create a gauge that shows the percentage of your services that are documented, as shown in figure 8.12.

After that I'll also show you how you can create a pie chart that shows the various lifecycle stages your services are in. Figure 8.13 shows the result you're going for.

A small note before you get started: If you run the WSO2 registry and the gadget server at the same time, you'll probably have a problem because both servers want

**Figure 8.12   Gauge showing
the percentage of your
services that are documented**

to bind to the same ports. To solve this problem, open the carbon.xml file in the <GADGET_SERVER_HOME>/repository/conf directory and look for the <Offset> XML element. If you add the value 100 here, all the ports the gadget server uses will be

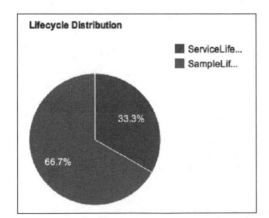

**Figure 8.13   Pie chart that shows the lifecycle
stages your services are in**

increased by 100. This will make sure you can run the gadget server at the same time as the registry.

In the next section we'll start with the gauge that shows the documentation percentage.

8.5.1　*Creating a gauge that shows the documentation percentage*

To get the documentation percentage, you need to take the following steps:

1 *Configure the processor to retrieve information from the repository*—You need to configure a processor that retrieves the information from the repository. Based on this information this processor must create an event that contains information about the various lifecycle stages the services are in.

2 *Add a gauge to the gadget server*—When the events are created, you can add a gauge gadget to the gadget server and configure it to show the information from the Bamos server.

The Bamos server provides a number of standard processors you can use and append to talk to the WSO2 registry. The following listing shows the configuration for the `DocumentationOverviewProcessor`.

Listing 8.10　Configuring the `DocumentationOverviewProcessor`

```
<bean id="DocumentationPoller"
    class="...processors.event.wso2.DocumentationOverviewProcessor">
        <property name="ttl" value="60"/>
        <property name="delay" value="5"/>
        <property name="initialDelay" value="5"/>
</bean>
```

For this processor you configure three properties. The `ttl` defines how long your events will be stored in the database, the `delay` value defines the interval (in seconds) that the repository should be queried, and the `initialDelay` determines how long this processor waits before it polls for the first time. I won't show you the code of this processor because it looks a lot like the code from listing 8.9. What this processor does is this:

1 Retrieve all the services from the repository (see listing 8.9).
2 Retrieve all the associations from each service.
3 Iterate over all the associations; if it finds an association with the name "Documentation," it means this service is documented (see chapter 4 for more information on this).
4 Calculate the percentage of services that have a documentation association.
5 Create and send an event containing this information.

The event that this processor creates looks like this:

```
{"event": {
    "timestamp": "1328179042700",
    "eventclass": "documentation",
    "documentationPercentage": "33.333336",
```

```
      "service": "services",
      "server": "wso2"
}}
```

Now all you need to do is add a gauge to the gadget server and configure it to display the information from this event. Open the gadget server, log in, and add the gauge gadget from URL http://localhost:9003/web/gadget/bamos-gauge.xml. Click the Settings icon for the gadget (in the upper-right corner) and configure the properties shown in table 8.5.

Table 8.5   Properties to set on the gauge gadget to show the documentation percentage

Property	Description
JSON URL	You want to get a single event with the `eventclass documentation`. `http://localhost:9003/services/event/list?class=documentation&count=1&reverse=true`
Lower Limit Gauge	You have a percentage you want to show; the lower limit should be set to 0.
Upper Limit Gauge	The upper limit should be set to 100.
Query Interval	This determines how often the gauge is updated. For this example set it to 1000, which will update the gauge every second.
Property Name	You want to show the value from the `documentationPercentage` property.
Label	The label to be shown in the gauge. In this case set it to `Doc: %`.

If you've set these properties, a gauge will be shown somewhat like the one in figure 8.14.

Next, you'll configure a gadget that shows an overview of the various lifecycles that services are in.

8.5.2   Creating a pie chart that shows the lifecycle stages

To create a pie chart with this information, you need to take the same steps as you did in the previous section. You'll configure a processor that gathers the information and a gadget that shows this information.

For this specific use case the Bamos server also provides a processor, the `LifeCycleOverviewProcessor`, out of the box that you can use. The configuration for this processor is shown in the following listing.

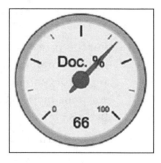

Figure 8.14   Gauge showing that two-thirds of your services have been documented

Listing 8.11   Configuring the `LifeCycleOverviewProcessor`

```
<bean id="LifeCyclePoller"
    class="...processors.event.wso2.LifeCycleOverviewProcessor">
        <property name="ttl" value="60"/>
```

```
        <property name="delay" value="5"/>
        <property name="initialDelay" value="5"/>
</bean>
```

These three properties are the same as you saw in listing 8.10 and can be used to configure the polling frequency of this processor and set how long the events will be stored in the datastore. This processor takes the following steps every time it's run:

1 Retrieve all the services from the repository (see listing 8.9).
2 Get all the properties from each resource.
3 From the properties get the property that identifies the lifecycle name and the stage of the lifecycle the service is in.
4 Count the number of services that are in a specific lifecycle stage.
5 Create and send an event that shows the aggregated count.

The event that this processor creates looks like this:

```
{"event": {
  "timestamp": "1328181657762",
  "eventclass": "lifecycle",
  "lc_ServiceLifeCycle.Development": "1",
  "lc_SampleLifeCycle.Development": "2",
  "service": "services",
  "server": "wso2"
}}
```

You can see in this event that the services are currently in two different stages. You have two services that are in the Development stage of the ServiceLifeCycle lifecycle and one service that's in the Development stage of the SampleLifeCycle lifecycle.

To show this in the gadget server, add the http://localhost:9003/web/gadget/bamos-piechart.xml gadget and open the settings for this gadget. Configure the settings from table 8.6.

Table 8.6 Properties to set on the gauge gadget to show the documentation percentage

Property	Description
JSON URL	You want to get a single event with the eventclass lifecycle: http://localhost:9003/services/event/list?class=lifecycle&reverse=true&count=1.
Query Interval	This determines how often the gauge is updated. For your example set it to 1000, which will update the gauge every second.
Prefix	You want to show all the values that start with the prefix lc_.
Hover Label	The label to be shown when you hover over the pie chart.

And with these settings a pie chart will be shown (figure 8.15).

In this section I showed you how you can integrate the Bamos server with the WSO2 registry to show information about objects registered in the repository. I explained how to do this for the service objects. This same principle can be applied to other registered objects such as policies, WSDLs, XSDs, and other content you want to store. If you want to create your own custom processors, it's a good idea to look at the sources of the `LifeCycleOverview-Processor` and the `Documentation-OverviewProcessor`. They can serve as a good starting point for creating your own processors that talk to the WSO2 registry.

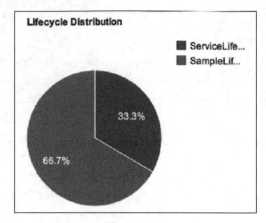

Figure 8.15   Pie chart gadget that shows the various lifecycle stages used by the services

8.6   Summary

In this chapter I've shown you the following:

- The importance of having a good service lifecycle
- A default configuration for a service lifecycle
- How to define a service lifecycle in the WSO2 registry
- How to extend the basic functionality of the WSO2 registry by using a custom UI element
- The various stages that make up a policy lifecycle
- How to define a policy lifecycle in the WSO2 registry
- How you can use the various search options available in the WSO2 registry to locate resources
- That you can use the registry client to browse through the repository from code and retrieve information about the stored objects
- The steps you need to take to show information from the registry as a gadget in the gadget server

Integrating SOA governance tools with existing tools and technologies

This chapter covers

- Integrating the governance tools with enterprise tools such as Mule, Activiti, and Spring
- Connecting to the registry and to Bamos using C#, Python, and Ruby
- Connecting Bamos to the open source monitoring tool Nagios

In the previous chapters we looked at how you can apply design-time governance and set up a runtime governance-monitoring environment. In this chapter I'll show you how to use the tools and environments we've discussed in this book to integrate with various other tools and servers.

We'll start by looking at how to integrate CXF, Spring, the Mule ESB, and the Nagios monitoring tool with the WSO2 governance repository and the Bamos server. Even though there are many other tools available, this set of tools should give you a good overview of how to integrate enterprise tools and frameworks. After that we'll look at how you can integrate a BPM engine, Activiti in this case, with these tools. Finally, I'll show you how to access the Bamos server and the WSO2 repository from some other languages: C#, Ruby, and Python.

9.1   Enterprise integration

In this first section we'll look a bit closer at how you can integrate the SOA governance tools you've seen so far with existing tools and technologies. In the next couple of sections you'll learn how to do the following:

- Provision a WSDL from the SOA governance repository
- Store and retrieve configuration files in the repository
- Integrate Mule with the Bamos event server
- Start Mule from a context stored in the repository
- Send events to Nagios from the Bamos event server

First, we'll look at how you can configure CXF to work with the SOA governance repository.

9.1.1   Provisioning a WSDL from the repository

In the previous chapters I've shown you how you can store WSDLs in the repository. A WSDL in a repository can easily be documented, found, versioned, and referenced by other artifacts. If you create a service that implements the contract defined by this WSDL, it's common practice to allow your consumers to access the WSDL for this service. Usually this is done by appending ?wsdl to the location of the service. For instance, if you have a service that can be accessed at http://localhost:9001/services/accountService, the WSDL for this service should be made available to your consumers at http://localhost:9001/services/accountService?wsdl. Normally, this WSDL will be deployed with your application, but it would be better if you could show the WSDL as it's stored in the repository. In that case the consumer will always be shown the latest version with the most up-to-date documentation. This would also mean that the WSDL used by the developers, for instance for code generation, should also be retrieved from the repository. In this section I'll show you how you can do this for CXF. I've chosen CXF because it's used often in open source projects and is also the web service library used by Jboss, as well as in the Mule and ServiceMix ESBs. The practices shown in this example could also easily be applied to other web service frameworks. For instance, Axis2 provides a WSDLSupplier interface for this that you can implement to tell Axis2 where to provision the WSDL description from.

SETTING UP WSDL IN THE REPOSITORY

For this example you need a WSDL in the repository. This is the WSDL you'll show when the consumer requests this by appending ?wsdl to the URL. In chapter 2 you created the AccountService, for which you defined a WSDL and an XSD. You'll now add these to the repository by taking the following steps:

- Create a zip file containing the WSDL and the XSD. You can find this zip file in the resources/contract directory of the chapter9-cxf project.
- Upload this zip file to the repository. This will create all the various resources in the correct location in the repository.

Figure 9.1   Upload the zip file containing the WSDL and schema.

To upload this zip file, log in to the repository and go to the Metadata > Add > WSDL menu option. This will show you the screen shown in figure 9.1. Click the Choose File button and browse to the source folder containing the service.zip file. After you've selected the file, click the Add button, which will add the WSDL and XSD to the repository.

Now go the Metadata > List > WSDLs menu option, and you should see the WSDL, as shown in figure 9.2.

Figure 9.2   The uploaded WSDL

Now that you have a WSDL in the repository that you can use, the next step is to look at how to modify CXF to show this WSDL instead of trying to retrieve one from the file-system or generating one from the Java interface.

EXPANDING CXF TO RETRIEVE A WSDL FROM THE REPOSITORY

CXF uses a specific class to handle ?wsdl requests. This class is called the WSDLQuery-Handler. Whenever the ?wsdl URL is requested, the writeResponse method of this class is called. In this method CXF checks whether a separate WSDL file was specified that needs to be shown or whether it should generate a WSDL from the Java interface. If you want to provide a WSDL from the repository, you need to extend this class and override the writeResponse method. In your implementation of this method, you'll use the name and the namespace of the service to determine where in the repository you can find the WSDL. After you know the location, you'll make an HTTP GET call to retrieve the WSDL and show it to the user. The code for this is shown in the following listing.

Listing 9.1   Extending the WSDL handler for CXF

```
public class MyWSDLQueryHandler extends WSDLQueryHandler {        Base location ❶
                                                                  of WSDLs

    private String baseLocation = "http://.../_system/governance/wsdls/";   ◁──┘
```

```
@override
public void writeResponse(String baseUri, String ctxUri,          ❷ Method
        EndpointInfo endpointInfo, OutputStream os) {                 to override
  QName qname = endpointInfo.getName();
  String qnameNs = qname.getNamespaceURI();

  String locationToQuery = baseLocation + qnameNs.replace('.', '/') +
      ctxUri + ".wsdl";                                         ❸ Create resource
                                                                   location
  InputStream is = getWSDL(locationToQuery);

    try {
      IOUtils.copy(is, os);                                     ❹ Get the WSDL
    } catch (IOException e) {
      // handle exception
    }
  }

  @Resource
  public void setQueryHandlerRegistry(QueryHandlerRegistry qhr) {
      qhr.registerHandler(this, 0);
  }                                                             Register this
                                                                handler in the
  private InputStream getWSDL(String location) {               ❺ registry
   HttpClient client = new HttpClient();
   client.getState().setCredentials(
       new AuthScope(null, -1, null),
       new UsernamePasswordCredentials("admin", "admin")
       );

   GetMethod method = new GetMethod(location);
   method.setDoAuthentication(true);
   return method.getResponseBodyAsStream();
  }
}
```

In this listing you've overridden the writeResponse method. In your implementation you determine ❸ the location of the WSDL using the baseLocation ❶ and information from the service that gets passed into this method ❷. You use the qnameNs for this and replace the . with /. You need to do this because the WSO2 repository stores WSDL files based on their namespace.

With this location you make an HTTP GET call ❹ and return the result as an InputStream. With this code, if a WSDL is requested, it's retrieved from the repository. The final step is tell CXF to use this class to handle the ?wsdl request ❺. Now run the repository and the chapter9-cxf example, and open http://localhost:9001/account Service?wsdl in your browser. You'll now be shown the WSDL from the repository.

9.1.2 *Provisioning the configuration from the repository*

When developing enterprise applications, you aren't finished when you've defined your service. You need to configure database access, integration with various other systems, and automatic jobs. All these parts have different properties that need to be defined correctly for a specific environment and are usually stored in the filesystem or in a directory service. Because you already have a repository where you store your contracts and schemas, why not store the configuration properties for a specific environment in this same repository? This will give you the advantages of using a repository and allow you to easily access all the properties from a centralized location. Note that you should take special care when you store passwords in property files. If you store property files that contain passwords in the repository, anyone who can access that part of the repository can see the passwords. If you do this, you have to make sure that the correct authentication and authorization have been set up in the repository, so that no unauthorized person can see the passwords or other sensitive information.

You'll first create a simple property file in the repository, and then I'll show you how to access this file from Spring. If you use a different framework or technology, you should be able to apply pretty much the same concepts. You'll store the following set of properties:

```
prop1=hallo
prop2=world
prop3=today
```

The first thing you do in the repository is create a collection where you'll store the configuration files. To do this, open the Resources > Browse menu item and navigate to the /_system/

Figure 9.3   Click Add Collection to create a new folder.

governance collection. If you click this link you'll be shown the details of this collection. From here you can add a new collection. Click the Add Collection button, as shown in figure 9.3.

In the form that opens enter `properties` as the new name for the collection and click Add. This will create the new collection with the name properties and open this collection. In this screen click the Add Resource button, and the screen in figure 9.4 will be shown.

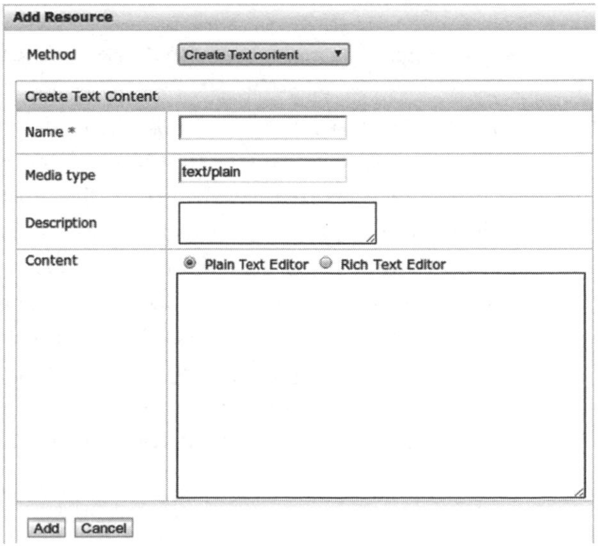

**Figure 9.4
Add a resource to the collection.**

In the Add Resource screen select Create Text Content for the Method field. This way you can add content directly through the repository, without having to create a separate text file first. Enter `example-properties.txt` as the name of the resource, and copy the three properties shown at the beginning of this section into the content area. Click Add and you'll have a set of properties stored in the repository. Now you'll extend Spring so that you can use these properties in your configuration files. For this you'll create a factory bean that returns a set of properties to Spring's default `PropertyPlaceHolderConfigurer`.

The following listing shows how to configure Spring to use a factory bean to provide properties to the `PropertyPlaceHolderConfigurer`.

Listing 9.2 Spring configuration

```
<bean id="propertyConfigurer"
    class="org...config.PropertyPlaceholderConfigurer">
  <property name="ignoreUnresolvablePlaceholders" value="true"/>
<property name="propertiesArray">
  <list>
    <bean factory-bean="propertiesHolder"           1  Call method
        factory-method="asProperties" />               of factory
  </list>
</property>
</bean>
                                                    2  Factory that
                                                       returns properties
                                                       from repository
<bean id="propertiesHolder" class="PropertiesHolder" >  ◁
  <property name="location"
          value="http://10.0.0.9:9763/registry/resource/_system/governance
                 /properties/example-properties.txt"/>
  <property name="username" value="admin"/>
  <property name="password" value="admin"/>
</bean>
                                                    3  Pojo to test with
<bean id="pojo" class="SimplePojo">                 ◁
  <property name="prop1" value="${prop1}" />
</bean>
```

In this configuration you define three beans. The first one is a standard `Property-PlaceholderConfigurer` that Spring uses to replace placeholders (see the `pojo` bean) with the values from a properties file. On this bean you configure a factory ❶ to provide a set of properties. This factory ❷ is a custom class, which I'll explain in a bit, that retrieves the properties from the repository. On this factory bean you configure the location of your properties file and the credentials that you'll use to connect to the repository. Finally in this configuration you define a simple bean ❸ with which to test whether the property gets correctly replaced.

In the `PropertiesHolder` class you make an HTTP call to the repository, retrieve the properties file, and return it as a Java `Properties` object. This is shown in the next listing.

Listing 9.3 PropertiesHolder configuration

```
public class PropertiesHolder {

  private String location;
  private String username;
  private String password;

  public Properties asProperties() {
    HttpClient client = new HttpClient();

    client.getState().setCredentials(                          ❶  Set the
            new AuthScope(null, -1, null),                         authentication
            new UsernamePasswordCredentials(username, password)    for the HTTP call
            );

    GetMethod method = new GetMethod(location);
    method.setDoAuthentication(true);

    Properties prop = new Properties();
    try {
      InputStream stream =null;                                 ❷  Get the response as
      client.executeMethod(method);                                an InputStream
      stream = method.getResponseBodyAsStream();
      prop.load(stream);                                           Fill the properties
                                                                ❸  from the
    } catch (Exception e) {
      // error while loading remote properties
      throw new IllegalArgumentException("Could not load properties from:"
                                          + location,e);
    }
      return prop;  |                                             Return the retrieved
  }                                                           ❹  properties
}
```

In listing 9.3 you use `HttpClient` to make an authenticated ❶ GET call to the URL specified in the configuration in listing 9.2. The result from this call is retrieved as an `Input-Stream` ❷ and is then used to fill the `Properties` object ❸. This object is returned ❹ and can be used by Spring to replace placeholders in its configuration files.

In this example you've stored a property file to be used by Spring. You can use the repository to store all different kinds of configuration files besides standard properties files and use this same mechanism to retrieve them.

9.1.3 Sending events from Mule

Mule is an open source ESB that you can use to easily integrate various systems. It provides a large list of connectors with which you can bridge various protocols and transports. In this section we'll look at how you can integrate Mule with the Bamos tools. I'll show you how to send events from Mule that can then be processed by the Bamos server. We won't dive too deeply into the specifics of Mule because that's out of scope for this book. If you want to know more, check out Manning's *Mule in Action* or *Open Source ESBs in Action*.

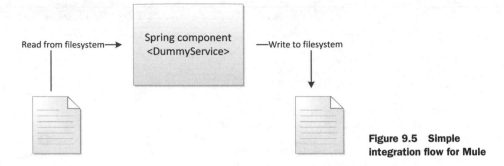

Figure 9.5   Simple integration flow for Mule

There are many different ways you can configure Mule. In this example you'll use flow-based configuration. With flow-based configuration you define the processing steps for each message in a simple XML format. For this example you'll use a configuration that reads a file from a specific directory, passes the content on to a custom component, and finally stores the file into a different directory. This flow is shown in figure 9.5.

To accomplish this you'll use the Mule flow configuration shown in the next listing.

Listing 9.4   Mule configuration to test with

```
<flow name="SimpleFlow">
    <file:inbound-endpoint address="file://target/in"                ❶ Read from
                           pollingFrequency="1000" />                    directory
    <custom-transformer class="chapter9.mule.AddTimestamp"/>
    <pooled-component>                                                ❸ Dummy
      <spring-object bean="dummyService"/>                               service
  </pooled-component>
  <file:outbound-endpoint address="file://target/out" />            ❹ Write to
</flow>                                                                 directory
```

❷ Custom transformer

Listing 9.4 creates a simple flow. This flow will read all the files put into the target/in directory ❶. It will then send these files to the custom transformer you defined ❷, which will add the current timestamp as a message property (see listing 9.5). In the next step a simple dummy service processes the message ❸ before it's passed to the final component, which writes the message to the target/out directory ❹. You can start this configuration from the sources in the chapter9-mule project.

You'll send an event that shows how long the dummyService took to process the message. To do this you'll do the following:

1   *Get the time when the message was received*—You need to know the time when the event was received by the component. In this case you do this in a custom transformer. This transformer sets a message property with the current time.

2   *Calculate the total processing time*—Once the dummyService is done processing, you calculate the time it took for this service to process the message. You do this by taking the timestamp that was set by the transformer and subtracting this from the current time.

3 *Send the event to the Bamos server*—To send the event to the Bamos server, use the Bamos client introduced in chapter 7. With this client you can send events in the format the Bamos server expects.

You use a transformer to set the time when the event was received. Listing 9.4 showed how to configure this in the flow. In the following listing you can see the implementation of this transformer.

Listing 9.5 `AddTimestamp` transformer

```
public class AddTimestamp extends AbstractTransformer {

  @Override
  public MuleEvent process(MuleEvent event) throws MuleException {
    event.getMessage().setProperty("START_TIME",                    ❶ Set the
        System.currentTimeMillis(), PropertyScope.INVOCATION);         current time
    return super.process(event);                                      as property
  }

  @Override
  protected Object doTransform(Object src, String enc)            ❷ Return the
      throws TransformerException {                                 original
    return src;                                                      content
  }
}
```

In listing 9.5 you get the message and set a custom property ❶. In the `doTransform` method ❷ you don't do anything; you just return the original message. With this configuration, for each message that's received by the dummy service, this `START_TIME` property is set. You can now use this property to calculate the processing time after the service is done processing. For this you could have created another transformer from which to send the event, but for this example you use Mule's notification mechanism. This allows you to configure which type of notifications you want to receive and how you want to process these notifications. For this example you'll listen to `COMPONENT-MESSAGE` notifications. These notifications are sent by Mule before and after a component processes a message. This configuration is shown in the next listing.

Listing 9.6 Notification configuration for Mule

```
<spring:beans>                                               ❶ To send events with
  <spring:bean name="bamosClient" class="org.bamos.client.BamosClient">
    <spring:property name="url"
                value="http://localhost:9003/services/event"/>
  </spring:bean>

  <spring:bean name="muleEventSender"                        ❷ Notification
            class="chapter9.mule.MuleEventSender" >            listener
    <spring:property name="client" ref="bamosClient"/>
  </spring:bean>
</spring:beans>
```

```
<notifications>
  <notification event="COMPONENT-MESSAGE" />
  <notification-listener ref="muleEventSender" />
</notifications>
```
❸ **Notification configuration**

You configure the notification in the Mule configuration ❸ so that the custom `mule-EventSender` will receive all the `COMPONENT-MESSAGE` notifications. This `muleEvent-Sender` is a simple Java class ❷ that gets a Bamos client injected ❶ with which it can send events. The code for the `muleEventSender` is shown in the next listing.

Listing 9.7   Sending events from Mule when a notification is received

```
public class MuleEventSender implements
        ComponentMessageNotificationListener<ComponentMessageNotification> {

    private BamosClient client;

    public void onNotification(
            ComponentMessageNotification compNotification) {
        if (compNotification.getAction() ==
            ComponentMessageNotification.COMPONENT_POST_INVOKE) {
            Object startTime =
                compNotification.getSource().getProperty("START_TIME",
                    PropertyScope.INVOCATION);
            if (startTime != null) {
                long processingTime = System.currentTimeMillis() -
                    ((Long)startTime).longValue();
                Map<String,Object> userData = new HashMap<String, Object>();
                userData.put("Processing_time", processingTime);
                client.sendEvent(compNotification.getServerId(),
                    compNotification.getServiceName(), "MULE_EVENT",
                    System.currentTimeMillis(), userData);
            }
        }
    }
}
```
❶ **Check the type of notification**

Determine processing time ❷

❸ **Send an event**

In this custom notification listener you first check ❶ the type of notification you've received. You're only interested in notifications that occur after the service has processed the message. Next, you calculate the processing time ❷ and use the Bamos client to send an event ❸. If the Bamos server is running, an event that looks something like this will be received:

```
{
"event":{
  "Processing_time":299,
  "timestamp":"1315053621563",
  "eventclass":"MULE_EVENT",
  "service":"SimpleFlow",
  "server":"jos-ubuntu"
  }
}
```

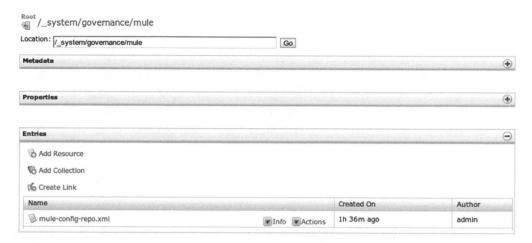

Figure 9.6 Mule config added to the repository

In this example you loaded the Mule configuration from the filesystem. In the next section I'll show you how to load the configuration from the repository, just as you did for the Spring properties and the WSDLs for CXF.

9.1.4 Loading the Mule configuration from the repository

When you run Mule in a distributed environment where you have multiple Mule instances running using the same configuration, it can be difficult to keep the various configurations of these instances consistent. In this section I'll show you how to store the Mule configuration in the repository and use that configuration to start Mule. In section 9.1.2 I showed you how to add properties files to the repository. Create a new collection named mule and add a resource with the name mule-config-repo.xml, just as you did in section 9.1.2. This is shown in figure 9.6.

Mule uses a configuration builder to load its configuration files. To load these configuration files from the repository, you need to extend Mule's SpringXmlConfigurationBuilder and override the loadConfigResources method. This is shown in the following listing.

Listing 9.8 LoadConfigResources builder that runs Mule with configuration from repo

```
@Override
protected ConfigResource[] loadConfigResources(String[] configs)
                                throws ConfigurationException {
  try {
    configResources = new ConfigResource[configs.length];
    for (int i = 0; i < configs.length; i++) {                    ❶ Create config
      configResources[i] = new ConfigResource(configs[i],             resource
                                getResource(configs[i]));         Fill with
    }                                                             config from
                                                                ❷ repository
    return configResources;
```

```
  } catch (IOException e) {
    throw new ConfigurationException(e);
  }
}
```

With this code fragment you create a `ConfigResource` based on the supplied URLs ❶. The normal behavior of this method is that the supplied URLs are retrieved from the filesystem or from the classpath. In this case you call the `getResource(configs[i])` ❷ method, which retrieves them from the repository. I won't show you the code for this method because it's almost the same as in listing 9.3; you can also look at the source code for the chapter9-mule project.

The final step is to tell Mule to use this new configuration builder. The code for this is shown in the next listing.

Listing 9.9   Launcher for configuration from repo

```
public class MuleLauncherFromRepo {

private static String config =
➥ "http://10.0.0.9:9763/registry/resource/_system/governance/mule/
➥ mule-config-repo.xml";

  public static void main(String[] args) throws Exception {
    DefaultMuleContextFactory muleContextFactory = new
        DefaultMuleContextFactory();
    RepoSpringConfigurationBuilder configBuilder = new
        RepoSpringConfigurationBuilder(config);
    MuleContext muleContext =
        muleContextFactory.createMuleContext(configBuilder);
    muleContext.start();
  }
}
```

If you run this code, Mule will start up and load its configuration from the repository. The last enterprise tool we'll look at is Nagios.

9.1.5   *Sending events to Nagios from the Bamos event server*

Nagios (http://www.nagios.org) is a monitoring tool that can be used to monitor IT infrastructure. It provides a simple dashboard that shows the state of various servers, services, applications, and other resources. If a problem is detected in one of the monitored solutions, Nagios can send an email or an SMS to the configured contact so downtime can be reduced. An example of what Nagios looks like is shown in figure 9.7.

Installing and configuring Nagios is different for each environment, so we won't dive into the details for that. To run this example make sure you have a Nagios instance running with the NSCA add-on on your local machine.

In this section I'll show how to send the events you processed in the Bamos server to Nagios, so that Nagios will pick them up and show them in its services overview. For this example we'll expand on an example from chapter 7. In chapter 7 you saw how to use an Esper-based processor to determine the average processing time of an event. In

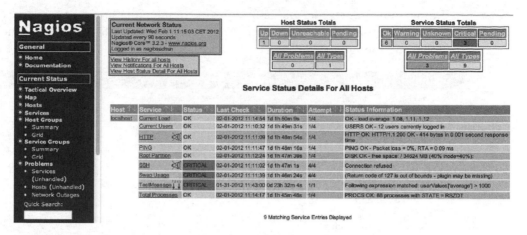

Figure 9.7   Nagios monitoring a set of services on localhost

this example I'll show you to receive notifications in Nagios when the average processing time passes a specific level.

To accomplish this take the following steps:

1   *Set up Nagios to support NSCA and your services*—NSCA is an add-on for Nagios that allows you to send events into Nagios from remote systems. You'll use this to send an event from the Bamos server to Nagios when a specific condition occurs. You also need to configure a service object inside Nagios that can be shown on the Nagios overview page.

2   *Configure a processor to check for conditions*—The normal behavior of the Bamos processors is to store an event in the datastore. For this example you'll add an additional processor that will send an event to Nagios.

3   *Test the configuration*—Finally, you'll send a couple of events to the Bamos server to see whether Nagios picks up the events and shows them in its overview.

CONFIGURING NSCA AND NAGIOS

The first thing to do is make sure that NSCA is configured correctly on your system. Open your nsca.cfg file and set the following values:

```
server_port=5667
password=secret
decryption_method=1
```

With these values you tell NSCA to use XOR (which is decryption method 1) as its decryption method and set the password to `secret`. You'll need to use the same values when you send a message from the Bamos server, as you'll see later in this section. With NSCA configured, the next thing to do is configure Nagios so that it will show a service object that represents the condition you're monitoring. For this you'll alter the templates.cfg, localhost.cfg, and commands.cfg files that can be found in the Nagios configuration directory.

In the templates.cfg file you define a set of common parameters for service definitions. You'll create a new template that can be used for the NSCA checks, as shown in the following listing.

Listing 9.10   Defining a service in the templates.cfg file

```
define service{
    use generic-service
    name passive_service                              ◁──┐  The name of
    active_checks_enabled 0                            ❶ this template
    passive_checks_enabled 1
    flap_detection_enabled 0
    register 0 # This is a template, not a real service
    is_volatile 0
    check_period 24x7
    max_check_attempts 1
    normal_check_interval 5
    retry_check_interval 1
    check_freshness 0
    contact_groups admins
    check_command check_dummy!0                        ◁──┐  The command this
    notification_interval 120                          ❷ template executes
    notification_period 24x7
    notification_options w,u,c,r
    stalking_options w,c,u
}
```

For more information about these properties see the Nagios documentation. The information that's important for you is the name ❶ of this service and the command it will execute ❷. Because this is just a template, you still need to configure the real service that will show in the Nagios overview. You do this in the localhost.cfg file, as shown in the following listing.

Listing 9.11   Defining a service in the localhost.cfg file

```
define service{
            use passive_service                   ◁─┐  ❶ Name of template
            service_description ProcessingTime     ◁──── ❷ Service name
            host_name localhost                    ◁─┐
}                                                     ❸ Server name
```

In listing 9.11 you define the service that will show up in the Nagios web application. You use the template ❶ you defined earlier and set the name of the service ❷ and the server ❸ this service is running on. You'll use these same values later on in your processors.

You still need to configure one more item in Nagios. Listing 9.10 referenced a check_command. You'll configure this command in the commands.cfg file, as shown in the next listing.

Listing 9.12 Defining the dummy command in commands.cfg

```
define command {
        command_name check_dummy
        command_line $USER1$/check_dummy $ARG1$
}
```

This command is defined as a dummy command, because you don't want Nagios to actively check this service. You'll let Nagios know when something interesting happens. After these configuration changes, restart Nagios. You should now see your new service listed, as shown in figure 9.8.

CONFIGURING THE PROCESSOR THAT SENDS INFORMATION TO NAGIOS

With Nagios configured you can look into configuring the Bamos server. For the Bamos server you'll configure two processors. The first one is the Esper-based processor from chapter 7 that shows the average processing time. The configuration for this processor is shown in the next listing.

Listing 9.13 Esper-based processor to calculate average processing time

```
<bean id="espereventprocessorAverageNagios"
  class="org.bamos.core.processors.event.esper.EsperEventProcessor">
  <property name="expression" value="serverName == 'localhost'"/>
  <property name="esperStatement" value="
      select avg(cast(userValues('processingTime'),double)) as average
                                  , serverName
                                  , serviceName from Event"/>     ❶ Process
  <property name="userClass" value="averageForNagios"/>              result
  <property name="storeDirectly" value="false"/>               ◁     completely
  <property name="ttl" value="30"/>                          ◁── Time this event
</bean>                                                        ❷ may live
```

This processor will process all the events that have the property `serverName` set to `localhost`. As you saw in chapter 7, you use the `esperStatement` to calculate the average processing time. This statement is modified a bit to also return the `serverName` and the `serviceName` of the original event. You do this so that you can use those values in the event you send to Nagios. In listing 9.13 you can see two options you haven't seen before. You set `storeDirectly` to `false` ❶. This tells the Bamos server to process the event this processor generates as if it was a new event. This means that for this new event you'll once again check to see if any of the processors you've defined match. You also

Host	Service	Status	Last Check	Duration	Attempt	Status Information
localhost	Current Load	OK	02-01-2012 11:19:54	1d 2h 48m 2s	1/4	OK - load average: 1.03, 1.13, 1.12
	Current Users	OK	02-01-2012 11:20:32	1d 2h 47m 24s	1/4	USERS OK - 12 users currently logged in
	HTTP	OK	02-01-2012 11:21:09	1d 2h 46m 47s	1/4	HTTP OK: HTTP/1.1 200 OK - 414 bytes in 0.001 second response time
	PING	OK	02-01-2012 11:21:47	1d 2h 46m 9s	1/4	PING OK - Packet loss = 0%, RTA = 0.09 ms
	ProcessingTime	PENDING	N/A	0d 0h 0m 23s+	1/1	Service is not scheduled to be checked...
	Root Partition	OK	02-01-2012 11:22:24	1d 2h 45m 32s	1/4	DISK OK - free space: / 34623 MB (40% inode=40%):
	Total Processes	OK	02-01-2012 11:19:17	1d 2h 43m 39s	1/4	PROCS OK 91 processes with STATE = RSZDT

Figure 9.8 Nagios service overview with your new custom NSCA service

set the `ttl` property ❷. With this property you define how long the event should be kept in the datastore. Because you use this event only for Nagios, there's no need to keep it in your datastore. With this configuration this event is removed after 30 seconds.

The second processor you define, shown in the following listing, processes the events the processor in listing 9.13 creates.

Listing 9.14 Processor that sends events to Nagios

```xml
<bean id="sendToNagiosProcessor"
    class="org.bamos.core.processors.event.common.SendToNagiosEventProcessor">
  <property name="expression"
    value="eventClass == 'averageForNagios'"/>

  <property name="errorExpression"
    value="userValues['average'] > 1000"/>
  <property name="warningExpression"
    value="UserValues['average'] &gt; 500"/>
  <property name="okExpression"
    value="UserValues['average'] &lt;= 500"/>

  <property name="nagiosHostName"
    value="userValues['serverName']"/>
  <property name="nagiosServiceName"
    value="userValues['serviceName']"/>

  <property name="nscaHost" value="localhost"/>
  <property name="nscaPort" value="5667"/>
  <property name="nscaPassword" value="secret"/>

</bean>
```

Process the events with this ❶ **eventClass**

❷ **What type of message to send**

❸ **Set values in event to Nagios**

❹ **Configures how to send**

Listing 9.14 shows the configuration of the processor that sends events to Nagios. You first define ❶ which type of events you want to process. This is the same class you set in listing 9.13. Next you define three different expressions ❷ that are executed on the received event. If the `errorExpression` matches, an error message is sent to Nagios; if the `warningExpression` matches, a warning message is sent, and if the `okExpression` matches, an OK message is sent. Nagios needs to know the server and service that the event belongs to. You use the expressions shown in ❸ to set these with information from the original event. Finally, you tell this processor where to send the message ❹. These values should match the settings you made in the nsca.cfg file in the beginning of this example.

TESTING THE CONFIGURATION

To test this configuration add the bamos-processors-nagios-integration.xml file from the chapter 9 sources to the /src/main/resources directory of the Bamos server and restart the server. You can use soapUI to send a message to the Bamos server and quickly test the configuration. This event should look something like this:

```
{"event":
    {"timestamp":"1310294128456",
        "service":"ProcessingTime",
```

```
        "processingTime":1300,
        "eventclass":"ev",
        "server":"localhost"
    }
}
```

This event will be first processed by the Esper-based processor and after that by the Nagios processor. Based on the result from this check, an event will be sent to Nagios. In this case, if this is the first event, a message will be sent to Nagios that results in the following Critical warning for your custom service, as shown in figure 9.9.

Host	Service	Status	Last Check	Duration	Attempt	Status Information
localhost	Current Load	OK	02-01-2012 13:29:54	1d 4h 7m 20s	1/4	OK - load average: 1.23, 1.20, 1.10
	Current Users	OK	02-01-2012 13:30:44	1d 4h 6m 42s	1/4	USERS OK - 12 users currently logged in
	HTTP	OK	02-01-2012 13:31:34	1d 4h 6m 5s	1/4	HTTP OK: HTTP/1.1 200 OK - 414 bytes in 0.002 second response time
	PING	OK	02-01-2012 13:22:17	1d 4h 5m 27s	1/4	PING OK - Packet loss = 0%, RTA = 0.08 ms
	ProcessingTime	CRITICAL	02-01-2012 13:32:05	0d 0h 0m 9s	1/1	Following expression matched: userValues['processingTime'] > 1000
	Root Partition	OK	02-01-2012 13:21:17	1d 4h 4m 50s	1/4	DISK OK - free space: / 34635 MB (40% inode=40%):
	Total Processes	OK	02-01-2012 13:19:17	1d 4h 2m 57s	1/4	PROCS OK: 78 processes with STATE = RSZDT

Figure 9.9 Nagios event overview that shows the status of the custom service

9.2   BPM engine integration

Part of business activity monitoring (BAM) is using the information that's gathered to determine how good the business processes are that you have in place. You want to know where steps can be made more effective and how resources can be better allocated. A good starting point for this is getting an insight into how much time a specific task in a business process takes. Remember that in chapters 2 and 3 we talked about the use case where people who drove outside the busiest hours of the days would be paid some small compensation. There's a business process in place to determine the amount of this compensation, transferring the money to the correct person and handling all the administration. If you could monitor the average time each of these steps takes, you could use that to determine possible improvements.

In the following examples I'll show you how to connect a BPM engine to the BAM tooling used in this book. For this you'll use the open source Activiti BPM engine, but the same principles shown here can also be applied to other BPM engines.

9.2.1   Monitoring average task execution

To monitor the average task execution you'll send events from your BPM engine, process them using the BAM tools, and create a gadget that shows the results. The result you want to see is shown in figure 9.10.

Figure 9.10   Pie chart showing the task execution times of a specific task

**Figure 9.11
BPMN process to monitor**

Before we start looking at the code and configuration, let's look at the business process that you'll monitor; see figure 9.11. This business process can be found in the samples from the Activiti distribution, and they're also included in the code for chapter 9.

In the process shown in figure 9.11, you can see two simple steps. In the first step you need to write a financial report, and in the next step someone else will verify this report.

As shown in chapter 6, the best first step is to define the event format that you want to send:

```
{"event":{
      "timestamp":"1312721382049",
      "eventclass":"ActivitiTaskCompletion",
      "service":"ActivitiTask",
      "server":"Activiti",
      "taskName":"Verify monthly financial report",
      "taskExecutionTime":593}
}
```

This event is fairly basic. The interesting parts here are the eventclass, which specifies the type of event being sent, and the taskName and taskExecution properties, which show how long it took to finish this specific task. You'll need to configure Activiti in such a manner that it will send an event whenever a task is finished. For this Activiti allows you to define a custom TaskListener, which gets invoked when a specific task event occurs. The following listing shows the code for the TaskListener implemented in this example.

Listing 9.15   TaskListener implementation that sends events to Bamos

```java
public class TaskCompleteListener implements TaskListener {

  private final static BamosClient client =                            ❶ Where to send
    new BamosClient("http://localhost:9003/services/event");              events

  public void notify(DelegateTask delegateTask) {
    long startTime = delegateTask.getCreateTime().getTime();           ❷ Determine
    long currentTime = System.currentTimeMillis();                       execution time

    Map<String,Object> userData = new HashMap<String, Object>();
    userData.put("taskName", delegateTask.getName());                  ❸ Set as data
    userData.put("taskExecutionTime", currentTime-startTime);            on event

    client.sendEvent("Activiti", "ActivitiTask",
                "ActivitiTaskCompletion",                              ❹ Send event
                  currentTime, userData);
  }
}
```

This listener sends an event whenever it's invoked using the Bamos client ❶. This client will contain the name of the task and the execution time ❸ which is calculated based on the time the task was created and the current time ❷. This example sets some static values on the event ❹, but these could also be provided by the Activiti engine, for instance. The last step to get Activiti to send these events is to configure the business process so that this `TaskListener` is executed for the user tasks shown in figure 9.7. This can be done by adding the following lines of code to the BPMN configuration of this process.

Listing 9.16 Adding an extension to the BPMN `userTask` for Activiti

```
<userTask id="writeReportTask" name="Write monthly financial report" >
  <documentation>
    Write monthly financial report for publication to shareholders.
  </documentation>
  <extensionElements>
    <activiti:taskListener                                     ❶ Add a taskListener
          event="complete"
          class="chapter9...TaskCompleteListener" />
  </extensionElements>
  ...
</userTask>
```

In listing 9.16 you add a `taskListener` element ❶ that points to your custom `Task-CompleteListener`. Note that this isn't standard BPMN functionality but specific activity functionality. You can see this from the `activiti` prefix. This listener now receives an event whenever a task is completed because you set the `event` attribute to `complete`. You now have the sending part ready. To show this event in a pie chart, you process this event in the Bamos server. In the server you'll do the following two things:

1 Calculate the average execution time based on this event and the events that have already been received. For this you'll be using an Esper-based processor.

2 Group all the events together and create a single event that can be processed by the pie chart gadget to show the average time per executed task.

Calculating the average execution time using Esper is easy. In the following listing you can see the configuration and Esper statement for this.

Listing 9.17 Esper processor configuration to calculate the average

```
<bean id="esperAverageTaskExection" class="org...EsperEventProcessor">
    <property name="expression" value="serverName == 'Activiti'"/>
    <property name="esperStatement" value=
        "select userValues('taskName') as taskname,
                avg(cast(userValues('taskExecutionTime'),double))
                    as processingTime
         from Event group by userValues('taskName')"/>
    <property name="userClass" value="esperAverageTaskExecution"/>
    <property name="shouldStoreOriginal" value="false"/>
    <property name="storeDirectly" value="false"/>
</bean>
```

The important part from listing 9.17 is the esperStatement. This statement does the following for each event it receives, as shown in table 9.1.

Table 9.1   Esper tasks

Esper fragment	Description
Select userValues('taskName') as taskname	Select the taskName property from the event. Because this is a custom property you need to retrieve this from the userValues map. In the new event this property will be known as taskname.
avg(cast(userValues ('taskExecutionTime'), double)) as processingTime	Also select the taskExecution property from the userValues map. Then cast it to a double, and determine the average value based on the other received events. In the new event this average is called processingTime.
from Event group by userValues('taskName')	Process all of the events received so far and group the events based on the taskName property. This will make sure that the average calculations are done on events with the same taskName.

With this configuration every time Esper receives a new event, Esper calculates the new average processing time for that specific task and sends out a new event based on the properties shown in listing 9.17. Because you don't want to show the average processing time of a single task, you need to group the tasks together. You do this using a custom Java-based processor as shown in chapter 6. This simple processor stores the latest received average time in Cassandra, and when it has processed a new event, it sends out an aggregated event that contains all the average processing times for all the tasks it has received so far. The event produced by this processor is the one you'll use to show the pie chart and is shown next:

```
{"event": {
    "taskname_Verify monthly financial report": "593.0",
    "timestamp": "1312721382067",
    "eventclass": "TaskAggregatorProcessor.class",
    "PROC_NAME": "TASKAGGREGATORPROCESSOR",
    "service": "TaskAggregatorProcessor.class",
    "server": "EsperServer",
    "taskname_Write monthly financial report": "315.0"
}}
```

If you set the jsonURL to this

```
http://localhost:9003/services/event/
    list?class=TaskAggregatorProcessor.class&reverse=true
```

and the prefix to taskname_, you'll see the pie chart that shows the average execution time (see figure 9.12).

To test this you can use a simple test case provided by Activiti that automatically starts a business process and completes a couple of user tasks. This test case can also be found in the source code for chapter 9.

9.2.2 Monitoring which processes are started

A business process is usually started from a specific trigger. A customer requests new insurance, an employee wants to take a class, or a resident wants to request a building permit. Depending on how many and when the processes are started, you might require additional resources to quickly and efficiently process the tasks resulting from these business processes. In this example

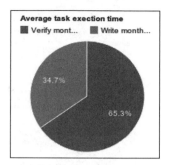

Figure 9.12   Pie chart showing the task execution times of a specific task

I'll show you how to extend Activiti so that it will send an event whenever a process is started. Based on these events you'll create a bar chart that shows the number of processes that have been started. The bar chart will look something like the one shown in figure 9.13.

You can, if you want, also render the same information in a pie chart (figure 9.14). To get these charts you need to take the following steps:

1 *Expand the processes in Activiti with an ExecutionListener*—Activiti allows you to add an ExecutionListener that's called whenever a process is started. You need to add a custom ExecutionListener to the Activiti process you want to monitor.

2 *Send events from Activiti whenever a process starts*—In this custom Execution-Listener you'll send an event with the name of the process that was started.

3 *Count the events based on process name*—In the Bamos server you'll keep track of how many processes with a specific name have been started.

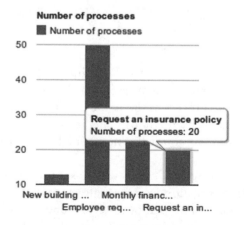

Figure 9.13   Bar chart showing number of processes that have been started

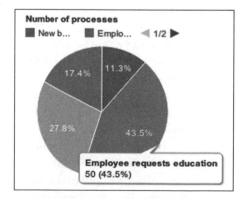

Figure 9.14   Pie chart showing number of processes that have been started

4   *Show the events in a bar or pie chart*—You'll define a gadget that retrieves an event containing an overview of how many processes of a specific type have been started.

To get information on when a process is started by Activiti, you'll use an `Execution-Listener` that listens for `start` events. For this you'll create a custom `Execution-Listener`, as shown in the following listing.

Listing 9.18   Extending the BPMN process with a custom `ExecutionListener`

```
<extensionElements>
  <activiti:executionListener
      class="chapter9....activiti.ProcessExecutionListener"
      event="start" />
</extensionElements>
```

With this code added to a process definition, Activiti will call your custom `Process-ExecutionListener` every time a process is started. This custom listener is shown in the next listing.

Listing 9.19   `ProcessExecutionListener` that sends events

```
public class ProcessExecutionListener implements ExecutionListener {

  private final static BamosClient client = new
    BamosClient("http://localhost:9003/services/event");

  public void notify(DelegateExecution execution) throws Exception {
    String name = ((ExecutionEntity)execution).getEventSource()          ❶ Get name
            .getProcessDefinition().getName();                              of process
    long currentTime = System.currentTimeMillis();

    Map<String,Object> userData = new HashMap<String, Object>();
    userData.put("processName", name);
    client.sendEvent("Activiti", name, "ActivitiProcessStart"            ❷ Send
                ,currentTime, userData);                                    an event
  }
}
```

The `notify` method is called each time a process is started. In this method you get the name of the process ❶ that was started and send an event ❷. Notice that when you send the event you use the name of the process as the name of the service in the event (the second parameter for the `sendEvent` method). This is done so that you can use the standard `CountEventProcessor` to count the number of processes that have been started.

   If you now start a couple of processes in Activiti, events will be sent to the Bamos server. Because you don't want to show information from a single event, but an overview of how many processes have been started grouped by process name, you need to process the incoming events. You do this, just as in chapter 6, with the `CountEvent-Processor`. This processor will keep track of how many events for a specific service have been received. And because you use the process name as the service name in these events, you can use this processor to group the events. The configuration for this processor is shown next.

Listing 9.20   Processor configuration to count the processes

```
<bean id="countProcesses"
      class="org.bamos.core.processors.event.common.CountEventProcessor">
  <property name="expression"
            value="eventClass == 'ActivitiProcessStart'"/>
  <property name="userClass" value="activityProcessCount'"/>
</bean>
```

Which events are processed

Identify the generated event

For more information on the configuration of this processor see chapter 6. You also saw in chapter 6 how to configure the various charts. To see the charts shown in the beginning of this section, configure a pie chart or a bar chart with the following URL and prefix:

- URL: `http://localhost:9003/services/event/list?service=CountEvent Processor.service&server=Activiti&count=1&reverse=true`
- Prefix: `countfor_`

That wraps up our BPMN examples. Activiti provides much more information that you can use in your charts than what we've shown here. These two examples, however, should show you how you can access and expose this information.

In the next section we'll look at how you can use various other languages to access the Bamos server and the WSO2 repository.

9.3   Language integration

The examples we've shown in this book use Java as programming language. You can also use other languages to connect to the various tools used in this book. In this section we'll look specifically at how you can use C#, Ruby, and Python to

- Send an event to the Bamos server
- Query the events stored in the Bamos server
- Retrieve an object from the repository

We'll start by showing you how to do this in C#.

9.3.1   C#

C# is a language created by Microsoft and has a C-like syntax. It provides many great libraries (open and closed source) and is one of the most popular languages on Windows platforms. You can also use C# on non-Windows platforms, by using the open source Mono implementation. The examples shown in this section should work with both the official C#/.NET implementation from Microsoft and the open source Mono implementation. To run these examples from the command line using Mono use the following commands:

- Compile: `gmcs <nameOfScript>.c`
- Run: `mono <nameOfScript>.exe`

SENDING EVENTS USING C#

If you want to send an event to the Bamos server using C#, you need to create a JSON request and make an HTTP POST call. You can use the `HttpWebRequest` object for this, as is shown in the following listing.

Listing 9.21 Sending an event to the Bamos server from C#

```csharp
using System;
using System.Net;
using System.IO;
using System.Web;
using System.Text;

public class PostEventUsingCSharp {

static string exampleEvent = @"{
""event"":{
  ""Processing_time"":299,
  ""timestamp"":""1315053621563"",
  ""eventclass"":""MULE_EVENT"",
  ""service"":""SimpleFlow"",
  ""server"":""test-server""
  }
}";


static public void Main () {
  Uri address = new Uri("http://localhost:9003/services/event");
  HttpWebRequest request = WebRequest.Create(address) as HttpWebRequest;

  request.Method = "POST";
  request.ContentType = "application/json";

  byte[] byteData = UTF8Encoding.UTF8.GetBytes(exampleEvent);

  request.ContentLength = byteData.Length;

  using (Stream postStream = request.GetRequestStream()) {
    postStream.Write(byteData, 0, byteData.Length);
  }
}
}
```

Listing 9.21 doesn't show you how to create a JSON object from scratch but rather how to send the `exampleEvent` string. There are a number of open source libraries available for C#/.NET that you can use to work with JSON objects. A good one to use is Json.NET, which you can find at http://james.newtonking.com/pages/json-net.aspx.

QUERYING EVENTS USING C#

If you want to use C# to query the Bamos server you need to make HTTP GET calls to the Bamos server. The following listing once again uses the HttpWebRequest for this.

Listing 9.22 C# code to query the events from the Bamos server

```
using System;
using System.Net;
using System.IO;

public class GetRepositoryResourceUsingCSharp {
    static public void Main () {
        string result = HttpGetAmount("http://localhost:9003/services/
     event/list",3);
      Console.WriteLine(result);
    }

    static string HttpGetAmount(string url, int count) {
            HttpWebRequest req = WebRequest.Create(url + "?count=" + count)
                as HttpWebRequest;
            string result = null;
            using (HttpWebResponse resp = req.GetResponse() as
                HttpWebResponse) {
              StreamReader reader = new
                  StreamReader(resp.GetResponseStream());
              result = reader.ReadToEnd();
            }
            return result;
        }
}
```

This listing doesn't show you how to parse the response. The response is a JSON array of events. Just as in the previous example, if you want to parse this you can use one of the available open source JSON libraries.

GETTING A RESOURCE FROM THE REPOSITORY USING C#

The last C# example shows how to access the WSO2 repository. If you have information stored in the repository that you want to access from C#, for instance a WSDL or documentation, you can do this with the code shown in the next listing.

Listing 9.23 Retrieve a resource from the WSO2 repository

```
using System;
using System.Net;
using System.IO;

public class GetRepositoryResourceUsingCSharp {
    static public void Main () {
        string result =
            HttpGet("http://10.0.0.9:9763/registry/resource/_system/" +
            "governance/mule/mule-config-repo.xml", "admin", "admin");
      Console.WriteLine(result);
    }
```

```
static string HttpGet(string url, string username, string password) {
        HttpWebRequest req = WebRequest.Create(url) as HttpWebRequest;
    req.Credentials = new NetworkCredential(username, password);
        string result = null;
        using (HttpWebResponse resp = req.GetResponse() as
            HttpWebResponse) {
          StreamReader reader = new
              StreamReader(resp.GetResponseStream());
          result = reader.ReadToEnd();
        }
        return result;
    }
}
```

The main difference between this piece of code and the one where you queried the Bamos server is that this time authentication is required. The WSO2 repository makes use of basic authentication. This is supported directly by C# using the `Network-Credential` object.

9.3.2 *Ruby*

Ruby became popular a couple of years ago when people started using Ruby on Rails for developing web applications. The Ruby language itself is a concise language with many interesting language features. It also has a great set of open source libraries that you can use in your development. If you want to run these examples from the command line, use the following command:

```
ruby <nameOfScript>.rb
```

SENDING EVENTS USING RUBY

Ruby has great support for HTTP and allows you to make HTTP calls with a minimal amount of effort. The code to send an event to Ruby is shown in the next listing.

Listing 9.24   Sending an event to the Bamos server from Ruby

```
require 'net/http'

jsondata = <<-eos
{
"event":{
  "Processing_time":299,
  "timestamp":"1315053621563",
  "eventclass":"MULE_EVENT",
  "service":"SimpleFlow",
  "server":"jos-ubuntu"
  }
}
eos

url = URI.parse('http://localhost:9003/services/event')
request = Net::HTTP::Post.new(url.path)
request.body = jsondata
response = Net::HTTP.start(url.host, url.port) {|http|
          http.request(request)}
```

Here I've only shown you how to make a POST call. If you want to work with JSON more easily, you can use the JSON library that's available for Ruby. This library can be installed using the command-line tool `gem` like this: `gem install json`.

QUERYING EVENTS USING RUBY

If you thought the code for sending data to the Bamos server was short and simple, the code for querying data is even simpler; see the following listing.

Listing 9.25 Ruby code to query the events from the Bamos server

```
require 'net/http'

url = "http://localhost:9003/services/event/list?count=3"

begin
   data = Net::HTTP.get_response(URI.parse(url)).body
   print data
rescue
   print "Connection error."
End
```

The code from listing 9.25 will make a call to the Bamos server and print out the results.

GETTING A RESOURCE FROM THE REPOSITORY USING RUBY

If you want to access the WSO2 repository from Ruby, you have to make a simple GET operation but this time with authentication. In the following listing you create a new HTTP object and a Get request. You set the authentication on this request and use the HTTP object to send the request.

Listing 9.26 Retrieving a resource from the WSO2 repository using Ruby

```
require 'net/http'

begin
   http = Net::HTTP.new('10.0.0.9', 9763)
   http.start do |http|
     req = Net::HTTP::Get.new('/registry/resource/
     ➥ _system/governance/mule/mule-config-repo.xml')
     req.basic_auth 'admin', 'admin'
     resp, data = http.request(req)
     print data
   end
end
```

If you run this script, you'll see the content of the specific object from the repository.

9.3.3 Python

The final language we'll discuss is Python. Python has been around for years and is used frequently on Unix-like environments. It's often called a "glue" language and is used for administrative programs such as package management. Running a Python script can be done by using the following command:

```
Python <nameOfScript>.py
```

SENDING EVENTS USING PYTHON

The first example we look at for Python is how to make an HTTP POST. For this you can use Python's urllib2 library, as shown in the following listing.

Listing 9.27 Sending an event to the Bamos server from Python

```
import urllib2

url = 'http://localhost:9003/services/event'
data = '''{"event":{
  "Processing_time":299,
  "timestamp":"1315053621563",
  "eventclass":"MULE_EVENT",
  "service":"SimpleFlow",
  "server":"jos-ubuntu"
  }
}'''

req = urllib2.Request(url, data)
response = urllib2.urlopen(req)
the_page = response.read()
```

Just like the other two languages we discussed so far, Python also has a number of open source JSON libraries you can use to make working with JSON easier. A good and easy-to-use JSON library for Python can be found here: http://pypi.python.org/pypi/simplejson/.

QUERYING EVENTS USING PYTHON

The same library you used for making a POST request in the previous example can be used to make a GET request. In the following listing you make a simple GET request and print out the results.

Listing 9.28 Python code to query the events from the Bamos server

```
import urllib2
import base64
import sys

# Where do we want to connect to
url = 'http://localhost:9003/services/event/list?count=3'
req = urllib2.Request(url)

# execute the GET method and print the result
try:
    handle = urllib2.urlopen(req)
except IOError, e:
    print "Is the server running?"
    sys.exit(1)
thepage = handle.read()
print(thepage)
```

In this example you didn't use authentication. In the following example you once again make a GET request, but this time you specify basic authentication.

GETTING A RESOURCE FROM THE REPOSITORY USING PYTHON

Unlike C# and Ruby, Python doesn't have a standard, easy way to specify basic authentication. For Python you have to manually add the authentication header to the HTTP request you're going to make. The next listing shows how you can do this.

> **Listing 9.29   Retrieving a resource from the WSO2 repository using Python**

```
import urllib2
import sys

# Where do we want to connect to
url = 'http://10.0.0.9:9763/registry/resource/
➥ _system/governance/mule/mule-config-repo.xml'
username = 'admin'
password = 'admin'

# set up basic authentication
req = urllib2.Request(url)
base64string = base64.encodestring('%s:%s' % (username, password))[:-1]
authheader =  "Basic %s" % base64string
req.add_header("Authorization", authheader)

# execute the GET method and print the result
try:
    handle = urllib2.urlopen(req)
except IOError, e:
    print "It looks like the username or password is wrong."
    sys.exit(1)
thepage = handle.read()
print(thepage)
```

In this and the previous sections I've shown you how you can access the WSO2 registry and the Bamos server from different languages. As you've seen, doing this is easy and straightforward. Both tools expose (most of) their functionality using open standards, in this case a REST-based approach.

9.4   *What you should remember from this book*

In the three parts of this book I showed you how you can apply SOA governance in a practical way. In this final section I'll give you a couple of important points to think about when you're applying the principles and concepts set out in this book:

- SOA governance is a broad subject. It involves setting up governance boards, determining the policy processes you want to follow, and defining the policies that describe how the various services and people working with these services should act. Technology, however, does play an important part in applying SOA governance in your organization. With technology you can easily create a centralized location that stores the various policies and provides information to the different parties involved in SOA governance.

- The two main parts of SOA governance that apply to service development are design-time governance and runtime governance. Design-time governance describes how the services should be developed, and runtime governance describes how they should act when deployed. In both parts it's important to use tools such as a repository and a BAM server to monitor compliance to the policies.

- There are many open source tools available that can help you in applying SOA governance or in conforming to specific policies. In this book you used identity management tools for dealing with security-related policies, used the WSO2 SOA governance repository as the central location to store policies and services, and used a number of other open source libraries and tools. The tools shown in this book aren't the only options. You should look closely at what's available, the maturity of a specific tool, and its functionality before making a choice. But remember that open source provides you with a lot of good tools, libraries, and frameworks that you can use to apply SOA governance within your organization.

- It's important to start small. It's hard, and sometimes nearly impossible, to get a large organization to use the practical aspects of SOA governance. Just start within your own department. Set up a registry where you store your services, define a versioning scheme you comply with, and set up monitoring for the services you provide to your customers. If your department is successful, others will surely follow.

- Apply the policies in this book to your own situation. I tried to show a set of common policies that you can use in your own organization. Don't be afraid to modify these policies so they better fit your environment. If you already have a repository, see if you can use it to store service information and documentation. Maybe it also provides an external API you can use to integrate various tools and products.

Before I finish up this book with the summary of this chapter, the final thing I'd like to say is to just start experimenting with the examples from this book. See if you can set up a simple SOA governance environment, define some simple policies, and start monitoring services!

9.5   Summary

The most important items discussed in this chapter are these:

- The WSO2 registry can be easily accessed using standard HTTP calls with basic authentication.
- You can use the WSO2 registry to store more than just WSDLs, service descriptions, and documentation. You can also store property files, ESB configurations, and BPM processes.
- You can easily integrate Spring to retrieve properties from the WSO2 registry.
- With the Bamos client you can quickly integrate various tools with the Bamos server.
- The Activiti BPM engine provides various extension points that you can use to provide task and process information to the Bamos server.
- Using the WSO2 repository and the Bamos server from languages other than Java is easy. You just have to be able to make HTTP GET and POST requests and support basic authentication.

appendix:
Installing tools, libraries, and frameworks

This appendix shows how to install the various tools and libraries used in the examples in this book. In this appendix you'll find how to install the following components:

- *Java*—The examples we use in this book are based on Java. Even though the concepts shown here can be applied to other languages, the environment we work with for our examples is Java.
- *Maven*—To make it easier to run the examples, Maven projects are provided for all the examples. This allows you to easily run the examples from the command line or from Eclipse.
- *Eclipse*—The development environment we work with is Eclipse. Eclipse is a great Java development environment with a lot of plug-ins and extensions.
- *Cassandra*—The data for our examples and for our BAM tools is stored in a NoSQL database. For this database we use Cassandra.
- *WSO2 Governance Registry*—We make heavy use of a registry in the examples in this book. For instance, we use this registry to store artifacts created in the examples and to look up resources programmatically.
- *WSO2 Gadget Server*—The WSO2 Gadget Server is used to represent our BAM gadgets.
- *OpenAM*—When we're working with security-related policies, we use a central identity provider. For the examples in this book we use the OpenAM identity server.
- *soapUI*—It's hard to test services. Usually there's no user interface or interactive shell to test your components. To facilitate testing I've provided a set of soapUI projects you can use to test the services you create in this book.

Before you start installing anything, create a directory named governance somewhere on your system. This is the directory where you'll install all the different tools you'll use for the examples in this book. For the rest of this book and for the installations I'll call this directory <GOV_HOME>.

A.1   Java

For Java we require an up-to-date version of the JDK. To download the JDK go to http://www.oracle.com/technetwork/java/javase/downloads/index.html and click the Download JDK button. This will bring you to a download page where you can select the JDK for your platform. Download this version and install it using the method specific to your platform. During installation, when you're asked for the directory in which to install the JDK, select the <OPEN_GOV>/jdk1.6.0_25 directory. This will install the JDK, which you'll use for the examples.

A.1.1   Adding JAVA_HOME in Windows

To make sure Maven can find your Java installation you need to add an environment variable named JAVA_HOME. Each platform has its own specific way to do this. For Windows you need to add this in the following manner:

1   Right-click the My Computer icon on your desktop or the Computer option in your Start menu and select Properties.
2   In the Properties screen that opens select the Advanced tab, or in newer versions of Windows select the Advanced System Settings tab.
3   Click the Environment Variables button.
4   Under System Variable, click New.
5   Enter the variable name as JAVA_HOME.
6   Enter the variable value as the full path to the installed JDK: <OPEN_GOV>/jdk1.6.0_25.
7   Click OK, as shown in figure A.1.
8   Click Apply Changes.

To check whether this was set correctly, you can open a console window and type echo %JAVA_HOME%; this should show the location you entered.

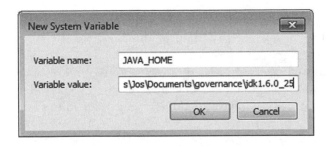

Figure A.1   Add the Windows system variable JAVA_HOME.

A.1.2 Adding JAVA_HOME in Linux

For those working with Linux, the easiest way to make sure the JAVA_HOME property is known from the command line is to add the following to the /etc/environment file:

```
JAVA_HOME=/home/jos/Books/governance/jdk1.6.0_25
```

This should work on most Linux systems. If this doesn't work for you, you could also try adding this to the /etc/profile or the /etc/bash.bashrc file. Testing this is very easy. Open a terminal window and run echo $JAVA_HOME, which should output the location you entered previously.

A.2 Maven

Maven is a tool with which you can easily build your project, manage its dependencies, generate documentation, and much more. You'll be using Maven in this book for all the different services you'll be building. Maven in itself is a command-line tool and, using the m2eclipse plug-in, which you'll install in the following section, it has great integration with Eclipse. Installing Maven is simple. First, get the download from the Apache site at http://maven.apache.org/download.html. Download the Maven 3.0.1 version and unpack it to the <GOV_HOME> directory. If you want to run the Maven (mvn) command, which can be found in the <GOV_HOME>\apache-maven-3.0.1\bin directory, without having to type in the complete path, add it to your system's Path variable. To add a directory to the path in Windows, open the environment variable's window, just as you did in the previous section. In the system variables list select the Path variable and click Edit. In the value field of this property you can see the current path. At the end of the path add a semicolon (;) and the full path to the <GOV_HOME>\apache-maven-3.0.1\bin directory and click OK. This will allow you to just type in mvn in the console to run Maven. For Linux, you can do pretty much the same as you did in the previous section for Java. In the /etc/environment file append <GOV_HOME>\apache-maven-3.0.1\bin to the Path variable.

To test whether Maven is correctly installed, run the mvn command from the command line. You should see output similar to the following:

```
[INFO] Scanning for projects...
[INFO] ----------------------------------------------------
[INFO] BUILD FAILURE
[INFO] ----------------------------------------------------
[INFO] Total time: 0.184s
[INFO] Finished at: Sun Dec 12 18:48:29 CET 2010
[INFO] Final Memory: 1M/59M
```

Don't worry about the BUILD FAILURE message shown here. This is to be expected because you haven't set up a project yet that Maven can work with.

A.3 Eclipse

The first thing you need to do is download an Eclipse installation. Go to http://www.eclipse.or/downloads and select the Eclipse IDE for Java Developers version. This

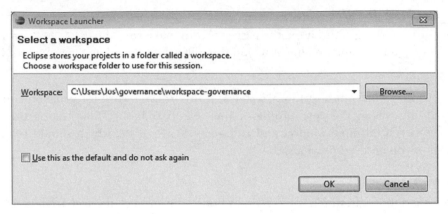

**Figure A.2   Set the default workspace location to the workspace-governance folder in the
<GOV_HOME> directory.**

will download a zip file (or a tar.gz for those on Linux). Copy this file to the
<GOV_HOME> directory and unpack it there. This will create an Eclipse directory in
the <GOV_HOME> directory.

Now go to the <GOV_HOME>/Eclipse directory and run `eclipse.exe` (or
`eclipse.sh`) to start up Eclipse. If you have a correct Java installation, you'll see an
Eclipse welcome screen, as shown in figure A.2.

Figure A.2 is the first screen you'll see when you start Eclipse. This screen lets you
specify where you want to store your Eclipse workspace (where all your projects are
kept). To keep the files together, set the location of the workspace to the
<GOV_HOME>\workspace-governance directory. If you don't want to select the work-
space each time you start Eclipse, you can check the check box in this window. Now
click OK, and you're finished with the basic Eclipse installation. The next step is installation of the plug-ins.

All the sources for this project are stored in an SVN repository. To access these you
can either install a command-line SVN client or integrate this with Eclipse. For now do
the latter. Start Eclipse if you don't have it running, and select the Install New Software option from the Help menu. A screen will pop up (see figure A.3), with which
you can install new software. In this screen at the top you'll find a Work With drop-
down menu. In that drop-down select the All Available Sites option. In the Type Filter
Text field enter svn and press Enter. Now wait a bit, and you'll see a set of plug-ins that
you can install.

Now check the Subversive SVN Team Provider (Incubation) option and click Next.
On the following screen click Next again, and you're shown the licenses. Select the I
Accept option and click Finish. This will start the download of the Subversion plug-in.
Once it's done downloading and installing, you're asked to restart Eclipse; do so by
choosing the Restart Now option. Once Eclipse is restarted, open the SVN Repository
Perspective (Window > Open Perspective; if you don't see this perspective choose the

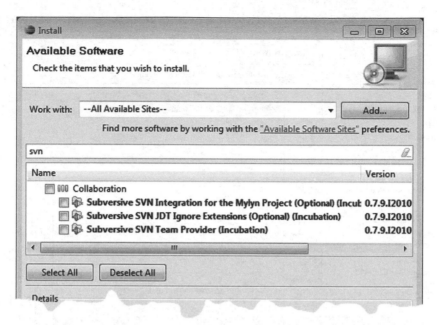

Figure A.3 Search for the SVN-related Eclipse plug-in by specifying a search filter.

Others menu option and select it from there). Now you'll get a pop up to select a Subversive connector. Select SVN-KIT 1.3.2 and click Next until you get to the license agreement. Accept this once again, and the install will start. You might get a pop up mentioning unsigned content; if so, select to trust this content. Now you'll have to restart Eclipse again, and the SVN connector will be up and running.

Now that you can get to the sources, you can install Maven, which is used for building the services and managing the dependencies.

You'll start in the same manner as you did for the SVN plug-in. Go to the Install New Software option of the Help menu. Since the m2eclipse plug-in isn't available from the standard Eclipse update sites, you have to add a custom one. For this click the Add button. On the screen that pops up, fill in the information as shown in figure A.4.

Once you've entered the values, click OK, wait a bit, and you're shown the contents of this update site, which is just a single item. Select the Maven Integration for Eclipse plug-in and click Next. On the following page click Next again, and accept the terms

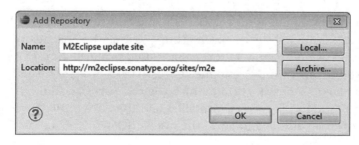

**Figure A.4
Add a new update site for
the M2Eclipse plug-in.**

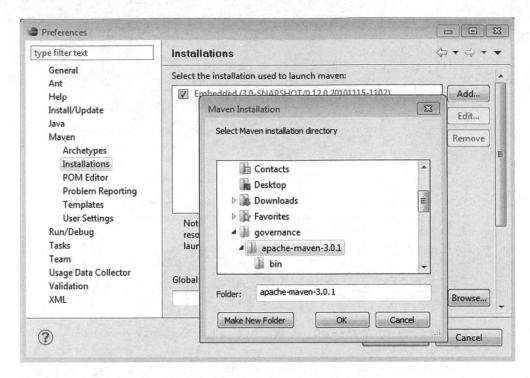

Figure A.5   Adding a custom Maven installation to the m2eclipse plug-in

of the license agreement. Finally, click Finish and you've finished installing this plug-in. Eclipse will once again ask you to restart, which you should do.

You're not completely finished with this step; you now need to make sure the plug-in uses the same configuration as the Maven installation you installed in the previous section. To do this, open the Preferences screen (from menu option Window select Preferences). In the screen that opens select the Maven > Installations option. Click the Add button and navigate to your Maven installation, as shown in figure A.5, and click OK.

This will add the installation and set it as default. Click OK once again to exit the Preferences screen.

A.4   *Cassandra*

Cassandra is used in our examples as the NoSQL data source. Installing Cassandra isn't difficult. Go to the Cassandra website at Apache (http://cassandra.apache.org/download/) and download Cassandra (the 0.7.x version is used in this book). Extract this file (using 7-Zip if you're on Windows) into the <GOV_HOME> directory. This will create an apache-cassandra-0.7.x directory from which you can start Cassandra.

To test whether Cassandra is correctly installed and the JAVA_HOME property has been set correctly, open a console and go to the <GOV_HOME>/cassandra-0.7.x/bin directory. From there run the Cassandra (.bat) file. This should start Cassandra in the console and show you output like this:

```
INFO 22:11:51,539 Cassandra version: 0.7.5
INFO 22:11:51,541 Thrift API version: 19.4.0
INFO 22:11:51,543 Loading persisted ring state
...
INFO 22:11:52,026 Listening for thrift clients...
```

If you want to start Cassandra without having to navigate to the installation directory, add this bin directory to your path, in the same manner as you did for Maven.

A.5 *WSO2 Governance Registry*

Installing the registry is very easy. Just head over to the WSO2 registry download site at http://wso2.org/downloads/governance-registry and select the binary distribution for download. Once this is downloaded, unzip this file into the <GOV_HOME> directory. This will create a wso2greg-3.6.0 folder, which contains the installation. The best way to check if everything is installed correctly is by trying to start the registry. To do this go to the <GOV_HOME>/wso2greg-3.6.0/bin directory and run wso2server.bat (or wso2server.sh on non-Windows systems). A lot of console output will scroll by; if all goes well, at the end of this output you should see something like this:

```
INFO -  Server :  WSO2 Governance Registry-3.6.0
INFO -  WSO2 Carbon started in 30 sec
```

When the registry is started, open up a browser and point it to http://localhost:9443. This will show you the login screen, shown in figure A.6, where you can log in with username admin and password admin.

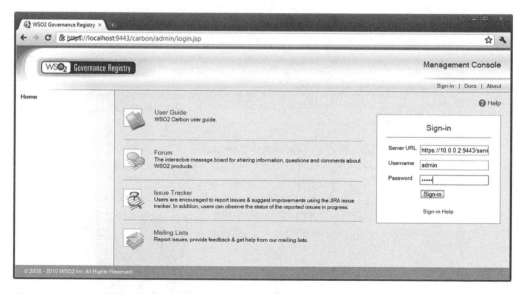

Figure A.6 The login page after you've installed the WSO2 service registry

A.6   *WSO2 Gadget Server*

You'll use the WSO2 Gadget Server as your tool to visualize your BAM monitoring widgets. The visualizations you make are made available as gadgets following the OpenSocial Specification (http://code.google.com/apis/opensocial/). This way you can run them locally for now, but you could also run them in a gadget container of your choosing. The WSO2 server is based on the Apache Shindig project and provides a lot of user-friendly features to make it easy to display your own gadgets.

Go to the WSO2 website at http://wso2.com/products/gadget-server/. Here you'll find a Download button for the gadget server. Download the latest stable version (version 1.3.0 is used in this book), which downloads a zip file to your local system. When the download has finished, unzip this file in the <GOV_HOME> directory. This will create a wso2gs-1.3.0 folder that contains the gadget server. As a final test to see if the installation was successful, go into the <GOV_HOME>/wso2gs-1.3.0/bin directory and execute the wso2server.bat file (or wso2server.sh for those not on Windows). This will start the Gadget Server, and in the console you'll eventually see something like this:

```
INFO Gadget Server Default Context : http://10.0.0.3:8080/portal
INFO Started Transport Listener Manager
INFO Server :  WSO2 Gadget Server-1.3.0
INFO WSO2 Carbon started in 35 sec
```

The interesting part here is the URL where the portal server can be accessed. If you now open a browser and navigate to http://localhost:8080/portal, you'll be presented with the home page of the Gadget Server, as shown in figure A.7.

A.7   *OpenAM*

OpenAM is the identity provider you'll use for a couple of your security-related policies. OpenAM is a web application that you can run in a servlet container such as Tomcat. To install OpenAM you'll first install Tomcat, and then I'll show you how to install and configure OpenAM.

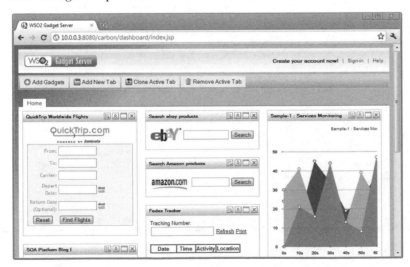

**Figure A.7
Welcome screen
of the WSO2
Gadget Server**

A.7.1 Downloading and installing Tomcat

You can download a recent version of Tomcat from the Apache website (http://tomcat.apache.org/download-60.cgi). For ease of use just download the zip version, which you find on this page under Binary Distributions/Core. Unzipping this file to the <GOV_HOME> directory will create an apache-tomcat-6.0.32 folder from which you can run Tomcat. To see if everything installed correctly, open a terminal and start Tomcat from the <GOV_HOME>/apache-tomcat-6.0.32/bin folder using the `startup(.sh)` command. When run, this command should output something like the following:

```
INFO: Deploying web application directory ROOT
May 14, 2011 3:24:58 PM org.apache.coyote.http11.Http11Protocol start
INFO: Starting Coyote HTTP/1.1 on http-8080
May 14, 2011 3:24:58 PM org.apache.jk.common.ChannelSocket init
INFO: JK: ajp13 listening on /0.0.0.0:8009
May 14, 2011 3:24:58 PM org.apache.jk.server.JkMain start
INFO: Jk running ID=0 time=0/48  config=null
May 14, 2011 3:24:58 PM org.apache.catalina.startup.Catalina start
INFO: Server startup in 2108 ms
```

Now run the `shutdown(.sh)` command from the same directory to stop Tomcat. The next step is to download and install the OpenAM web application.

A.7.2 Downloading and installing OpenAM

OpenAM can be downloaded as a zip file containing the web application from the ForgeRock site at http://forgerock.com/downloads.html. Download this zip to a temporary directory and unzip this to the <GOV_HOME>/opensso directory. In this directory you'll find a subdirectory with the name deployable-war. From this directory copy the file opensso.war to the <GOV_HOME/apache-tomcat-6.0.32/webapps directory. If you now start Tomcat, the opensso.war web application will be automatically deployed.

The next step is to set up the default configuration for OpenAM. This can be done through the OpenAM web console, which can be found at http://localhost:8080/opensso. Figure A.8 shows this welcome screen.

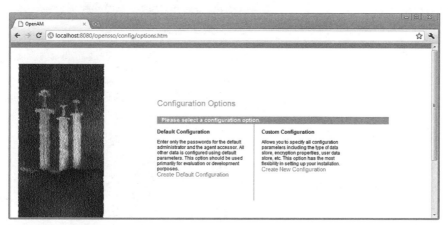

Figure A.8 OpenAM welcome screen, the first time it's started

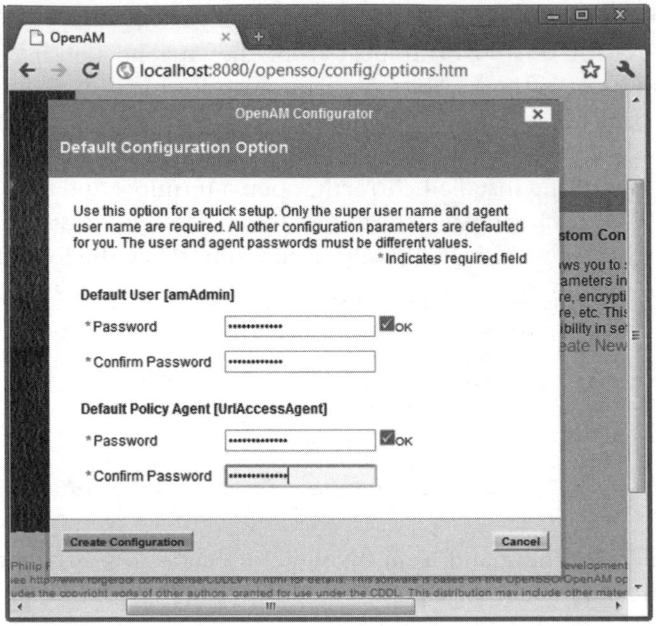

Figure A.9   Enter passwords for the OpenAM default users.

On this screen select the Create Default Configuration option. This will present you with the screen shown in figure A.9, where you'll need to enter passwords for the system users.

Finally, click the Create Configuration option, and you're finished. To check whether everything went OK, you can log in as the default admin user. The username of this user is amadmin and the password is the one you entered previously. After logging in you're presented with the OpenAM welcome screen, where you can configure the rest of the environment. This configuration will be shown in the policies that use OpenAM for authentication and authorization.

A.8   soapUI

To download soapUI go to the download page at http://sourceforge.net/projects/soapui/files/. This page will have a link to the latest version for your specific operating system. I used the 3.6.1 version for this, but newer versions will work in pretty much the same manner. After you've downloaded the installation file, run this file and follow the instructions; it's

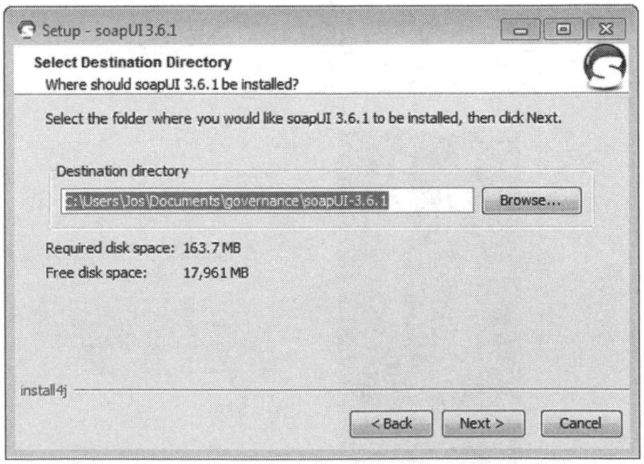

Figure A.10   Install soapUI into the <GOV_HOME> location.

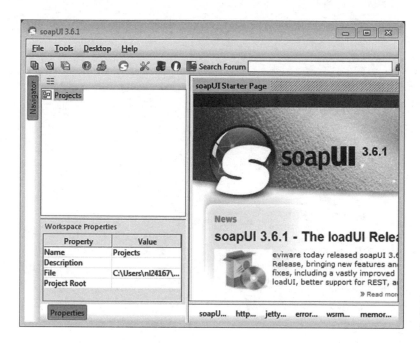

**Figure A.11
Startup screen
of soapUI**

pretty straightforward. When asked to specify a directory, specify one inside the <GOV_HOME> folder, as shown in figure A.10. That way you'll keep all the tools used for this book central.

For all the other questions you can just click Next. Doing so will select the default options for soapUI and install it in the specified location inside <GOV_HOME>.

After the installation is complete, go to the installation directory at <GOV_HOME>/soap-UI-3.6.1 and double-click the soapUI 3.6.1 icon to start soapUI. This should start soapUI and present you with the screen shown in figure A.11.

index

Symbols

@afterClass annotation 160
@beforeClass annotation
    160–161, 163–165
@service annotation 41
@TestCase annotation 164
@WebService annotation 48

A

Access Control tab 133
access token, for OAuth
    getting 147
    using 147–149
Account object 160
account.getSsn() method 159
Account.registerCar(Car
    toRegister) method 37
account.validate() method 159
accountRepository.getAccount
    .account.getSsn()
    method 159
AccountRepository()
    method 161
AccountService 164–168, 236
AccountServiceImpl()
    method 159
accumulated events 203
action property 124
Add Association button 94
Add button 93–94
Add Collection button 93, 239
Add Document button 93
Add Gadgets button 57

Add New Lifecycle button 216
Add New Policy page 222
Add New Tab button 57
Add Resource button 239
Add Service option 51
addPolicyBean operation 223
AddPolicyUtil class 220–221,
    223
advantages, of SOA 6–7
Amazon cloud 176–185
    data layer 177–180
    deploying to 182
    remoting layer 180–182
    testing 182
Amazon Web Service. *See* AWS
AmazonImageComment-
    Repository 178–179, 182
AmazonSimpleDBClient
    179–180
Analytics department 62
ApplicationContext 164, 166
applicationcontext.xml file 56,
    119, 123, 130, 138, 140,
    162–163
applying policies 11–12
architecture 28–31
    data layer 29–30
    logic layer 30
    service remoting 30–31
assemble phase, lifecycle of
    services 213–214
assertEquals.getTestAccount()
    method 166
association.getAssociation-
    Type() method 106
association.getDestination-
    Path() method 106

association.getSourcePath()
    method 106
Associations tab 94
Atom Syndication Format 86
authenticateThroughOpenAM
    135, 138
authentication façade 134–137
    authenticating user 134–135
    validating token 135–137
authentication filter 133,
    137–141
    REST authentication
        filter 138–139
    WS-* authentication
        filter 139–141
authentication provider
    132–133, 137
    configuring 133–134
    installing 133
authentication, failed
    attempts 208–210
authenticationcount class
    209–210
authenticationFailure
    event 208–210
authorization filter 153
authorization services 149–155
    authorization filter for 153
    OpenAM entitlement
        service 150–152
    configuring
        application 151–152
    creating policies 152
authorization, failed
    attempts 208–210
authorizationcount class 209

authorizationFailure event 209
Authorize method 154–155
average response time
  event 196–199
AWS (Amazon Web
  Services) 127
AWS Management Console 182

B

backup policies 176
BAM (business activity
  monitoring) 28, 251
BAM application 53–58
  attaching event sender to
    service 54–57
  installing tools for 53–54
  setting up widget to visualize
    statistics 57–58
BAM Gadgets 57
BAM tools 25
Bamos 189–211
  average response time
    event 196–199
  documentation
    compliance 211
  event processor in 194–195
  event producer in 192–193
  event service in 193–194
  failed authentication and
    authorization 208–210
  gadget in 191
  number of requests per time
    period 206–207
  report usage based on
    location 202–206
  report usage based on
    service 199–202
Bamos event server, sending
  events to Nagios from
  246–251
  configuring NSCA and
    Nagios 247–249
  configuring processor
    249–250
  testing configuration 250–251
bamos-extensions-services-
  ipinfodb project 204
bamos-processors-nagios-
  integration.xml file 250
baseLocation 237–238
benefits, of SOA 13–14
  keeping track of how services
    are used 13–14

keeping uniformity among
  services 14
bottom-up contract design 44
BPM engine integration
  251–257
  monitoring average task
    execution 251–255
  monitoring which processes
    are started 255–257
breaking changes 81, 106–109,
  111–113
BUILD FAILURE message 267
business activity monitoring. *See*
  BAM
business services 103

C

C# 257–260
  getting resource from reposi-
    tory using 259–260
  querying events using 259
  sending events using 258
CA (certificate authority) 118
Car entity 35–37
carbon.xml file 230
CarService operation 162–163,
  167–168
cassandra-cli tool 35
Cassandra, installing 270–271
CassandraServiceDataCleaner()
  method 160
centralized identity system
  131–141
  authentication façade 134–137
    authenticating user
      134–135
    validating token 135–137
  authentication filter 137–141
    REST authentication
      filter 138–139
    WS-* authentication
      filter 139–141
  authentication provider
    configuring 133–134
    installing 133
CEP (complex event
  processing) 191, 195
certificate authority. *See* CA
check_command 248
class property 194
cleaner.cleanupDataDirectories()
  method 160
client-side SSL, and HTTPS with
  Jetty 119–120

client.createAccount.getTest-
  Account() method 166
client.getState() method 238,
  241
client.sendEvent.comp-
  Notification.getServerId()
  method 244
clientAuthentication
  element 120
cloud computing 63–64
cloud, developing for 174–185
  Amazon cloud 176–185
    data layer 177–180
    deploying to 182
    remoting layer 180–182
    testing 182
  choosing provider 175–176
  types of cloud services
    174–175
col.getChildren() method 229
ColumnFamily 36
commands.cfg file 247–249
comment.getComments()
  method 179
comment.getLocation()
  method 179
comment.getUserdata()
  method 180
CompanyRegistrationService 68
complex event processing. *See*
  CEP
compNotification.getService-
  Name() method 244
compNotification.getSource()
  method 244
COMPONENT-MESSAGE
  notifications 243–244
components.xml file 219–220
ConfigResource 245–246
configuration, provisioning
  from repositories 238–241
Configure Widgets link 173
consumerKey 145, 148
consumerSecret 145
ContactInformationService 69
content search, searching repository from web application
  227
Content-MD5 header 127, 129
Content-Type header 127
contract design 44
conversion, testing 166–167
ConvertUtil class 164, 166
corporate governance 7
CountEventProcessor 256–257

Create Default Configuration option 274
createAccount () method 159–161, 164, 166, 168–169
createRepository() method 161
createTestAccount() method 159, 161
custom pages 219
custom view, for policies 217–225
    creating logic 220–222
    creating pages 222–223
    defining format 219–220
    deploying pages 224–225
    linking media type 220
Customer Support department 62
customUI element 220
CustomUIServiceClient 221–222
CXF, retrieving WSDL in repositories with 237–238
CXFBasedJettyLauncher class 41, 48

D

data initiatives 68
data layer 29–30, 35–37, 157–158
    for Amazon cloud 177–180
    testing 160–161
data model 34–35
data security 176
Date header 127, 131
Date() method 129–130
DDD (domain-driven design) 30
decryptionPropFile property 123–125
DefaultMuleContextFactory() method 246
defining policies 10–11
delegateTask.getCreateTime() method 252
delegateTask.getName() method 252
deploy phase 214
deploying, to Amazon cloud 182
describing resources 91
design policies 21
design time, applying policies at 17–18
Development manager 63, 71, 74, 77

digest.digest() method 155
digest.update.msg.trim() method 155
discovering resources. *See* searching repository
documentation compliance, and Bamos open source project 211
documentation policies 82–95
    and reusable services 106–107
    for OpenGov example 70
    for REST-based service 83–88
        human-readable documentation 86–88
        referenced resources 85
        report resource 84–85
        using links 85–86
    for service repository 92–95
    for WS-* based service 88–92
        generating from WSDL 91–92
        WSDL for PermitService 89–91
DocumentationOverviewProcessor 231, 234
documentationPercentage property 231–232
Domain Services department 62
domain-driven design. *See* DDD
doTransform method 243
DSL (domain-specific language) 197

E

Eclipse
    in environment 31–32
    installing 267–270
    welcome screen 268
Elastic Beanstalk tab 182
embedded.setup() method 160
EmbeddedServerHelper .teardown() method 160
EmbeddedServerHelper() method 160
Enable Dependency Management option 32
encryption 121
encryptionPropFile property 124–125
encryptionUser property 124–125
endpointInfo.getName() method 238
enforcing policies 12–13

enterprise integration 236–251
Mule
    loading configuration from repository 245–246
    sending events from 241–245
    provisioning configuration from repository 238–241
    provisioning WSDL from repository 236–238
        expanding CXF to retrieve WSDL from 237–238
        setting up WSDL in repository 236–237
    sending events to Nagios from Bamos event server 246–251
        configuring NSCA and Nagios 247–249
        configuring processor 249–250
        testing configuration 250–251
enterprise service bus. *See* ESB
entrySet() method 145, 147
errorExpression 250
ESB (enterprise service bus) 192
Esper statement 195, 198, 206, 209, 253
EsperEventProcessor 197–199, 206–207, 209–210
EsperProcessor property 195
esperStatement 249, 253–254
event processor, in Bamos open source project 194–195
event producer, in Bamos open source project 192–193
event sender, attaching to service 54–57
event service, in Bamos open source project 193–194
event.getMessage() method 243
event.getServerName() method 203–204
event.getServiceName() method 203
event.getUserValues() method 203
eventclass 193, 198, 201, 244, 254, 258, 260, 262
Eventclass property 193
EventCountProcessor property 195

EventProcessor 196–197, 200, 203, 206, 209
events
  querying
    with C# 259
    with Python 262
    with Ruby 261
  sending
    from Mule 241–245
    to Nagios 246–251
    with C# 258
    with Python 262
    with Ruby 260–261
example-properties.txt 240
exampleEvent string 258
ExampleTag 105
ExecutionListener 255–256
expect() method 160

F

filter property 198
FindRoadWorks operation 96
from property 193

G

gadget server 190–191, 199, 231
gadget, in Bamos open source project 191
GET method 84, 101, 127, 135, 138, 262–263
GET operation 39, 53
GET request 42, 262
getAccessToken 147
getAccount operation 159–161
getAllAssociations operation 106
getMainWindow() method 146
GetMethod() method 135, 137, 154, 238, 241
getObjectContent() method 180
GetPolicyUtil class 220–221
getResourcePathWithTag method 105
getSecret() method 131
getStatus() method 56
getUserClass() method 204
getUserDetails operation 136
<GOV_HOME> directory 267–268, 270–273
GovData 67–68
governance 7–13
  corporate governance 7

IT governance 7–10
policies for
  applying 11–12
  defining 10–11
  enforcing 12–13
governanceFolder.getDescription() method 52
GovForms application 65, 88
GovMobile 66–67
GovPortal 67
GovTraffic 66
GPS data points 33, 40
GPSData object 40, 162
granularity, defining correct level of 103–104
Groups tab 150

H

handle.read() method 262–263
handleMessage operation 140–141
handleRequest 130, 139, 153
handleResponse operation 56
Hash-based Message Authentication Code. See HMAC
header.getObject() method 140
Hector library 29, 36
HMAC (Hash-based Message Authentication Code) 126–131
  client code for 128–131
  fields to use for 127–128
HMACTest class 129
href attribute 92
HTTP method 127, 144, 154
HTTP object 261
HttpClient() method 129, 135, 154, 163–164, 238, 241
HTTPS with Jetty 118–119
HttpWebRequest 258–260
human-readable documentation, for REST-based service 86–88

I

IaaS (infrastructure as a service) 175
IDE (integrated development environment) 28
identity theft 73
IllegalArgumentException() method 128
ImageComments 180–181

ImageCommentService 177
Implementation Support department 62
info.getBaseUriBuilder() method 40, 162
infodbservice service 204
infrastructure as a service. See IaaS
inInterceptor 140
init() method 179
initialDelay 231, 233
initialize() method 52, 105, 229
InputStream 177–178, 180, 238, 241
installing
  Cassandra 270–271
  Eclipse 267–270
  Maven 267
  OpenAM 273–274
  soapUI 274–275
  Tomcat 273
  WSO2 Gadget Server 272
  WSO2 Governance registry 271
integrated development environment. See IDE
integrating SOA
  governance 235–264
  BPM engine integration 251–257
    monitoring average task execution 251–255
    monitoring which processes are started 255–257
  enterprise integration 236–251
    loading Mule configuration from repository 245–246
    provisioning configuration from repository 238–241
    provisioning WSDL from repository 236–238
    sending events from Mule 241–245
    sending events to Nagios from Bamos event server 246–251
  language integration 257–263
    C# 257–260
    Python 261–263
    Ruby 260–261
integration layer 157
integration testing 167–170
  running from Maven 169–170
  using SOAPUI 167–169

integrityFilter element 130
Interval property 199
iplanet attribute 152
iPlanetDirectoryPro 153, 155
isUserAuthenticated
   operation 135, 137
IT governance 7–10

J

Java class 192, 196, 220, 244
Java interface 97, 191, 237
JAVA_HOME
   in Linux 267
   in Windows 266
JAVA_HOME property 267, 270
jaxrs:providers element 56
jaxrs:server configuration 56
JSON object 40, 56, 258
JSON schema 91
JSONObject() 181
jsonURL 199, 201, 205, 207, 210
JUnit tests 155

K

Keyspace 37
keytool command 118–119,
   122–123

L

language integration 257–263
   C# 257–260
      getting resource from repo-
         sitory using 259–260
      querying events using 259
      sending events using 258
   Python 261–263
      getting resource from
         repository using 263
      querying events using 262
      sending events using 262
   Ruby 260–261
      getting resource from
         repository using 261
      querying events using 261
      sending events using
         260–261
Launch Application button 183
Lead analyst 63
Legal department 61, 73
lifecycle
   of OpenGov service 214–217

of policy 225–227
of service 213–217
   assemble phase 213–214
   manage phase 214
   model phase 213
LifeCycleOverviewProcessor
   232, 234
limit property 194
<link> tag 86
links, documenting REST-based
   service 85–86
Linux, JAVA_HOME in 267
List Services button 93
listAllLifecycles() method 229
loadConfigResources
   method 245
localhost.cfg file 247–248
locationData.size() method 203
LocationProcessor property 195
logic layer 30, 37–38, 157–158
logical layer, decoupling from
   transport layer 104
Lower LimitGauge 199

M

m.getExchange() method 55
MAC (message authentication
   code) 126
mac.doFinal.data.getBytes()
   method 128
makeHTTPCallUsingHMAC()
   method 129
manage phase, lifecycle of
   services 214
Maven
   installing 267
   running integration testing
      from 169–170
   running Sonar from 172–174
Maven command 170
Maven plug-in 31, 47
Media type 86, 88, 101, 113
message.getHeaders()
   method 140
metadata search, searching
   repository from web
   application 228–229
method.getName() method 129
method.getPath() method 129
method.getResponseBodyAs-
   Stream() method 238, 241
method.getResponseBodyAs-
   String() method 135–136,
   138

method.getResponseHeader(
   164
MIME type 40
Mobile Services department 62
mock objects, testing using
   159–160
mockRepository() method 159
model phase, lifecycle of
   services 213
Mule
   loading configuration from
      repository 245–246
   sending events from 241–245
mule-config-repo.xml file
   245–246, 259, 261, 263
muleContext.start()
   method 246
muleEventSender 243–244
Mutator 36–37
mutator.execute() method 37
mvn command 267

N

Nagios, sending events to
   configuring NSCA 247–249
   configuring processor 249–250
   from Bamos event
      server 246–251
   testing configuration 250–251
NagiosProcessor property 195
name.getLocalPart()
   method 140
NewsService 69
node.getTextContent()
   method 140
nonbreaking changes 107–109,
   112
NoSQL database 27, 30, 35, 160,
   265
Not invented here pattern 82
notify method 256
nsca.cfg file 247, 250

O

OAuth 141–149
   authorizing consumer
      146–147
   getting access token 147
   getting request token 144–145
   registering consumer with ser-
      vice provider 143–144
   using access token 147–149

oauth_callback property
    145–147
oauth_consumer_key 144
oauth_nonce 144
oauth_signature_method 144
oauth_timestamp 144
oauth_verifier 147
oauth_version 144
oauthclient 147
OAuthMessage 145, 147–148
oAuthMessage.getConsumer-
    Key() method 148
oAuthMessage.getSignature-
    Method() method 148
oAuthMessage.getToken()
    method 148
OAuthServlet() method 148
<Offset> element 230
OMAbstractFactory.get-
    OMFactory() method 221
open data initiatives 68
open source 22–25
    BAM tools 25
    defined 22–24
    SOA repositories 24
OpenAM 150–152
    configuring application
        151–152
    creating policies 152
    installing 273–274
OpenDataService 69, 95
OpenGov example 60–78
    documentation policies 70
    organizational chart for
        61–62
    performance policies
        measuring performance in
            real time 75–76
        processing GPS data within
            10 ms 75
    products 64–68
        GovData 67–68
        GovForms 65
        GovMobile 66–67
        GovPortal 67
        GovTraffic 66
    security policies 72–75
        complying with
            legislation 72–73
        simpler authentication and
            authorizations
            mechanisms 74–75
        verifying GPS data 73–74
    service design policies
        multiple services that han-
            dle accounts 71–72

support for multiple
    versions 72
using generally accepted
    data models 71
services available from 68–69
stakeholders of 63–64
testing policies
    horizontally scaling
        services 76–77
    reporting on overview of
        different permit applica-
        tions from last day 76
    users find many bugs in
        services 77
opengov_hmac header 131
opengov_token 138–139
opengovHeader.size()
    method 139, 153
OpenSearch specification 95,
    99–101
org.bamos.core.launcher.Bamos
    Launcher class 54
organizational chart, for Open-
    Gov example 61–62
otherData.keySet() method 180

P

PaaS (platform as a service) 63,
    175
package command 224
ParkingPermitService 69, 149,
    151–153, 155
passwordCallbackClass
    property 123–125
PeopleRegistrationService 68
performance policies, for Open-
    Gov example
    measuring performance in
        real time 75–76
    processing GPS data within
        10 ms 75
performance, running Sonar
    from Maven 172–174
Permit Bureau 149–150
PermitService 89–90, 93–94,
    104–106, 120
PermitSystem 90
pitfalls, for SOA 14–15
platform as a service. See PaaS
pojo bean 240
polElement.toString()
    method 221
policies 20–22
    applying 11–12

at design time 17–18
at runtime 18
creating policies 16–17
custom view for 217–225
    creating logic 220–222
    creating pages 222–223
    defining format 219–220
    deploying pages 224–225
    linking media type 220
defining 10–11
design policies 21
documentation policies 21
enforcing 12–13
of lifecycle 225–227
performance policies 22
security policies 21–22
testing policies 22
policy format 219–220
policy_add_handler_ajaxprocess
    or.jsp 222–223
pom.xml file 98, 170, 172
portType 90–91, 97, 110–111
POST method 39, 84, 163, 193,
    262
PostMethod method 129
process services 103
processes, monitoring which are
    started 255–257
processingTime event 196–198,
    244, 249, 251, 253–254
Product Development
    department 62
Product Support
    department 62, 76
Product Support manager 63,
    75, 77
products, for OpenGov
    example 64–68
    GovData 67–68
    GovForms 65
    GovMobile 66–67
    GovPortal 67
    GovTraffic 66
ProductsService 69
Properties object 240–241
Properties() method 241
PropertiesHolder class 240
PropertyPlaceHolderConfigurer
    240
props.keySet() method 229
providers, for cloud
    services 175–176
public data 68, 73, 78
PublicSpaceRegistrationService
    68

PUT method 38–40, 84
putAttributes method 180
PutMethod method 163–164
putObject.bucket.getName()
    method 179
Python 261–263
    getting resource from reposi-
        tory using 263
    querying events using 262
    sending events using 262
Python script 261

Q

QAService 69
qname.getNamespaceURI()
    method 238
qnameNs 238
query.execute() method 37

R

Raw tab 43
RDF (Resource Description
    Framework) 86
RDS (Relation Database
    Service) 178
reader.readLine() method 136
reader.ReadToEnd()
    method 259–260
receivedDate.getTime()
    method 130
ReferenceDataService 69
Register button 143
registerGPSData operation 162
registering service, in WSO2
    Governance Registry 50–51
registry, visualizing information
    from 230–234
    using gauge that shows docu-
        mentation percentage
        231–232
    using pie chart that shows
        lifecycle stages 232
Relation Database Service. See
    RDS
remoting layer, for Amazon
    cloud 180–182
report resource 84, 87
ReportService 69, 83–84, 93, 123
repositories
    getting resource from
        with C# 259–260
        with Python 263
        with Ruby 261

loading Mule configuration
    from 245–246
provisioning configuration
    from 238–241
searching 227–230
    from repository client
        229–230
    from web application
        227–229
WSDL in
    retrieving with CXF
        237–238
    setting up 236–237
req.GetResponse()
    method 259–260
request token, for OAuth
    144–145
request.GetRequestStream()
    method 258
request.getRequestURL()
    method 154
RequestHandler interface 56,
    139
requesttoken 146
requirements, for SOA 15–18
    applying policies at design
        time 17–18
    applying policies at
        runtime 18
    creating policies 16–17
Resource Description Frame-
    work. See RDF
resource.getContent()
    method 229
Response object 40
Response.created 40, 162
Response.ok() method 101, 181
response.read() method 262
REST authentication filter, for
    centralized identity
    system 138–139
REST interface 38, 55, 67, 132,
    134, 144, 178, 211
REST resource, XML schema
    in 98–99
REST services 38–43
    documentation policies
        for 83–88
        human-readable docu-
            mentation 86–88
        referenced resources 85
        report resource 84–85
        using links 85–86
    implementing 40–41
    overview 38–39

testing 41–43, 162–164
versioning 111–115
REST-based interface 133
REST-based search
    definition 99–103
REST-soapui-project.xml file 42
result.getRoadEvent()
    method 99
result.getSsn() method 47, 164
reusable services 103–107
    and documentation 106–107
    and using standards 106–107
    and versioning 106–107
    decoupling transport layer
        from logical layer 104
    defining correct level of
        granularity 103–104
    service discovery 104–106
reverse property 194
RoadEventMessage 96, 99
RoadEventStructure 96–97
RoadWorksSearchService
    101–102
RoadWorksService 96–97, 99
Ruby 260–261
    getting resource from reposi-
        tory using 261
    querying events using 261
    sending events using 260–261
runtime governance, Bamos
    open source project
    189–211
    and documentation
        compliance 211
    average response time
        event 196–199
    event processor in 194–195
    event producer in 192–193
    event service in 193–194
    failed authentication and
        authorization 208–210
    gadget in 191
    gadget server in 191–192
    number of requests per time
        period 206–207
    report usage based on
        location 202–206
    report usage based on
        service 199–202
runtime, applying policies at 18

S

S3 (Simple Storage Service) 178
s3.putObject 179

SaaS (software as a service) 63,
    175
Sales department 62–63
Sales manager 63, 71–72, 75–76
SavePolicyUtil class 220–221
scalability 176
Search property 228
searching repository 227–230
    from repository client
        229–230
    from web application
        227–229
        content search 227
        metadata search 228–229
searchRoadWorks
    operation 101
{searchTerms} parameter 101
SecretKeySpec.secret.getBytes()
    method 128
security policies 21–22, 116–155
    centralized identity
        system 131–141
        authentication façade
            for 134–137
        authentication filter
            for 137–141
        authentication provider
            for 133–134
    for OpenGov example 72–75
        complying with
            legislation 72–73
        simpler authentication and
            authorizations
            mechanisms 74–75
        verifying GPS data 73–74
    reusing authorization
        services 149–155
        authorization filter for 153
        OpenAM entitlement
            service 150–152
    using HTTPS with Jetty
        118–119
    using OAuth 141–149
        authorizing consumer
            146–147
        getting access token 147
        getting request token
            144–145
        registering consumer with
            service provider
            143–144
        using access token 147–149
    validating message
        integrity 120–131
        using HMAC 126–131

    using WS-Security with
        SOAP messages 121–126
self linking 86
self-documenting services 79,
    82, 85, 106
sendEvent method 256
server property 193–194
server.keystore 118–120
serverName property 249–250,
    253
Service Consumer Name
    field 143
service design policies
    following existing
        standards 95–103
        REST-based search
            definition 99–103
        XML schema in REST
            resource 98–99
        XML schema in WSDL
            95–98
    for OpenGov example
        multiple services that han-
            dle accounts 71–72
        support for multiple
            versions 72
        using generally accepted
            data models 71
    reusable services 103–107
        and documentation 106–107
        and using standards 106–107
        and versioning 106–107
        decoupling transport layer
            from logical layer 104
        defining correct level of
            granularity 103–104
        service discovery 104–106
    versioning services 107–115
        REST service 111–115
        WS-* based service 107–111
service discovery 104–106
service property 193–194
service remoting 30–31, 157
service repository, documenta-
    tion policies for 92–95
service-level agreement. See SLA
service-oriented architecture. See
    SOA
service.getProperties()
    method 229
serviceKeystore.jks 122, 125
ServiceLifeCycle 233
services, lifecycle of 213–217
    assemble phase 213–214
    manage phase 214
    model phase 213

sessionAwareFunction()
    method 222
setup() method 159–160, 163,
    165
Sign-in button 50
Sign-in link 57
signaturePropFile
    property 123–125
signing 121
Simple Storage Service. See S3
SimpleDB 178–180
SimpleOAuthValidator()
    method 148
single sign-on. See SSO
SLA (service-level
    agreement) 75
SliceQuery 37
smartphones 66
SOA (service-oriented architec-
    ture)
    advantages of 6–7
    and governance 7–13
        applying policies 11–12
        corporate governance 7
        defining policies to
            apply 10–11
        IT governance 7–10
        monitoring and enforcing
            policies 12–13
    and open source 22–25
        BAM tools 25
        defined 22–24
        SOA repositories 24
    benefits of 13–14
        keeping track of how ser-
            vices are used 13–14
        keeping uniformity among
            services 14
    defined 4–7
    pitfalls for 14–15
    policies in 20–22
        design policies 21
        documentation policies 21
        performance policies 22
        security policies 21–22
        testing policies 22
    requirements of 15–18
        applying policies at design
            time 17–18
        applying policies at
            runtime 18
        creating policies 16–17
SOA repositories 24
SOAP button 168
SOAP messages, WS-Security
    with 121–126

SOAP services 43–49
  implementing 47–48
  overview 43–44
  testing 48–49
  WSDL contract for 44–47
SOAPAction mapping 47
SOAPUI, integration testing
    using 167–169
  installing 274–275
software as a service. *See* SaaS
Sonar, running from
    Maven 172–174
sonar.host.url 172
SpringXmlConfigurationBuilder
    245
src/test/resources folder 35, 48
SSO (single sign-on) 131
stakeholders, of OpenGov
    example 63–64
standards, following 95–103
  and reusable services 106–107
  REST-based search
      definition 99–103
  XML schema in REST
      resource 98–99
  XML schema in WSDL 95–98
START_TIME property 243
statement element 220
statistics queries 53
storeDirectly 249, 253
storeImageComment
    operation 178–179, 181
Subjects tab 133
submitPolicyForm() method 223
Subversive SVN Team Provider
    option 268
super.getURL() method 145, 147
SuperColumn 36
SuperColumnFamily 36
SVN plug-in 31
SVN Repositories view 32

T

TaskCompleteListener 252–253
taskExecution property 252, 254
TaskListener 252–253
taskName property 252–254
teardown() method 160
technical services 103
Technical Support
    department 62
templates.cfg file 247–248
TestCase editor 168

testCreateAccount() method 161
TestCreateAccountWithValid-
    Account() method 159
testing 157–170
  conversion 166–167
  data layer 160–161
  in Amazon cloud 182
  integration testing 167–170
    running from Maven
        169–170
    using SOAPUI 167–169
  policies 22
    for OpenGov example
      horizontally scaling
          services 76–77
      reporting on different
          permit applications 76
      users find many bugs in
          services 77
  REST services 41–43, 162–164
  SOAP services 48–49
  using mock objects 159–160
  WS-* based service 164–166
testInvalidMessage()
    method 163
testResponseContentType()
    method 163
testValidCall() method 166
timestamp property 192–194,
    196, 198, 201, 203–204
tlsServerParameters element 119
to property 193
token validity 134
Tomcat, installing 273
tools, for BAM application
    53–54
top-down contract design 44
traffic avoidance example, over-
    view 32–34
TrafficAccountService 69
TrafficDataService 69
transport layer, decoupling from
    logical layer 104
trustManagers element 120
ttl property 250
Type Filter Text field 268
types:account 45

U

UBL (Universal Business
    Language) 95
uniform resource identifier. *See*
    URI

uniformity, among services 14
Universal Business Language. *See*
    UBL
updateAccount operation 168
Upper LimitGauge 199
URI (uniform resource
    identifier) 84
Url type 100
URLEncoder.encode.super
    .getURL() method 146
User data property 193
user identification 121
userClass property 197–198,
    200, 205–206, 209
userValues 197–198, 209
UUID.randomUUID()
    method 179

V

validating message
    integrity 120–131
  using HMAC 126–131
    client code for 128–131
    fields to use for 127–128
  using WS-Security with SOAP
      messages 121–126
verify () method 159–160, 166
versioning services 107–115
  and reusable services 106–107
  REST service 111–115
  WS-* based service 107–111
visualizing information, from
    registry 230–234
  using gauge that shows docu-
      mentation percentage
      231–232
  using pie chart that shows life-
      cycle stages 232
vnd prefix 87

W

warningExpression 250
web application, searching
    repository from 227–229
  content search 227
  metadata search 228–229
Web Service Definition Lan-
    guage. *See* WSDL
widgets, for BAM
    application 57–58
Windows, JAVA_HOME in 266

writeResponse method 237–238
WS-* authentication filter, for
    centralized identity
    system 139–141
WS-* based service
    documentation policies
        for 88–92
        generating from WSDL
            91–92
        WSDL for
            PermitService 89–91
    testing 164–166
    versioning 107–111
WS-Remoting layer 47
WS-Security, with SOAP
    messages 121–126
WSDL (Web Service Definition
    Language)
        for SOAP services 44–47

generating documentation
    from 91–92
in repository
    retrieving with CXF
        237–238
    setting up 236–237
XML schema in 95–98
WSDL file 89, 108, 237–238
WSDL option 51
wsdl-viewer.xsl file 92
wsdl:definitions 89
wsdl:documentation tag 89
wsdl:operation 90
wsdl:porttype 90
wsdl:types 45, 90
WSDLQueryHandler class 237
wsdlResource object 53
WSDLSupplier interface 236
WSO2 Gadget Server 191, 272

WSO2 Governance Registry 49–53
    accessing 51–53
    registering service in 50–51
    running 49–50
WSO2 governance registry 216
WSO2 Governance registry,
    installing 271
WSRegistryServiceClient 51–52

X

XML file 91–92, 100
XML parsing 47
XML schema
    in REST resource 98–99
    in WSDL 95–98
XML type 45
XSD file 89
XSD type 45, 90

Activiti in Action
Executable Business Processes in BPMN 2.0
by Tijs Rademakers

    ISBN: 978-1-617290-12-1
    456 pages, $49.99
    July 2006

SOA Patterns
by Arnon Rotem-Gal-Oz

    ISBN: 978-1-933988-26-9
    250 pages, $49.99
    August 2012

Camel in Action
Enterprise AOP with Spring Applications
by Claus Ibsen and Jonathan Anstey

    ISBN: 978-1-935182-36-8
    552 pages, $49.99
    December 2010

Open Source ESBs in Action
Example Implementations in Mule and ServiceMix
by Tijs Rademakers and Jos Dirksen

    ISBN: 978-1-933988-21-4
    528 pages, $44.99
    September 2008

For ordering information go to www.manning.com

YOU MAY ALSO BE INTERESTED IN

Spring Integration in Action
by Mark Fisher, Jonas Partner,
   Marius Bogoevici, and Iwein Fuld

   ISBN: 978-1-935182-43-6
   400 pages, $49.99
   July 2012

RabbitMQ in Action
Distributed Messaging for Everyone

by Alvaro Videla and Jason J.W. Williams

   ISBN: 978-1-935182-97-9
   312 pages, $44.99
   April 2012

ActiveMQ in Action
by Bruce Snyder, Dejan Bosanac,
   and Rob Davies

   ISBN: 978-1-933988-94-8
   408 pages, $44.99
   March 2011

Specification by Example
How Successful Teams Deliver the Right Software

by Gojko Adzic

   ISBN: 978-1-617290-084
   296 pages, $49.99
   June 2011

For ordering information go to www.manning.com